Jung on Astrology

Jung on Astrology brings together C.G. Jung's thoughts on astrology in a single volume for the first time, significantly adding to our understanding of his work.

Jung's *Collected Works*, seminars, and letters contain numerous discussions of this ancient divinatory system, and Jung himself used astrological horoscopes as a diagnostic tool in his analytic practice. Understood in terms of his own psychology as a symbolic representation of the archetypes of the collective unconscious, Jung found in astrology a wealth of spiritual and psychological meaning and suggested it represents the "sum of all the psychological knowledge of antiquity."

The selections and editorial introductions by Safron Rossi and Keiron Le Grice address topics that were of critical importance to Jung – such as the archetypal symbolism in astrology, the precession of the equinoxes and astrological ages, astrology as a form of synchronicity and acausal correspondence, the qualitative nature of time, and the experience of astrological fate – allowing readers to assess astrology's place within the larger corpus of Jung's work and its value as a source of symbolic meaning for our time.

The book will be of great interest to analytical psychologists, Jungian psychotherapists, and academics and students of depth psychology and Jungian and post-Jungian studies, as well as to astrologers and therapists of other orientations, especially transpersonal.

Safron Rossi, PhD, is a Professor of mythology and depth psychology in the Jungian and Archetypal Studies specialization at Pacifica Graduate Institute, California. For many years she was curator of the Joseph Campbell and James Hillman manuscript collections. She writes in the fields of archetypal psychology, mythology, and astrology.

Keiron Le Grice, PhD, is a Professor of depth psychology and program chair in the Jungian and Archetypal Studies specialization at Pacifica Graduate Institute, California, and co-founder of the Institute of Transpersonal and Archetypal Studies (ITAS). He is the author of several books and a founding editor of *Archai: The Journal of Archetypal Cosmology.*

Also published by Routledge in this series

Jung on the East, edited by J. J. Clarke

Jung on Alchemy, edited by Nathan Schwartz-Salant

Jung on Evil, edited by Murray Stein

Jung on Astrology

C. G. Jung

Selected and Introduced by
Safron Rossi and Keiron Le Grice

LONDON AND NEW YORK

First published 2018
by Routledge
2 Park Square, Milton Park, Abingdon, Oxon OX14 4RN

and by Routledge
711 Third Avenue, New York, NY 10017

Routledge is an imprint of the Taylor & Francis Group, an informa business

British Library Cataloguing-in-Publication Data
A catalogue record for this book is available from the British Library

Library of Congress Cataloging-in-Publication Data
A catalog record for this book has been requested

ISBN: 978-1-138-23072-9 (hbk)
ISBN: 978-1-138-23073-6 (pbk)
ISBN: 978-1-315-30451-9 (ebk)

Typeset in Times New Roman
by Apex CoVantage, LLC

Contents

Figures

Acknowledgments

We are indebted to the Jung family whose support and permission to gather Jung's writings on astrology in one place made this volume possible. We also would like to thank our colleague Susan Rowland, for making our introduction to Routledge, and Susannah Frearson, our editor at Routledge, who shepherded this project with grace and ease. Thanks also goes to the Graduate Research Library at Pacifica Graduate Institute, California, who made Jung's *Collected Works* available to us in electronic form, and to Toni D'Anca for the photo of the Orphan Stone.

Safron would like to personally thank Keiron Le Grice, her co-editor in this project, and her husband, Glen Slater. Keiron expresses his thanks to Safron Rossi for collaborating on the project and for the original idea for the book and to his wife, Kathryn Le Grice, for her ongoing support.

Safron Rossi
Keiron Le Grice

Abbreviations

The reader will find three kinds of numbered notes at the end of each chapter. This is due to the material being mainly drawn from Jung's previously published works. All notes without brackets are Jung's original notes from the *Collected Works* or original notes by the editors of *C. G. Jung Letters*, the three volumes of Jung's seminars or the *Red Book*. Notes that are followed by [EDITORS] or placed entirely in square brackets are by the original editors of the *Collected Works*. Last, notes by the editors of this current work are indicated by their initials in brackets, Keiron Le Grice [KLG] and Safron Rossi [SR]. Works by Jung are identified by the following abbreviations.

CW *The Collected Works of C. G. Jung*. Edited by Gerhard Adler, Michael Fordham, and Herbert Read; William McGuire, Executive Editor; translated primarily by R.F.C. Hull. Princeton (Bollingen Series XX) and London (Routledge), 1953–1983. 21 volumes.

Letters *C. G. Jung Letters*. Selected and edited by Gerhard Adler in collaboration with Aniela Jaffé; translations by R.F.C. Hull. Princeton (Bollingen Series XCV) and London (Routledge), 1973, 1975. 2 volumes.

Works by other authors cited in the endnotes are identified by title, author, or both. For more information on Jung's sources, see bibliographies at the end of the *CW* volumes.

Introduction

The astrological horoscope, Carl Jung observed in a letter of 1954, "corresponds to a definite moment in the colloquy of the gods, that is to say the psychic archetypes."[1] This statement, one of many similar assertions made throughout his life, is illustrative of Jung's belief that astrology can provide symbolic insight into the workings of the human psyche. Astrological charts, cast for specific moments in time, might be construed as something like a symbolic portrayal of the universal principles, or archetypes, once personified by the gods and goddesses of ancient myth. Indeed, astrology, Jung remarked in a letter to Sigmund Freud, "seems indispensable for a proper understanding of mythology."[2] However, despite Jung's abiding personal interest in astrology, and his serious exploration of it, his views on the subject have received scant attention from scholars in the field of depth psychology. By contrast, Jung's ideas have been readily embraced by many practicing astrologers and authors of astrology books, perhaps in the hope that the association with Jung might lend to astrology a degree of credibility otherwise lacking, given the natural affinity between the two fields. This book – a compilation of Jung's writings in this area – is intended for readers in both depth psychology and astrology. Yet the ideas explored herein are also relevant to any of us searching for deeper life meaning and a greater sense of order in life or for a way to explore the mysteries of human experience.

Questions of the human being's place within the cosmos, of the limits of rationality and causal determinism, and of the scope of human free will and the existence of what was once recognized as the workings of fate or destiny remain critically relevant to us today. Now, as in other periods of our recent past, the challenges of our historical moment impress upon us the need to better recognize and work in harmony with the greater forces, both psychological and physical, shaping our lives. "We know nothing of man," Jung proclaimed in an interview near the end of this life, and it is this unconsciousness of human nature, especially our capacity for destruction and evil, that, he believed, poses the greatest threat to our existence – and perhaps today even to the planet's.[3] No less significant is the need to find sources of individual life meaning and orientation for our future direction, given the increasing secularism of the modern world, with the much-discussed absence of myth and decline in religious belief. In giving his attention to the symbolism, practice, and theoretical understanding of astrology, Jung grappled with each of these concerns. The results of his exploration of astrology, recorded in various places in his *Collected Works* and his other less formal writing, are set before you in this volume.

Astrology held Jung's interest throughout most of his life, evident as early as 1911 in correspondence with Freud ("my evenings are taken up very largely with astrology"[4]) to his many letters on this topic from the late 1950s. Jung's writing in this area is of historical import too, revealing Jung's engagement with astrology as one notable element of a burgeoning cultural interest in the irrational and psychological exploration in the late nineteenth and early twentieth centuries, a movement out of which depth psychology itself arose. At a biographical level, Jung's fascination with astrology, and with other aspects of the occult, was a contributory factor in his professional and personal break from Freud in early 1913. Jung's interest in matters astrological was to continue in the decades to follow and is especially evident in seminars given in the late 1920s and 1930s, and then in letters and formal writing from the 1950s, in connection with synchronicity (the phenomenon of "meaningful coincidence"), modern physics, and reflections on the mind-matter relationship. Although not treated in a dedicated volume of the *Collected Works*, astrology occupied Jung's attention for a fifty-year period as he ruminated on its workings and applied it to illuminate both individual psychology and the evolution of mythic symbolism within Western civilization.[5]

Such is the interconnection between astrology and Jungian ideas that the compilation of Jung's writings on this topic also constitutes an excursion into many, if not all, of the central aspects of his psychology, encompassing his theories of archetypes and the collective unconscious, individuation, synchronicity, the self and mandala symbolism, alchemy, myth, the evolution of the God-image, and more. Perhaps this range is not so surprising when we take into account Jung's view that astrology represents "the sum of all the psychological knowledge of antiquity."[6] For it could be argued that in certain respects Jungian psychology represents a modern articulation of the concerns of symbolic systems and practices omitted from the modern scientific worldview – astrology and alchemy chief among them. At root, both astrology and Jungian psychology might be seen as being engaged with the critical task of developing greater self-knowledge, of bringing to awareness the unconscious factors underlying our life experience. In Jung's view, astrology – whatever else it might be – is a symbolic language of archetypes, the formative principles and patterns in the depths of the unconscious mind.

While numerous astrological books have drawn on perspectives and ideas in Jungian psychology, as noted far less is known about Jung's own thoughts on astrology, which are often buried within discussions of other ideas and scattered throughout his many publications. This book is intended to address the need for an exposition of his ideas within a single volume, allowing Jung to speak for himself, as it were, and thus perhaps to allow us to extricate Jung's own thoughts on astrology from the ways Jungian ideas have been used by astrological writers. It is hoped that the book will allow readers to see for themselves Jung's enduring fascination with the topic and to read firsthand his own reflections on it, so as to be able to evaluate astrology's significance within the larger corpus of his work and assess its potential relevance for our time.

WHAT IS ASTROLOGY?

Simply stated, astrology is the practice of interpreting the meaning of observed correlations between human experience and the positions, interrelationships, and cycles of the planets (including the sun and the moon) in the solar system. The movements and positions of the planets are plotted against the zodiac, a symbolic frame of reference based on the ecliptic, the line formed by the apparent movement of sun around the Earth over the course of a year – this apparent movement, of course, as astronomers have known since the Copernican Revolution, is a result of the Earth's orbit around the sun. In astrology, the ecliptic forms the center-line of an imaginary band, extending eight to nine degrees above and below it. The zodiacal band, as it is called, is divided into twelve thirty-degree segments, which comprise the well-known signs of the zodiac: Aries, Taurus, Gemini, Cancer, Leo, Virgo, Libra, Scorpio, Sagittarius, Capricorn, Aquarius, and Pisces. The signs belong to one of four elements – Fire, Earth, Air, and Water – and are thought to possess qualities in keeping with the nature of the element. For example, Fire signs (Aries, Leo, and Sagittarius) are deemed to be energetic, warm, enthusiastic, inspirational, and often extraverted, whereas Water signs (Cancer, Scorpio, and Pisces) are associated with emotional sensitivity, compassion, inwardness, and depth of feeling. The qualities of the signs are thought to influence the astrological meanings and principles associated with each of the orbiting planets as they appear to move around the zodiac through each sign in turn. The planets themselves are symbolically associated with certain dynamic principles and powers. Jung likened them to gods and archetypes, whereas the signs might be construed as something like modes of being or archetypal styles manifest in enduring personality traits. Traditional astrology was concerned only with the seven "planets" known to classical antiquity – the sun, the moon, Mercury, Venus, Mars, Jupiter, and Saturn. Contemporary astrology, in many of its forms, has incorporated into its symbolism and practice the so-called modern planets, discovered since the late eighteenth century: Uranus, Neptune, and Pluto.[7]

As seen from any viewpoint on Earth, each planet in its orbit appears to pass in turn through each sign of the zodiac such that at any given moment a planet will be positioned in one particular sign, forming a configuration of relationships with the other planets, known as aspects. For instance, if two planets appear close to each other in the zodiac, within a range of about ten to twelve degrees (a conjunction), this is deemed significant, indicating that the principles and qualities associated with those planets are in a powerful, dynamic relationship, stimulating and blending with each other. Similarly, two planets approximately opposite each other in the zodiac are also considered to be in a potent, challenging, and often antagonistic relationship (an opposition), as are those planets close to 90 degrees apart (a square). Other geometric relationships, such as those based on 120 degrees (trine) and 60 degrees (sextile), are also considered. All the planets and their interrelationships are depicted in an astrological chart calculated for any given moment in time.

Alongside the annual passage of the sun around the zodiac, astrology utilizes another frame of reference based upon our experience of the sun's apparent daily motion across the sky, generated by the Earth's daily rotation on its axis. The line of the sun's journey over the course of a day forms a circle, which is divided into twelve equal sections known as houses, with each house designating a different field of experience or area of life. For example, the second house is traditionally thought to relate to finances, the sixth house to health, the eight to death, and the ninth house to travel. In casting an astrological chart – or horoscope, as it is known – the moment of sunrise on the eastern horizon determines the sign of the ascendant (the start of the first house); sunset, the western horizon, correlates with the descendant or start of the seventh house, with the *medium coeli* (the midheaven), the highest point of the chart, and *imum coeli*, the lowest point, symbolically representing noon and midnight, respectively.[8] Although astrology incorporates a vast and complex array of variables, the planets, signs of the zodiac, houses, and aspects are usually considered to be the most significant factors in astrological interpretations, or chart readings, as they are commonly known.[9]

Perhaps the most popular form of astrology practiced today, outside of newspaper horoscope columns, is natal astrology – astrological horoscopes cast for the moment of birth. Based on the relative positions and placements of the planets at birth, the astrologer synthesizes the meaning of the various factors in the chart to give a portrait of the individual's character and biographical experiences. The birth-chart reading is often augmented by the study of the ongoing movements of the planets in relation to each other as they traverse the zodiac, using methods known as transits and progressions. These methods can be used to gain insight into the qualities of particular periods of time – past, present, or future – and to understand the kinds of experiences and events one might encounter at these times. Historically, astrology has often been used for prediction, most famously, of course, by Nostradamus, whose prophecies were considered by Jung in a chapter in *Aion*, which is included in Part III of this book.

ASTROLOGY IN THE WESTERN WORLD

Western astrology, with which Jung was concerned almost exclusively, is thought to have originated in Mesopotamia, the "cradle of civilization," around 3400 BCE.[10] From there, it was transmitted to Egypt and to Greece and Rome, assimilating the character of the deities of these traditions in a form of mythic syncretism, with the planets ultimately taking on the names of the well-known Roman gods and goddesses – Mercury, Venus, Mars, Jupiter, and Saturn.[11] After a period of suppression by the Church, when Christianity became established as the official religion of the Roman Empire, astrology underwent a revival during the Middle Ages and flourished again during the Renaissance, with Marsilio Ficino (1433–1499) an influential figure, before its exclusion from serious intellectual thought after the Enlightenment and the rise of science.

The beginnings of modern Western astrology have been traced to the British theosophist Alan Leo (1860–1917), writing at the turn of the twentieth century (indeed, Jung notes the close connection between astrology and theosophy around that time). The theosophical influence on the direction of modern astrology continued with the work of Marc Edmund Jones (1888–1980) and then Dane Rudhyar (1895–1985), whose astrological writings date from the 1930s, following his emigration from France to the U.S.[12] All three figures were influential in the formation of a psychological or spiritual approach to astrology, in distinction to those forms of practice concerned with the literal prediction of events. Today, psychological astrology, which possesses the most explicit connections to Jungian thought, is one of multiple forms of contemporary astrological practice. Astrology is variously characterized by a range of descriptors, designating its distinct approaches and applications, including mundane (the astrology of world events), horary (answering specific questions), electional (finding the best time for a planned event), traditional, predictive, divinatory, psychological, evolutionary, spiritual, and most recently archetypal. For some practitioners, astrology is to be viewed as a divinatory method akin to the *I Ching* and Tarot. For others, it is a way to develop psychological insight and a source of mythic meaning. Some commentators see it primarily of interest historically, for understanding connections to our cultural past; others see certain forms of astrology as critically relevant today, both in preserving the psychological wisdom of previous eras and in offering an alternative to the disenchanted worldview of modernity.

Especially in academia and science, the prevailing view today, however, is that astrology is a pseudoscience whose premises are incompatible with the accepted scientific understandings of the nature of reality. Although three of the progenitors of the modern scientific era, Copernicus, Galileo, and Kepler, were themselves involved in astrology (in the period of the sixteenth and early seventeenth centuries in which astronomy and astrology were still a single discipline), the direction of scientific development thereafter pushed astrology outside the margins of the accepted paradigmatic boundaries of intellectual discourse, where it remains.[13] One central element in the debunking of astrology is the absence of a satisfactory causal explanation, in terms of known forces, as to how planets could influence human beings on Earth. Other critiques concern the apparent lack of empirical evidence to substantiate astrology's truth-claims, a critique Jung himself made and sought to address.

More broadly, with its apparent perpetuation of archaic notions of fate and predestination, astrology is at odds with a number of foundational assumptions of the modern worldview, such as the belief in rational self-determination and causality. If we are self-determining agents, with the capacity to shape the future through acts of free will, how can our lives be fated and controlled by the movements of the planets in the solar system? If our lives can be understood through the study of prior causes (such as genetics, early conditioning, and the environment), how can astrology also influence our experience, especially given that there is no significant demonstrable causal connection between the planets and human beings? Moreover, how can the signs of the zodiac, arbitrarily derived from a physically non-existent frame of reference, and no longer in alignment with the constellations of stars after which they were named, have any bearing on events and experiences on Earth? Astrology's apparent assumption of a geocentric rather than a heliocentric cosmology also seemingly places it at odds with the findings of science since the Copernican Revolution, although astrologers stress that adopting a geocentric perspective does not contradict the astronomical reality of a sun-centered solar system but only symbolically reflects the vantage point of individuals on Earth.

Taken together, such objections constitute a formidable barrier to the consideration of astrology, not only in terms of appraising the intellectual argument for its validity, but also because of the emotional investment in assumptions at the core of the consensus understanding of the nature of reality in the modern West, assumptions that astrology appears to flagrantly contradict. Astrology, as Richard Tarnas has noted, is today often seen as the "gold-standard of superstition."[14] For all the seeming irrationality of astrology, though, Jung believed it to be of great value, for he was struck most of all that astrology, however it might ultimately be conceptualized and explained, somehow *works*, in that it discloses, in a symbolic celestial language, information and insights about the psychology, and thus the "fates," of human beings.

THE SIGNIFICANCE OF JUNGIAN PSYCHOLOGY IN ASTROLOGY

The influence of Jungian thought in psychological astrology has been pivotal. It has provided a theoretical orientation for its practitioners that includes a recognition of the reality of the unconscious and the importance of the symbolic for understanding the psyche, giving access to the archetypal imagination and its divine data. Jungian psychology has recovered the value of mythological ideas and revived a sense of cosmological meaning. When the celestial realm is held as a meaningful mirror to the soul, there one experiences a sense of alignment with the deeper levels of life, as well as a sense of being a small part of a greater consciousness.

Prominent psychological astrologers and authors who cite Jung as an authority and have used Jungian ideas in their work include Liz Greene, Stephen Arroyo, Karen Hamaker-Zondag, Alice O. Howell, and Richard Tarnas. Whereas these astrologers each have their unique approaches to articulating Jung's thought in relation to astrology, generally speaking we find there are three main ways in which Jungian psychology has been employed: as a guide to psychological interpretation of astrological factors; as a way to emphasize psychological development (rather than offer prediction, as in traditional astrology); and for setting forth the theoretical assumptions behind astrology.

That Jung's analytical psychology has become a touchstone for the interpretation of astrological factors is evidenced by the many books that attempt to synthesize the two fields. One place where the fields meet is in the supposed manner astrological elements and zodiac signs correspond to Jung's four psychological types. Whereas Jung opened the door between typology and other ancient theories of character classification, he didn't pursue the typological correlation to astrology, yet surprisingly this is perhaps the primary way Jungian ideas have shaped modern astrological thought. Writing in the mid-1970s, Stephen Arroyo was one of the first astrologers to link Jung's psychology of archetypes and astrology, as well as Jung's theory of psychological types and the four astrological elements. Jung's theory of typology was also correlated to the astrological elements by Jungian analyst and astrologer Liz Greene in her book *Relating*. She writes, "Jung's four function types fit hand in glove with astrology's ancient division of the four elements. It is not a case of one being explained away by, or derived from, the other; rather, each is a distinct way of describing the empiric observations of the same phenomena."[15] Like Arroyo, Greene relates the element Air to the thinking type, Water to the feeling type, Earth to the sensation type, and Fire to the intuitive type. These type-to-element correlations have become canonical in psychological astrology. Karen Hamaker-Zondag, also a Jungian analyst and astrologer, has likewise written in depth on the correspondence between Jung's typology and the elements.

Jung's concept of the shadow and its relation to the planet Saturn is another example of psycho-astrological synthesis. Personifying the negative side of the personality, the shadow is composed of those aspects that one represses and hides from oneself, often experienced in projection. Jung said that owning one's shadow, and reconciling to it in some manner, is the first step of psychological work, for within the darkest aspects of our nature lies the potential for integration and wholeness. Saturn is associated with the processes of contraction and limitation, as well as discipline, fear, and the *prima materia* of alchemical work. At the same time, Saturn is the wise old one, the master, the great teacher. Both of these faces can be seen in the concept of the shadow. The correspondences are most notably explored in two of Liz Greene's books, *Saturn: A New Look at an Old Devil* and *Relating: An Astrological Guide to Living with Others on a Small Planet*. She writes,

> The position of Saturn on the birth chart suggests a sphere of the individual's life in which he has been somehow stunted, or arrested in growth, in which he may well feel inadequate, oversensitive or clumsy . . . [as] the unconscious side of personality is built up partially of those qualities which belong to us but which we cannot, or dare not, express. We may thus infer from the placement of Saturn that area where the shadow will express itself most readily, where one is perhaps the most defensive and critical of others, and where one is most liable to attract the hostility and opposition of the environment because of one's own unconscious attitude of inferiority.[16]

Alice O. Howell, Jungian analyst and astrologer, has also written about the relationship between the darker and repressed aspects of the psyche and Saturn's archetypal influence:

> When Saturn pairs up with any other planetary process and furthers its negative expression you will find one of the "seven deadly sins" or, psychologically expressed, one of the repressed or suppressed complexes. . . . Complexes

> are not in themselves sins but the results of processes which have been in intense internal conflict, for one reason or another, causing the ego to suffer a lack of harmony and self-acceptance.[17]

While these darker faces of Saturn signify its importance in a chart, its role in individuation is paramount. It is through Saturn that we learn what the soul most deeply needs, and Saturn as the wise old man is also the teacher whose lessons bring opportunities for profound growth and maturity.[18] Saturn is both what is working us and that part of our psyche that must be worked. As Jung often noted, the shadow is the doorway into the unconscious. In metaphorical terms, it is lead (Saturn) that is transformed into gold by those arduous and wondrous alchemical processes with which Jung was so concerned.

Astrology, as a guide to psychological development, is expressed in a number of ways, foremost being the perspective that the birth chart is symbolic of an individual's character structure, revealing how people experience life, the nature of their complexes, and their calling. Alice Howell writes that the birth chart

> is, *in potentia*, a treasure map to the individuation process or greater awareness of the Self, and I am using Self in Jung's definition of the word as meaning the center and totality of the psyche. The chart will impel us unconsciously, as do our complexes, until we become more conscious.[19]

Thus working with one's chart as a symbol becomes a tool for psychological growth for one can explore with some objectivity one's character, wounds, challenges, and calling. Furthermore, from this perspective the regular transits (and progressions) that one experiences, particularly transits of the outer planets, are understood to function as thresholds of transformations of consciousness. Correlating in some instances to natural stages of aging and development, the planetary transits reflect psychological stages and opportunities for growth. This is related to Jung's concept of individuation, which is often imagined as a spiritual journey wherein unconscious and conscious elements of the psyche become integrated.

Last, some of Jung's ideas have become critical in working with the theoretical assumptions behind astrology. The influence of Jung's ontological understanding of the archetypal basis of reality and the role of synchronicity in the emerging astrological worldview is best articulated currently in archetypal cosmology and archetypal astrology, a field pioneered by Richard Tarnas. In *Cosmos and Psyche*, Tarnas draws on these two foundational Jungian concepts and outlines a worldview anchored in archetypal patterns and their synchronistic informing of life. This worldview is easily merged with the astrological paradigm: "Between the astronomical and human is an archetypally informed synchronicity."[20] This emphasis on synchronicity is one of the most important contributions of Jung's thought to contemporary development and research in astrology, one which is introduced in greater detail in Part IV of this volume.

Arroyo's thoughts on what astrology offers summarizes the main sensibilities of a Jungian psychological approach to astrology. Contemporary Western people, he observes, have "lost touch with the archetypal foundation of [their] being and with the source of support and spiritual-psychological nourishment which they provide. Astrology can be used as a way of reuniting man with his innermost self, with nature, and with the evolutionary process of the universe."[21] In this respect, psychological astrology is broadly consistent with the aims of Jungian analytical psychology.

ORGANIZATION OF THE BOOK

Among the possible ways the material might have been presented to the reader, we chose to organize by theme rather than chronologically or by reproducing Jung's writings on astrology as they appear volume by volume. In many of his reflections, scattered throughout the *Collected Works* and elsewhere, Jung proffers an eclectic assortment of thoughts on the topic, intermingled with reflections on other subjects. On occasion, he even shifts his position on explanations of astrology within the space of a single chapter or section. While such fluctuations are of themselves noteworthy, they are not conducive to clear understanding, and there is little in the way of a consistent evolution of his ideas on astrology leading to a settled position, which might have justified placing the ideas in strict chronological sequence. Thus, rather than presenting Jung's words in the entire context in which they appear in the source texts, we extracted particular sentences or paragraphs, where appropriate, in order to arrange the material in discrete themed parts and chapters, although material in one section unavoidably overlaps with that in other sections. The reader can refer to the original sources if a fuller appreciation of original context is needed. In organizing the material by theme, we hoped to achieve a logical continuity of ideas and as much coherence as possible.

Although certain passages have been omitted to minimize repetition, almost all of Jung's writing on astrology is incorporated into this volume, sourced from the *Collected Works*, his transcribed seminars (*Visions*, *Nietzsche's Zarathustra*, and *Dream Analysis*), *C. G. Jung Speaking*, the two volumes of *C. G. Jung Letters*, the *Freud-Jung Letters*, the *Red Book*, and Jung's autobiography, *Memories, Dreams, Reflections*. One omission is the statistical data and results from Jung's ill-conceived astrology experiment, which is presented in full in the monograph "Synchronicity: An Acausal Connecting Principle." Rather than repeat in its entirety the description of the experiment, which is notable primarily for its methodological flaws and statistical errors, we chose instead to include only select material on the rationale behind the experiment and the conclusions Jung drew from it.

More material from the volumes on alchemy might have been included in this book, too, but in our estimation astrological symbolism in alchemy can be more appropriately approached through a study of the latter; in most cases, Jung's astrological references in his alchemical writings can only be adequately appreciated in the context of the often complicated exegeses and interpretations in *Psychology and Alchemy*, *Alchemical Studies*, and *Mysterium Coniunctionis*. Nonetheless, we have included here select material from these books, such as Jung's reflections on *heimarmene* as astrological fate and archetypal compulsion.

The four parts of the book are ordered such that foundational and contextual material is given first (Part I), followed by Jung's writing on astrological symbolism (Part II), next focusing on Jung's extensive treatment of the significance of the precession of the equinoxes in *Aion* and elsewhere (Part III), and turning last to a systematic exposition of Jung's multiple and sometimes conflicting explanations of astrology (Part IV). The Appendix contains an astrological interpretation of Jung's birth chart written by his second-eldest daughter, Gret Baumann-Jung. Each part opens with an editor's introduction, giving some orientation to the material to follow, accompanied where necessary by explanatory comments and analysis.

What emerges, in bringing together Jung's reflections, is a more complete sense of the significant place astrology occupied in his thinking. In a letter to Freud in 1911, Jung promised that he would return from his explorations of astrology and the occult "laden with rich booty for our knowledge of the human psyche."[22] The compilation of writings in this book shows the extent to which Jung was able to realize this intention.

Keiron Le Grice and Safron Rossi
December 2016

NOTES

1 Jung to André Barbault, 26 May 1954, in *Letters II*, pp. 175–177.
2 Jung to Sigmund Freud, 8 May 1911 (254J), in *Freud/Jung Letters*, p. 183.
3 Jung, "Face to Face Interview," with John Freeman, in *C. G. Jung Speaking*, p. 436.
4 Jung to Sigmund Freud, 12 June 1911, in *Letters I*, p. 24.
5 For a detailed study of the sources from which Jung developed his understanding of astrology, and the figures who influenced his views, see Liz Greene's forthcoming monograph *Jung's Studies in Astrology*. For a companion volume discussing Jung's use of astrological symbolism as a method of hermeneutics in *The Red Book*, see Greene, *The Astrological World of Jung's Liber Novus*.
6 Jung, "Richard Wilhelm: In Memoriam" (1930) in *Spirit in Man, Art, and Literature* (*CW* 15), p. 81.
7 In astronomy, following the discovery of Eris and other planet-like bodies in the outer reaches of the solar system, Pluto was reclassified as a dwarf planet in 2006, although this change of status is not considered to affect its significance in astrology. See Le Grice, *Discovering Eris*.
8 Jung employs variant spellings of the terms *ascendant* and *descendant* in his writing.
9 There are references to each of these factors in the chapters to follow, although Jung, it should be noted, does not always use the terms accurately.
10 Jung admits, "I know far too little about Indian and Chinese astrology" (Jung, *Aion*, p. 93).
11 For detail on the origins and history of Western astrology, see Campion, *History of Western Astrology*; Tester, *History of Western Astrology*; Whitfield, *Astrology*; Barton, *Ancient Astrology*; and Bobrick, *Fated Sky*.
12 Rudhyar's *The Astrology of Personality*, synthesizing Jungian ideas, the philosophy of holism, and theosophy, was published in 1936.
13 For a discussion of the astrological interests of Copernicus, Galileo, and Kepler, see Campion, *History of Western Astrology*, vol. 2.
14 Tarnas, cited in Le Grice, "Birth of a New Discipline," p. 7.
15 Greene, *Relating*, p. 53.

16 Ibid., p. 99.
17 Howell, *Jungian Symbolism in Astrology*, p. 176.
18 See Rossi, "Saturn in C. G. Jung's Liber Primus."
19 Howell, *Jungian Symbolism in Astrology*, p. 6.
20 Tarnas, *Cosmos and Psyche*, p. 69.
21 Arroyo, *Astrology, Psychology, and the Four Elements*, p. 29.
22 Jung to Sigmund Freud, 8 May 1911 (254J), in *Freud/Jung Letters*, p. 183.

BIBLIOGRAPHY

Arroyo, Stephen. *Astrology, Psychology, and the Four Elements*. Sebastopol, CA: CRCS, 1975.

Barton, Tamsyn. *Ancient Astrology*. London: Routledge, 1995.

Bobrick, Benson. *The Fated Sky: Astrology in History*. New York: Simon & Schuster, 2006.

Campion, Nicholas. *The History of Western Astrology*. 2 vols. London: Continuum Books, 2009.

Freud, Sigmund, and Carl Gustav Jung. *The Freud/Jung Letters: The Correspondence between Sigmund Freud and C. G. Jung*. Edited by William McGuire. Translated by Ralph Manheim and R.F.C. Hull. Princeton, NJ: Princeton University Press, 1974.

Greene, Liz. *The Astrological World of Jung's Liber Novus: Daimons, Gods, and the Planetary Journey*. Abingdon, UK: Routledge, 2018.

———. *Jung's Studies in Astrology: Prophecy, Magic and the Qualities of Time*. Abingdon, UK: Routledge, 2018.

———. *Relating: An Astrological Guide to Living with Others on a Small Planet*. York Beach, ME: Samuel Weiser, 1978.

———. *Saturn: A New Look at an Old Devil*. York Beach, ME: Samuel Weiser, 1976.

Hamaker-Zondag, Karen. *Psychological Astrology: A Synthesis of Jungian Psychology and Astrology*. 1980. Reprint, York Beach, ME: Samuel Weiser, 1990.

Howell, Alice O. *The Heavens Declare: Astrological Ages and the Evolution of Consciousness*. Second Edition. Wheaton, IL: Quest Books, 2006.

———. *Jungian Symbolism in Astrology*. Wheaton, IL: Quest Books, 1987.

Jung, Carl Gustav. *Aion*. 2nd Edition. Vol. 9, part II of *The Collected Works of C. G. Jung*. Translated by R.F.C. Hull. Princeton, NJ: Princeton University Press, 1968.

———. "An Astrological Experiment." 1958. In *The Symbolic Life*, 494–501. Vol. 18 of *The Collected Works of C. G. Jung*. Translated by R.F.C. Hull. London: Routledge & Kegan Paul, 1977.

———. *C. G. Jung Letters I: 1906–1950*. Edited by Gerald Adler and Aniela Jaffé. Translated by R.F.C. Hull. London: Routledge & Kegan Paul, 1973.

———. *C. G. Jung Letters II: 1951–1961*. Edited by Gerald Adler and Aniela Jaffé. Translated by R.F.C. Hull. London: Routledge & Kegan Paul, 1973.

———. *The Collected Works of C. G. Jung*. 19 vols. Bollingen Series XX. Translated by R.F.C. Hull. Princeton, NJ: Princeton University Press and London: Routledge & Kegan Paul, 1953–1979.

———. "Richard Wilhelm: In Memoriam." 1930. In *The Spirit in Man, Art, and Literature*, 53–62. Vol. 15 of *The Collected Works of C. G. Jung*. Translated by R.F.C. Hull. Reprint, Princeton: Princeton University Press, 1966/1971.

Jung, Carl Gustav, and John Freeman. "The Face to Face Interview." 1959. In *C. G. Jung Speaking*, 424–439. Edited by William McGuire and R.F.C. Hull. Princeton, NJ: Princeton University Press, 1977.

Le Grice, Keiron. "The Birth of a New Discipline: Archetypal Cosmology in Historical Perspective." *The Birth of a New Discipline. Archai: The Journal of Archetypal Cosmology*, Number 1 (2009). Edited by Keiron Le Grice and Rod O'Neal. Reprint, San Francisco, CA: Archai Press, 2011: 3–29.

——— *Discovering Eris: The Symbolism and Significance of a New Planetary Archetype*. Edinburgh, UK: Floris Books, 2012.

Rossi, Safron. "Saturn in C.G. Jung's Liber Primus." *Jung Journal: Culture & Psyche*. Volume 9, Number 4 (2015): 38–57.

Rudyhar, Dane. *The Astrology of Personality*. Santa Fe, NM: Aurora Press, 1936.

Tarnas, Richard. *Cosmos and Psyche: Intimations of a New World View*. New York: Viking, 2006.

Tester, Jim. *A History of Western Astrology*. Woodbridge, UK: Boydell Press, 1987.

Whitfield, Peter. *Astrology: A History*. New York: Harry N. Abrams, 2001.

Part I

Contexts and opinions

INTRODUCTION

The material in Part I addresses Jung's views of astrology – its place in the modern West, its personal and practical significance to him, and its relationship to his theory of the archetypes and the collective unconscious.

Chapter 1 situates astrology within the context of the cultural transformation of Western civilization since the late eighteenth century. Included here are passages from Jung's stirring commentary "The Spiritual Problem of Modern Man" (1928–1931) written almost in parallel with Freud's *Civilization and Its Discontents* (1929–1930). Jung draws attention to the ascent of reason and science in the modern West, displacing Christian faith as the primary modes of understanding the world, and on the compensatory resurgence of the seemingly irrational and unscientific fascination with psychic phenomena, evidenced by the widespread interest in Gnosticism, theosophy, anthroposophy, astrology, and more. Jung himself played no small part in this movement, of course, in that his work helped bring back into the light of day subjects excluded from the modern scientific view of the world – not least alchemy, mythology, and mysticism.

We read here too of Jung's insistence that the modern individual yearns for direct experience of the numinous depths of the psyche rather than accepting second-hand truths inherited from the doctrines of religion, to be followed as a matter of faith. "Modern man abhors faith and the religions based upon it," Jung claims, at the risk of overstatement. "He holds them valid only so far as their knowledge-content seems to accord with his own experience of the psychic background. He wants to *know* – to experience for himself."[1] Astrology seems to offer a path to self-knowledge in accordance with one's own experience, perhaps accounting in part for its popularity in our time – and perhaps accounting too for Jung's own abiding interest in it.

For Jung, then, the recovery of ancient symbolic wisdom and occult knowledge might be viewed as a response to the profound spiritual and psychological transformation of our time – the "metamorphosis of the gods," as he termed it, bringing a fundamental reorientation in the primary symbols by which each civilization gives expression to the numinous psychological powers that he called the archetypes of the collective unconscious.[2] Drawing on the power of the instincts, these formative archetypal principles, Jung believed, unconsciously animate and direct the human imagination, giving shape to the myths, religions, and cultural forms that provide a source of individual and collective life meaning.

For many in the West, the transition out of the Christian era has wrought psychological and spiritual confusion, and even psychopathology born of an unshakeable sense of meaninglessness and existential disorientation, as the old symbolic forms pass away. Indeed, Jung noted that the psychological suffering experienced by all of his patients over the age of thirty-five ultimately arose from the loss of a religious outlook on life.[3] In the modern era, he observed, spirit has "fallen" from the fiery empyrean above and has become "water," evoking the sense that the metaphysical realm of the heavenly powers of old and even of the Kingdom of God are now to be found submerged in the oceanic depths of the unconscious.[4] The "stars have fallen from heaven," he proclaimed in a similar vein; they have fallen into the unconscious, for neither celestial powers of astrology nor the mythic pantheon of an Olympian host have a place in the prevailing understanding of reality in the modern world.[5]

For all its seeming irrationality, astrology represents a still-vital perspective, living on in the collective unconscious, that repository of forms and archetypal patterns that is the source of our psychological and instinctual history. As an historical precursor to depth psychology, with roots in the ancient, classical, and medieval worlds, astrology preserves and carries forth other modes of interpreting reality to those pursued in science, offering a counterpoint to mechanistic determinism, atomistic reductionism, and a narrow scientific empiricism that excludes the experience of meaning. It is a perspective, Jung thought, that is based on the recognition of "meaningful coincidences" (synchronicities, as he called them) between external facts and inner experiences, in this case between planetary positions and constellated archetypal themes in human experience. In Jung's view, astrology is an example of "synchronicity on a grand scale," potentially providing an opening to a deeper background order of meaning.[6] He returns to consider such matters in detail in the selections included in Part IV.

Chapter 2 contains Jung's personal views of astrology, including observations on its value for illuminating the workings of the psyche and critical comments on its shortcomings and misconceptions. We see evidence here of Jung's willingness to turn to astrology as an aid to analytical work with his patients. For instance, in a letter to astrologer B. V. Raman in 1947, Jung comments: "In cases of difficult psychological diagnosis I usually get a horoscope in order to have a further point of view from an entirely different angle. I must say that I very often found the astrological data elucidated certain points which I otherwise would have been unable to understand."[7] Yet we also see Jung adopting a critical stance towards astrology, targeting especially the lack of statistical studies to provide evidence in support of it; astrologers, he notes, "prefer to swim in intuition"[8] rather than conduct empirical research.[9] Jung also takes issue with the prevailing approaches to astrological interpretations at the time, noting that they were "sometimes too literal and not symbolic enough, also too personal" in that astrology is to do with "impersonal, objective facts" and multi-leveled rather than singular meanings.[10]

Jung, as we discover in Chapter 3, "Planets and Gods: Astrology as Archetypal," understands astrology as a symbolic representation of the archetypal dynamics of the unconscious psyche. As such, astrology pertains to universal motifs and general themes and traits rather than the specific concrete particulars of life. Accordingly, we see here Jung introduce the term *planetary archetype* to describe the universal principles associated with each of the planets in astrology. His "planet simile," extracted from his alchemical writings in *Mysterium Coniunctionis*, strikingly portrays the symbolic relationship between the planets and archetypes, with the conscious ego standing in relation to the archetypes, as the sun does to the orbiting planets. Included here too is mention of Jung's view that the psychology of archetypes can help account for the "inner connection between historical events" and the "general laws" underlying individual development, which are two of the primary areas of application of astrology.[11]

Keiron Le Grice

NOTES

1 Jung, "Spiritual Problem of Modern Man," in *Civilization in Transition* (*CW* 10), p. 84, par. 171.
2 Jung, "Undiscovered Self," in *Civilization in Transition* (*CW* 10), p. 304, par. 585.
3 Jung, "Psychotherapists or the Clergy," in *Psychology and Religion: West and East (CW* 11), p. 334, par. 509.
4 Jung, "Archetypes of the Collective Unconscious," in *Archetypes and the Collective Unconscious (CW* 9i), pp. 18–19, par. 40.
5 Ibid., pp. 23–24, par. 50.
6 Jung, "Richard Wilhelm: In Memoriam" (1930), in *Spirit in Man, Art, and Literature* (*CW* 15), p. 56, par. 81.
7 Jung to B. V. Raman, 6 September 1947, in *Letters I*, pp. 475–476.
8 Jung, *Dream Analysis*, 20 November 1929, pp. 392–393.
9 Recent studies, such as the extensive survey of astrological correlations with patterns of cultural history undertaken by Richard Tarnas, have sought to put astrology on firmer empirical ground. See Tarnas, *Cosmos and Psyche*. See also the research in *Archai: The Journal of Archetypal Cosmology*.
10 Jung to André Barbault, 26 May 1954, in *Letters II*, pp. 175–177.
11 Jung to Karl Schmid, 26 January 1957, in *Letters II*, p. 345.

BIBLIOGRAPHY

Freud, Sigmund. *Civilization and Its Discontents*. 1929–1930. The Standard Edition. Translated by James Strachey. New York: W. W. Norton & Company, 1989.

Jung, Carl Gustav. "Archetypes of the Collective Unconscious." 1954. In *The Archetypes and the Collective Unconscious*, 3–41. 2nd Edition. Vol. 9, part I of *The Collected Works of C. G. Jung*. Translated by R.F.C. Hull. Princeton, NJ: Princeton University Press, 1968.

———. *C. G. Jung Letters I: 1906–1950*. Edited by Gerald Adler and Aniela Jaffé. Translated by R.F.C. Hull. London: Routledge & Kegan Paul, 1973.

———. *C. G. Jung Letters II: 1951–1961*. Edited by Gerald Adler and Aniela Jaffé. Translated by R.F.C. Hull. London: Routledge & Kegan Paul, 1973.

———. *Dream Analysis: Notes on the Seminar Given in 1928–1930*. Bollingen Series XCIX. Edited by William McGuire. Princeton, NJ: Princeton University Press, 1984.

———. "Psychotherapists or the Clergy." 1932. In *Psychology and Religion: West and East*, 327–347. Vol. 11 of *The Collected Works of C. G. Jung*. Translated by R.F.C. Hull. London: Routledge & Kegan Paul, 1958.

———. "Richard Wilhelm: In Memoriam." 1930. In *The Spirit in Man, Art, and Literature*, 53–62. Vol. 15 of *The Collected Works of C. G. Jung*. Translated by R.F.C. Hull. Reprint, Princeton, NJ: Princeton University Press, 1966/1971.

———. "The Spiritual Problem of Modern Man." 1928/1931. In *Civilization in Transition*, 74–94. 2nd Edition. Vol. 10 of *The Collected Works of C. G. Jung*. Translated by R.F.C. Hull. Princeton, NJ: Princeton University Press, 1970.

———. "The Undiscovered Self." 1957. In *Civilization in Transition*. 2nd Edition. Vol. 10 of *The Collected Works of C. G. Jung*. Translated by R.F.C. Hull. Princeton, NJ: Princeton University Press, 1970.

Tarnas, Richard *Cosmos and Psyche: Intimations of a New World View*. New York: Viking, 2006.

1 Astrology's place in the modern West

From: "Archetypes of the Collective Unconscious" (1934/1954) (*CW* 9i), par. 50

50 Since the stars have fallen from heaven and our highest symbols have paled, a secret life holds sway in the unconscious. That is why we have a psychology today, and why we speak of the unconscious. All this would be quite superfluous in an age or culture that possessed symbols. . . . Heaven has become for us the cosmic space of the physicists, and the divine empyrean a fair memory of things that once were. But the "heart glows," and a secret unrest gnaws at the roots of our being.

From: "The Spiritual Problem of Modern Man" (1928/1931) (*CW* 10), pars. 167–176

167 The rapid and worldwide growth of a psychological interest over the last two decades shows unmistakably that modern man is turning his attention from outward material things to his own inner processes. Expressionism in art prophetically anticipated this subjective development, for all art intuitively apprehends coming changes in the collective unconsciousness.

168 The psychological interest of the present time is an indication that modern man expects something from the psyche which the outer world has not given him: doubtless something which our religion ought to contain, but no longer does contain, at least for modern man. For him the various forms of religion no longer appear to come from within, from the psyche; they seem more like items from the inventory of the outside world. No spirit not of this world vouchsafes him inner revelation; instead, he tries on a variety of religions and beliefs as if they were Sunday attire, only to lay them aside again like worn-out clothes.

169 Yet he is somehow fascinated by the almost pathological manifestations from the hinterland of the psyche, difficult though it is to explain how something which all previous ages have rejected should suddenly become interesting. That there is a general interest in these matters cannot be denied, however much it offends against good taste. I am not thinking merely of the interest

taken in psychology as a science, or of the still narrower interest in the psychoanalysis of Freud, but of the widespread and ever-growing interest in all sorts of psychic phenomena, including spiritualism, astrology, Theosophy, parapsychology, and so forth. The world has seen nothing like it since the end of the seventeenth century. We can compare it only to the flowering of Gnostic thought in the first and second centuries after Christ. The spiritual currents of our time have, in fact, a deep affinity with Gnosticism. There is even an "Église gnostique de la France," and I know of two schools in Germany which openly declare themselves Gnostic. The most impressive movement numerically is undoubtedly Theosophy, together with its continental sister, Anthroposophy; these are pure Gnosticism in Hindu dress. Compared with them the interest in scientific psychology is negligible. What is striking about these Gnostic systems is that they are based exclusively on the manifestations of the unconscious, and that their moral teachings penetrate into the dark side of life, as is clearly shown by the refurbished European version of *Kundalini-yoga*. The same is true of parapsychology, as everyone acquainted with this subject will agree.

170 The passionate interest in these movements undoubtedly arises from psychic energy which can no longer be invested in obsolete religious forms. For this reason such movements have a genuinely religious character, even when they pretend to be scientific. It changes nothing when Rudolf Steiner calls his Anthroposophy "spiritual science," or when Mrs. Eddy invents a "Christian Science." These attempts at concealment merely show that religion has grown suspect – almost as suspect as politics and world-reform.

171 I do not believe that I am going too far when I say that modern man, in contrast to his nineteenth-century brother, turns to the psyche with very great expectations, and does so without reference to any traditional creed but rather with a view to Gnostic experience. The fact that all the movements I have mentioned give themselves a scientific veneer is not just a grotesque caricature or a masquerade, but a positive sign that they are actually pursuing "science," i.e., *knowledge*, instead of *faith*, which is the essence of the Western forms of religion. Modern man abhors faith and the religions based upon it. He holds them valid only so far as their knowledge-content seems to accord with his own experience of the psychic background. He wants to *know* – to experience for himself.

172 The age of discovery has only just come to an end in our day, when no part of the earth remains unexplored; it began when men would no longer *believe* that the Hyperboreans were one-footed monsters, or something of that kind, but wanted to find out and see with their own eyes what existed beyond the boundaries of the known world. Our age is apparently setting out to discover what exists in the psyche beyond consciousness. The question asked in every spiritualistic circle is: What happens after the medium has lost consciousness? Every Theosophist asks: What shall I experience at the higher levels of consciousness? The question which every astrologer asks is: What are the operative forces that determine my fate despite my conscious intention? And

every psychoanalyst wants to know: What are the unconscious drives behind the neurosis?

173 Our age wants to experience the psyche for itself. It wants original experience and not assumptions, though it is willing to make use of all the existing assumptions as a means to this end, including those of the recognized religions and the authentic sciences. The European of yesterday will feel a slight shudder run down his spine when he gazes more deeply in to these delvings. Not only does he consider the subject of this so-called research obscure and shuddersome, but even the methods employed seem to him a shocking misuse of man's finest intellectual attainments. What is the professional astronomer to say when he is told that at least a thousand times more horoscopes are cast today than were cast three hundred years ago? What will the educator and advocate of philosophical enlightenment say about the fact that the world has not grown poorer by a single superstition since the days of antiquity? Freud himself, the founder of psychoanalysis, has taken the greatest pains to throw as glaring a light as possible on the dirt and darkness and evil of the psychic background, and to interpret it in such a way as to make us lose all desire to look for anything behind it except refuse and smut. He did not succeed, and his attempt at deterrence has even brought about the exact opposite – an admiration for all this filth. Such a perverse phenomenon would normally be inexplicable were it not that even the scatologists are drawn by the secret fascination of the psyche.

174 There can be no doubt that from the beginning of the nineteenth century – ever since the time of the French Revolution – the psyche has moved more and more into the foreground of man's interest, and with a steadily increasing power of attraction. The enthronement of the Goddess of Reason in Notre Dame seems to have been a symbolic gesture of great significance for the Western world – rather like the hewing down of Wotan's oak by Christian missionaries. On both occasions no avenging bolt from heaven struck the blasphemer down.

175 It is certainly more than an amusing freak of history that just at the time of the Revolution a Frenchman, Anquetil du Perron, should be living in India and, at the beginning of the nineteenth century, brought back with him a translation of the *Oupnek'hat*, a collection of fifty Upanishads, which gave the West its first deep insight into the baffling mind of the East. To the historian this is a mere coincidence independent of the historical nexus of cause and effect. My medical bias prevents me from seeing it simply as an accident. Everything happened in accordance with a psychological law which is unfailingly valid in personal affairs. If anything of importance is devalued in our conscious life, and perishes – so runs the law – there arises a compensation in the unconscious. We may see in this an analogy to the conservation of energy in the physical world, for our psychic processes also have a quantitative, energic aspect. No psychic value can disappear without being replaced by another of equivalent intensity. This is a fundamental rule which is repeatedly verified in the daily practice of the psychotherapist and never fails. The doctor in me

refuses point blank to consider the life of a people as something that does not conform to psychological law. For him the psyche of a people is only a somewhat more complex structure than the psyche of an individual. Moreover, has not a poet spoken of the "nations of his soul"? And quite correctly, it seems to me, for in one of its aspects the psyche is not individual, but is derived from the nation, from the collectivity, from humanity even. In some way or other we are part of a single, all-embracing psyche, a single "greatest man," the *homo maximus*, to quote Swedenborg.

176 And so we can draw a parallel: just as in me, a single individual, the darkness calls forth a helpful light, so it does in the psychic life of a people. In the crowds that poured into Notre Dame, bent on destruction, dark and nameless forces were at work that swept the individual off his feet; these forces worked also upon Anquetil du Perron and provoked an answer which has come down in history and speaks to us through the mouths of Schopenhauer and Nietzsche. For he brought the Eastern mind to the West, and its influence upon us we cannot as yet measure. Let us beware of underestimating it! So far, indeed, there is little of it to be seen on the intellectual surface: a handful of orientalists, one or two Buddhist enthusiasts, a few sombre celebrities like Madame Blavatsky and Annie Besant with her Krishnamurti. These manifestations are like tiny scattered islands in the ocean of mankind; in reality they are the peaks of submarine mountain-ranges. The cultural Philistines believed until recently that astrology had been disposed of long since and was something that could safely be laughed at. But today, rising out of the social deeps, it knocks at the doors of the universities from which it was banished some three hundred years ago.

From: "The Structure of the Unconscious" (1916) (*CW* 7), pars. 494–495

494 No one who is concerned with psychology should blind himself to the fact that besides the relatively small number of those who pay homage to scientific principles and techniques, humanity fairly swarms with adherents of quite another principle. It is entirely in keeping with the spirit of our present-day culture that one can read in an encyclopaedia, in an article on astrology, the following remark: "One of its last adherents was I. W. Pfaff, whose *Astrologie* (Bamberg, 1816) and *Der Stern der Drei Weisen* (1821) must be called strange anachronisms. Even today, however, astrology is still highly regarded in the East, particularly in Persia, India, and China." One must be smitten with blindness to write such a thing nowadays. The truth is that astrology flourishes as never before. There is a regular library of astrological books and magazines that sell for far better than the best scientific works. The Europeans and Americans who have horoscopes cast for them may be counted not by the hundred thousand but by the million. Astrology is a flourishing industry. Yet the encyclopaedia can say: "The poet Dryden (d. 1701) still had horoscopes cast for his children." Christian Science, too, has swamped Europe and America.

Hundreds and thousands of people on both sides of the Atlantic swear by theosophy and anthroposophy, and anyone who believes that the Rosicrucians are a legend of the dim bygone has only to open his eyes to see them as much alive today as they ever were. Folk magic and secret lore have by no means died out. Nor should it be imagined that only the dregs of the populace fall for such superstitions. We have, as we know, to climb very high on the social scale to find the champions of this other principle.

495 Anyone who is interested in the real psychology of man must bear such facts in mind. For if such a large percentage of the population has an insatiable need for this counterpole to the scientific spirit, we can be sure that the collective psyche in every individual – be he never so scientific – has this psychological requirement in equally high degree. A certain kind of "scientific" scepticism and criticism in our time is nothing but a misplaced compensation of the powerful and deep-rooted superstitious impulses of the collective psyche.

From: "Flying Saucers: A Modern Myth" (1958) (*CW* 10), par. 700

700 . . .The heyday of astrology was not in the benighted Middle Ages but is in the middle of the twentieth century, when even the newspapers do not hesitate to publish the week's horoscope. A thin layer of rootless rationalists read with satisfaction in an encyclopaedia that in the year 1723 Mr. So-and-so had horoscopes cast for his children, and yet do not know that nowadays the horoscope has attained the rank of a visiting card. Those who have even a nodding acquaintance with this background and are in any way affected by it obey the unwritten but strictly observed convention: "One does not speak of such things." They are only whispered about, no one admits them, for no one wants to be considered all that stupid. In reality, however, it is very different.

From: "A Psychological Theory of Types" (1931) (*CW* 6), pars. 916–917, 934

916 The psyche is still a foreign, barely explored country of which we have only indirect knowledge, mediated by conscious functions that are open to almost endless possibilities of deception.

917 This being so, it seems safer to proceed from outside inwards, from the known to the unknown, from the body to the psyche. Thus all attempts at characterology have started from the outside world; astrology, in ancient times, even started from interstellar space in order to arrive at those lines of fate whose beginnings lie in the human heart. To the same class of interpretations from outward signs belong palmistry, Gall's phrenology, Lavater's physiognomy, and – more recently – graphology, Kretschmer's physiological types, and Rorschach's klexographic method. As we can see, there are any number of paths leading from outside inwards, from the physical to the psychic, and it is necessary that research should follow this direction until the elementary

psychic facts are established with sufficient certainty. But once having established these facts, we can reverse the procedure. We can then put the question: What are the bodily correlatives of a given psychic condition? Unfortunately we are not yet far enough advanced to give even an approximate answer. The first requirement is to establish the primary facts of psychic life, and this is far from having been accomplished. Indeed, we have only just begun the work of compiling an inventory of the psyche, not always with great success.

934 This historical retrospect may serve to assure us that our modern attempts to formulate a theory of types are by no means new and unprecedented, even though our scientific conscience does not permit us to revert to these old, intuitive ways of thinking. We must find our own answer to this problem, an answer which satisfies the need of science. And here we meet the chief difficulty of the problem of types – that is, the question of standards or criteria. The astrological criterion was simple and objective: it was given by the constellations at birth. As to the way characterological qualities could be correlated with the zodiacal signs and the planets, this is a question which reaches back into the grey mists of prehistory and remains unanswerable. The Greek classification according to the four physiological temperaments took as its criteria the appearance and behaviour of the individual, exactly as we do today in the case of physiological typology. But where shall we seek our criterion for a psychological theory of types?

From: "Synchronicity: An Acausal Connecting Principle" (1952) (*CW* 8), par. 944

944 The idea of synchronicity and of a self-subsistent meaning, which forms the basis of classical Chinese thinking and of the naïve views of the Middle Ages, seems to us an archaic assumption that ought at all costs to be avoided. Though the West has done everything possible to discard this antiquated hypothesis, it has not quite succeeded. Certain mantic procedures seem to have died out, but astrology, which in our own day has attained an eminence never known before, remains very much alive. Nor has the determinism of a scientific epoch been able to extinguish altogether the persuasive power of the synchronicity principle. For in the last resort it is not so much a question of superstition as of a truth which remained hidden for so long only because it had less to do with the physical side of events than with their psychic aspects. It was modern psychology and parapsychology which proved that causality does not explain a certain class of events and that in this case we have to consider a formal factor, namely synchronicity, as a principle of explanation.

2 Jung's views on astrology

From: "Archaic Man" (1931) (*CW* 10), par. 121

121 Astrology and other methods of divination may certainly be called the science of antiquity.

From: "Richard Wilhelm: In Memoriam" (1930) (*CW* 15), par. 81

81 Its value is obvious enough to the psychologist, since astrology represents the sum of all the psychological knowledge of antiquity.

From: "4 December 1929," *Dream Analysis*

. . . [A]strology was the first form of psychology, which is an extremely young science, dating from the end of the nineteenth century only. Of course, there was a beginning of psychological technique at about the time of the decay of Christianity and the period of the French enlightenment. Voltaire would be one of the first psychologists, and La Rochefoucauld, and Fénelon.[1] But it was not yet science. It consisted more of intellectual aphorisms. It was essentially a critique. One might say that Nietzsche had a psychological approach to his material.

But inasmuch as the human soul has always existed, there must have been at all times an equivalent of psychology. Philosophy would be such an equivalent, but it is merely intellectual, or a metaphysical projection. Religion would be an equivalent also, one could say, yet it is metaphysical concretism. Then there was astrology, which was legitimate up to the seventeenth century and was used by doctors in universities, together with dreams, as aids in diagnosing disease. Palmistry also was so used. I have a little text-book of medicine written by a famous Würzburg professor towards the end of the sixteenth century.[2] It deals with astrology, phrenology, palmistry, and physiognomy, and was especially for the use of doctors. The author was practically the last of the official professors of astrology, which was a sort of psychology but with the qualities and peculiar character of projection. It was our psychology in its oldest form. Our modern science began with astronomy. Instead of saying that a man was led by psychological motives, they formerly said he was led by his stars.

In Schiller's *Wallenstein* there is a conversation between Wallenstein and the astrologer in which the latter says, "In thy heart are the stars of thy fate."[3] That is a translation of astrological into psychological terms. But this was very late, in the beginning of the nineteenth century. Until then, people assumed that it was not psychological motivation but the movement of the stars which caused the personal reactions, as if the direction of their lives was created by the vibrations of the planets. The puzzling thing is that there is really a curious coincidence between astrological and psychological facts, so that one can isolate time from the characteristics of an individual, and also, one can deduce characteristics from a certain time.

From: "Archetypes of the Collective Unconscious" (1934/1954) (*CW* 9i), par. 9

9 "The stars of thine own fate lie in thy breast,"[4] says Seni to Wallenstein – a dictum that should satisfy all astrologers if we knew even a little about the secrets of the heart. But for this, so far, men have had little understanding. Nor would I dare to assert that things are any better today.

From: "To L. Oswald, 8 December 1928," *Letters I*

You are quite right in supposing that I reckon astrology among those movements which, like theosophy, etc., seek to assuage an irrational thirst for knowledge but actually lead it into a sidetrack. Astrology is knocking at the gates of our universities: a Tübingen professor has switched over to astrology and a course on astrology was given at Cardiff University last year.[5] Astrology is not mere superstition but contains some psychological facts (like theosophy) which are of considerable importance. Astrology has actually nothing to do with the stars but is the 5000-year-old psychology of antiquity and the Middle Ages. Unfortunately I cannot explain or prove this to you in a letter.

From: "To Sigmund Freud, 8 May 1911 (254J)," *Freud-Jung Letters*

Occultism is another field we shall have to conquer[6] – with the aid of the libido theory, it seems to me. At the moment I am looking into astrology, which seems indispensable for a proper understanding of mythology. There are strange and wondrous things in these lands of darkness. Please don't worry about my wanderings in these infinitudes. I shall return laden with rich booty for our knowledge of the human psyche. For a while longer I must intoxicate myself on magic perfumes in order to fathom the secrets that lie hidden in the abysses of the unconscious.

From: "6 June 1934," *Nietzsche's Zarathustra I*

On the idea that the moment of creation, whether a work of art or person, carries the uniqueness of the moment in its character:

> This is substantiated in a way by the very awkward fact that the uniqueness of the particular moment in time in which a thing is created is characterized by certain qualities, as is proved by the fact that the horoscope can give the character of an individual.[7] If it were impossible to deduce a human character from a horoscope, then of course that whole idea of the identity of the uniqueness of the self with the uniqueness of the moment when a thing comes into existence would not be valid; but as a matter of fact you can deduce from a horoscope, you can show the character of an individual to an amazing extent.

From: "To Sigmund Freud, 12 June 1911," *Letters I*

My evenings are taken up very largely with astrology. I make horoscopic calculations in order to find a clue to the core of psychological truth. Some remarkable things have turned up which will certainly appear incredible to you. In the case of one lady, the calculation of the positions of the stars at her nativity produced a quite definite character picture, with several biographical details which did not belong to her but to her mother – and the characteristics fitted the mother to a T. The lady suffers from an extraordinary mother complex. I dare say that we shall one day discover in astrology a good deal of knowledge that has been intuitively projected into the heavens. For instance, it appears that the signs of the zodiac are character pictures, in other words libido symbols which depict the typical qualities of the libido at a given moment.

From: "Synchronicity: An Acausal Connecting Principle" (1952) (*CW* 8), pars. 895 and 904

895 . . . According to tradition the ascendent or "horoscopus," together with sun and moon, forms the trinity that determines fate and character.

904 . . . The three main components of the horoscope . . . [are] the ascendent, or rising degree of a zodiacal sign, which characterizes the moment, the moon, which characterizes the day, and the sun, which characterizes the month of birth.

From: "To Robert L. Kroon, 15 November 1958," *Letters II*

Astrology is a naïvely projected psychology in which the different attitudes and temperaments of man are represented as gods and identified with planets and zodiacal constellations. While studying astrology I have applied it to concrete cases many times.

There are remarkable coincidences, e.g., the position of Mars in the zenith in the famous horoscope of Wilhelm II, the so-called "Friedenskaiser." This position is said already in a medieval treatise to mean always a *casus ab alto*, a fall from the height.

From: "To B.V. Raman, 6 September 1947," *Letters I*

Since you want to know my opinion about astrology I can tell you that I've been interested in this particular activity of the human mind for more than 30 years.[8] As I am a psychologist I'm chiefly interested in the particular light the horoscope sheds on certain complications in the character. In cases of difficult psychological diagnosis I usually get a horoscope in order to have a further point of view from an entirely different angle. I must say that I very often found that the astrological data elucidated certain points which I otherwise would have been unable to understand. From such experiences I formed the opinion that astrology is of particular interest to the psychologist, since it contains a sort of psychological experience which we call "projected" – this means that we find the psychological facts as it were in the constellations. This originally gave rise to the idea that these factors derive from the stars, whereas they are merely in a relation of synchronicity with them. I admit that this is a very curious fact which throws a peculiar light on the structure of the human mind.

What I miss in astrological literature is chiefly the statistical method by which certain fundamental facts could be scientifically established.

From: "To André Barbault, 26 May 1954," *Letters II*

In response to the following question: What is your attitude to the positions taken by astrologers who admit the existence of a psychological field from birth on, and by psychoanalysts who explain the aetiology of neuroses in terms of the earliest life experiences?

3. *Attitude to positions taken by astrologers* [etc.]. The first experiences in life owe their specific (pathogenic) effect to environmental influences on the one hand, and on the other to the psychic predisposition, i.e., to heredity, which seems to be expressed in a recognizable way in the horoscope. The latter apparently corresponds to a definite moment in the colloquy of the gods, that is to say the psychic archetypes.

In response to the following question: In the course of analytical treatment, have you observed typical phases of either resistance or progress which would coincide with certain astrological constellations, e.g., transits?

5. I have observed many cases where a well-defined psychological phase, or an analogous event, was accompanied by a transit (particularly when Saturn and Uranus were affected).[9]

In response to the following question: What are your main criticisms of astrologers?

6. *My main criticisms of astrologers*. If I were to venture an opinion in a domain with which I am only very superficially acquainted, I would say that the astrologer does not always consider his statements to be mere possibilities. The interpretation is sometimes too literal and not symbolic enough, also too personal. What the zodiac and the planets represent are not personal traits; they are impersonal and objective facts. Moreover, several "layers of meaning" should be taken into account in interpreting the Houses.

From: "To Upton Sinclair, 25 February 1955," *Letters II*

The ruler of my birth, old Saturnus, slowed down my maturation process to such an extent that I became aware of my own ideas only at the beginning of the second half of my life, i.e., exactly with 36 years.[10] I beg your pardon for using old astrological metaphors. "Astrology" is another of those "random phenomena" wiped off the desk by the idol of the average, which everybody believes to be reality itself while it is a mere abstract. Soon a little book of mine which I have published with the physicist Prof. W. Pauli will come out in English.[11] It is even more shocking than *Job*, but this time to the scientist, not the theologian.

From: "To Robert L. Kroon, 15 November 1958," *Letters II*

The [astrological] experiment [included in "Synchronicity: An Acausal Connecting Principle"] is most suggestive to a versatile mind, unreliable in the hands of the unimaginative, and dangerous in the hands of a fool, as intuitive methods always are. If intelligently used the experiment is useful in cases where it is a matter of an opaque structure. It often provides surprising insights. The most definite limit of the experiment is lack of intelligence and literal-mindedness of the observer. It is an intelligent *aperçu* like the shape of the hand or the expression of the face – things of which a stupid and unimaginative mind can make nothing and from which a superstitious mind draws the wrong conclusions.

Astrological "truths" as statistical results are questionable or even unlikely . . .

The superstitious use (prediction of the future or statement of facts beyond psychological possibilities) is false.

Astrology differs very much from alchemy, as its historical literature consists merely of different methods of casting a horoscope and of interpretation, and not of philosophical texts as is the case in alchemy.

There is no psychological explanation of astrology yet, on account of the fact that the empirical foundation in the sense of a science has not yet been laid. The reason for this is that astrology does not follow the principle of causality, but depends, like all intuitive methods, on acausality. Undoubtedly astrology today is flourishing as never before in the past, but it is still most unsatisfactorily explored despite very frequent use. It is an apt tool only when used intelligently. It is not at all foolproof and when used by a rationalistic and narrow mind it is a definite nuisance.

From: "20 November 1929," *Dream Analysis*

Astrology . . . presents amazing suggestions which would be important if verified, but that has never been done. They ought to work out their researches statistically.

A Frenchman, Paul Flambart, made an attempt to verify certain irrational statements.[12] He has done some scientific research work in connection with the so-called aerial trigon: If the whole zodiac is designed in sections of a circle, then the three points, the months represented by Gemini, Libra, and Aquarius, form the aerial trigon. These are air-signs and air means mind or spirit. The old saying was that one born under these signs was apt to be spiritual or intellectual; that quality was given him at birth. So Flambart took one hundred nativities of men remarkable for their intelligence, and found that, though the birth-dates were everywhere on the circle, there was an extraordinary accumulation on each point of the trigon, so one could say that the majority of such nativities were associated with the corners of the aerial trigon, with intelligence. This is of the nature of a scientific truth, but astrologers are proverbially reluctant to make such researches. They prefer to swim in intuition. To work scientifically is too much trouble; each horoscope would take three hours and one would need thousands of them. Astrology is a dark science, a Hecate science.[13]

From: "27 November 1929," *Dream Analysis*

Now we cannot scientifically prove that our functioning is coincidental with the functioning of the sun and the moon. We observe the similarity between the periodicity of woman and the moon, but they do not coincide, it is merely the same rhythm. So also, metaphorically, we could say that the active principle in man is like the sun.

In astrology we have another consideration, a bit uncanny and therefore particularly hated by scientists. You remember my telling you that birthdates of important men tended to accumulate around the three points of the aerial trigon.[14] If this were confirmed, we might go further and make statistics about suicides, lunacy, epilepsy, etc. That might lead to tangible results, and then astrology would be a very serious consideration. I have suggested to astrologers that we should have more scientific statements. Sometimes people without knowing one's birthdate can make remarkable guesses as to where one's signs are. Twice it has happened to me, once in England and once in America. I was told that my sun was in Leo and my moon in Taurus, Aquarius rising. This made a great impression on me. How the devil did they know? Did they see it in my face? But when one once knows a little about these things, they do not appear so mysterious, and one can easily discover certain characteristics – anatomical, for instance. Or sometimes things come out in a negative way. For instance, I think a certain man is quite certainly not Scorpio, and then I find that he is just that. So I have often heard someone say, "Surely I will not marry that one!" – and then he does. Or a patient will say, "All that you say is true, but this is not true," and then I find it to be the closest truth.

Now that is where astrology is today. It enables certain people to make verifiable diagnoses; and sometimes certain guesses, intuitive shots, are peculiarly adequate, quite astonishing. For instance, I was in touch with an astrologer who knew my birth-date but nothing about my personal life, and I got reports from him occasionally – "on such and such a day you must have felt so and so" – but always in the past, so that I could verify the truth of it. Upon one of these occasions he wrote that on the 31st of March, let us say, two years ago, I must have had the feeling of being reborn, for such and such a planet passed over such and such a place in my nativity. At that time I had in my psychological diary accurate records of everything that happened. So I looked up that date and I had written, "Today I have a most unaccountable feeling of being reborn." I could tell you other irrational facts, certain evidences. But if one once takes it for granted that these things are true, one is confronted with the terribly serious question, what have *we* to do with the stars? Is there any connection between our miserable little everyday condition and these stars, great Jupiter and Saturn travelling through incredible cosmic distances? Moreover, the moment of birth is so accidental, the doctor is late, the midwife is clumsy, the mother is a little too impetuous. How could one assume such a connection? If you put it like that, it remains unanswerable. Astrologers are influenced by theosophy, so they say, "That is very simple, it is just vibration!" One astrologer after reading *Psychology of the Unconscious* wrote me, "Why do you bother about developing a libido concept? It is only vibration." But what is vibration? They say it is light energy, perhaps electricity, they are not quite informed. At all events the vibrations that could influence us have never been seen, so it remains just a word.

Now I will give you another wrinkle which is quite horrible. I hope you will be able to follow. You see, the astrologer says one was born when the sun was in such and such a degree of Libra, and the moon in such and such a degree of Scorpio, etc., and he bases the reading of one's horoscope entirely upon that position of the planets. For instance, he says, "Today Jupiter is passing over its own place in your nativity, therefore it is in the same degree in which it was at the moment of your birth." You take your telescope and you find the zodiacal constellation and Jupiter is not there at all! Then again the astrologer will inform you that the spring equinox is in zero degrees Aries and you naturally expect the sun to be rising at six o'clock in the morning, precisely at zero degrees Aries. But you find something entirely different, it is perhaps at 28 degrees Pisces. In the spring equinox the sun doesn't rise in Aries. You look it up in history and find that in 100 B.C. the sun[15] left the constellation of Aries and went into Pisces. Then the astrologer royal of Ptolemy said, "Now, we can't let that happen, we will fix that fact for always as it was in 2000 B.C. when the sun did the same thing – left Taurus and crossed over into Aries." You see, the spring-point moves back, there is a regression. That is the so-called precession of the equinoxes, moving 55 seconds each year, going back from the spring signs into the winter signs. Now this astronomer stopped that. He simply made it consistent. Otherwise the clocks would all go wrong each year by 55 seconds. So since 100 B.C. (Academy of Alexandria) we call the spring-point zero degrees Aries. We have kept our astronomical faith, but the heavens have moved on and we are simply out of time with the universe. If a man in 2000 B.C. said one was born in 25 degrees Sagittarius, it was true, but a hundred years later it was not quite true for it has already moved on 100 x 55 seconds and the horoscope is no longer exact. An astrologer perhaps says, "No wonder you have such a temperament, or such a royal gesture, because your sun is in the beginning of Leo; when the sun looked at you out of its own house at the moment of your nativity, naturally you were made into a little lion." But it *didn't* look out at you from its own house,[16] for in reality it was in Gemini. Nevertheless you can prove that the man whose sun is said to be in Taurus gets the bull neck, or the woman in Libra gets the qualities of the sun from the heights of Libra, or the one whose sun is in Sagittarius has intuition, and you are quite right. Yet the sun was not in those positions. So that destroys any hope of vibration! I told you of the statistics connected with the aerial trigon, and yet those men of superior mentality were not born when the sun was in those signs. It is an extraordinary puzzle, and there are astrologers who don't even know it; they are theosophists and they say, "It is quite easy, it is just vibrations." But, you see, when it comes to our Western mind, we must think. How then do we account for the fact that our peculiar characteristics can be explained by our planets? One says, "Venus is very clearly your sign."[17] How do you explain that *as if* when it is not?

NOTES

1 François de La Rochefoucauld (1613–80), whose *Réflexions et maximes morales* was first published in 1665. François de Salignac de la Mothe Fénelon (1651–1715), churchman and theologian, wrote mystical and quietest works.

2 Rodolphus Goclenius, *Uranuscopiae, chiroscopiae, metaposcopiae et ophthalmascopiae contemplatio* (Frankfurt, 1608), cited in Jung's foreword to Julius Spier, *The Hands of Children* (London, 1944; and edn., 1955); in CW 18, par. 1818.

3 Friedrich von Schiller (1759–1805), *Wallenstein* (1798–99), which is divided into three separate dramas; the quotation is from the second, *Die Piccolomini*, II, 6. Cited in CW 5, par. 102, n. 52 (as in 1912 edn.).

4 [Schiller, *Piccolomini,* II, 6. – EDITORS.]

5 Evening lectures by J.M. Thorburn, B.Sc., M.A., then lecturer in philosophy. The course continued for several years. Cf. Thorburn, 6 Feb. 52 [in *Letters II*]

6 While in Munich, Freud and Jung had discussed Ferenczi's experiences (see above, 158 F n. 8). After he got this letter, Freud wrote to Ferenczi: "Jung writes to me that we must conquer the field of occultism and asks for my agreeing to his leading a crusade. . . . I can see that you two are not to be held back. At least go forward in collaboration with each other; it is a dangerous expedition and I cannot accompany you." (11 May 11; see Jones, III, p. 415/387.) See also below, 293 F n. 6.

7 Jung expressed varying opinions about astrology. See below 13 Feb 1935, for a relatively negative account, but for a much more positive view of astrological phenomena treated not causally but synchronistically, see CW 8, pars. 872–915.

8 Cf. Freud, 12 June 11.

9 [KLG: Jung's specific reference to Saturn and Uranus might have been elicited by Barbault's question ("have you observed typical phases of either resistance or progress . . . ?"), since Saturn has been observed to correlate with the experience of resistance and Uranus with progress and breakthroughs. It is significant that Jung includes mention of Uranus here, for it demonstrates that his use and understanding of astrology was not limited to the seven traditional "planets" recognized in ancient astrology (the sun through Saturn). We do not know if Jung also used Neptune (discovered in 1846) or Pluto (discovered in 1930) in his astrological interpretations.]

10 The original version of *Symbols of Transformation* appeared in 1911/1912 and marked the beginning of the break with Freud. The onset of the second half of life often marks a turning-point. Cf. "The Stages of Life," CW 8, par. 773. [KLG: In citing "Saturnus" as the "ruler of his birth," Jung is presumably referring to the fact that his Ascendant or rising sign, as it is also known, is Aquarius. The ancient ruler of Aquarius is the planet Saturn. The "ruler" or "ruling planet" of one's birth chart is deemed to be the planet associated with the sign on the Ascendant. Jung also has Saturn in the first house.]

11 *The Interpretation of Nature and the Psyche* (1955). Jung's part, the essay on synchronicity, is in CW 8.

12 Flambart's researches were published in his *Preuves et bases de l'astrologie scientifique* (Paris, 1921), pp. 79ff. Cf. "Synchronicity: An Acausal Connecting Principle," CW 8, par, 869, n. 64.
13 [KLG: Jung had earlier compared lunar consciousness to the goddess Hecate. For a further discussion of Flambart's research, see Jung, *Visions*, pp. 1329–1330.]
14 Gemini, Libra, and Aquarius.
15 [KLG: i.e., the sun's position at the spring equinox.]
16 [KLG: Jung appears to be using the term *house* here in reference to what astrologers would call *signs*.]
17 [KLG: Here Jung uses the word *sign* when he is actually referring to a planet – Venus, in this case.]

3 Planets and gods

Astrology as archetypal

From: "To André Barbault, 26 May 1954," *Letters II*

In response to the following question: What connections do you see between astrology and psychology?
1. *The connections between astrology and psychology.* There are many instances of striking analogies between astrological constellations and psychological events or between the horoscope and the characterological disposition. It is even possible to predict to a certain extent the psychic effect of a transit. For example [. . .].[1] One may expect with a fair degree of probability that a given well-defined psychological situation will be accompanied by an analogous astrological configuration. Astrology, like the collective unconscious with which psychology is concerned, consists of symbolic configurations: the "planets" are the gods, symbols of the powers of the unconscious.

In response to the following question: What orientation of astrological thought do you consider desirable?
7. Obviously astrology has much to offer psychology, but what the latter can offer its elder sister is less evident. So far as I can judge, it would seem to me advantageous for astrology to take the existence of psychology into account, above all the psychology of the personality and the unconscious. I am almost sure that something could be learnt from its symbolic method of interpretation; for that has to do with the interpretation of the archetypes (the gods) and their mutual relations, the common concern of both arts. The psychology of the unconscious is particularly concerned with archetypal symbolism.

From: "To Karl Schmid, 26 January 1957," *Letters II*

I found your differential definition of the historical and psychological approach [of Jung's work, treated in Schmid's rectoral address of 1957, entitled "Recent Aspects of Spiritual History"] most illuminating, and I can only agree with what you say. I must add, however, that this applies only to a psychology which is still exclusively concerned with culture-promoting personalities and is therefore restricted to the sphere of individual phenomena. This is an aspect of psychology which affords us the greatest insight and is at the same time the unavoidable path leading down to the deeper levels from which those biological masterpieces we call personalities are produced. At these greater depths more general laws become discernible and more comprehensive figures stand out which eliminate the divisive factor of individual development and give psychology a homogeneity or inner coherence which raises it to the rank of a biological science.

By these deeper levels I mean the determining archetypes which are supradordinate to, or underlie, individual development and presumably are responsible for the supreme meaning of individual life. Seen from this level, not only is psychological experience a continuum, but the psychological approach also enables us to gain some knowledge of the inner connection between historical events. The archetypes have a life of their own which extends through the centuries and gives the aeons their peculiar stamp. Perhaps I might draw your attention to my historical contribution in *Aion*, where I have attempted to outline the evolutionary history of the Anthropos, which begins with the earliest Egyptian records. The material I have presented there may serve to illustrate these remarks of mine.

From: *Mysterium Coniunctionis* (1955–1956) (*CW* 14), pars. 501–502, 504

501 The starting point for our explanation is that the king is essentially synonymous with the sun and that the sun represents the daylight of the psyche, consciousness, which as the faithful companion of the sun's journey rises daily from the ocean of sleep and dream, and sinks into it again at evening. Just as in the round-dance of the planets, and in the star-strewn spaces of the sky, the sun journeys along as a solitary figure, like any other one of the planetary archons, so consciousness, which refers everything to its own ego as the centre of the universe, is only one among the archetypes of the unconscious. . . . This is what the complex of consciousness would look like if it could be viewed from one of the other planets, as we view the sun from the earth. The subjective ego-personality, i.e., consciousness and its contents, is indeed seen in its various aspects by an unconscious observer, or rather by an observer placed in the "outer space" of the unconscious. That this is so is proved by dreams, in which the conscious personality, the ego of the dreamer, is seen from a standpoint that is "toto coelo" different from that of the conscious mind. Such a phenomenon could not occur at all unless there were in the unconscious other standpoints opposing or competing with ego-consciousness. These relationships are aptly expressed by the planet simile. The king represents ego-consciousness, the subject of all subjects, as an object. His fate in mythology portrays the rising and setting of this most glorious and most divine of all the phenomena of creation, without which the world would not exist as an object. For everything that is only is because it is directly or indirectly known, and moreover this "known-ness" is sometimes represented in a way which the subject himself does not know, just as if he were being observed from another planet, now with benevolent and now with sardonic gaze.

502 This far from simple situation derives partly from the fact that the ego has the paradoxical quality of being both the subject and the object of its own knowledge, and partly from the fact that the psyche is not a unity but a "constellation" consisting of other luminaries besides the sun. The ego-complex is not the only complex in the psyche.[2]

504 Pitilessly it is seen from another planet that the king is growing old, even before he sees it himself: ruling ideas, the "dominants," change, and the change, undetected by consciousness, is mirrored only in dreams. King Sol, as the archetype of consciousness, voyages through the world of the unconscious, one of its multitudinous figures which may one day be capable of consciousness too. These lesser lights are, on the old view, identical with the planetary correspondences in the psyche which were postulated by astrology. When, therefore, an alchemist conjured up the spirit of Saturn as his familiar, this was an attempt to bring to consciousness a standpoint outside the ego, involving a relativization of the ego and its contents. The intervention of the planetary spirit was besought as an aid. When the king grows old and needs renewing, a kind of planetary bath is instituted – a bath into which all the planets pour their "influences."[3] This expresses the idea that the dominant, grown feeble with age, needs the support and influence of those subsidiary lights to fortify and renew it. It is, as it were, dissolved in the substance of the other planetary archetypes and then put together again. Through this process of melting and recasting there is formed a new amalgam of a more comprehensive nature, which has taken into itself the influences of the other planets or metals.[4]

From: "8 February 1939," *Nietzsche's Zarathustra II*

If you simply destroy it, you create a ghost of the old value and you are possessed by that thing. So when we destroyed Christianity – of course it just happened that it was destroyed, to a great extent it destroyed itself – the ghost of Christianity was left, and we are now possessed. The Christian sacrifice is now produced in actuality, in the flesh. And so it was when the people threw away the old gods. They then had the conflict of their emotions in themselves, and had to assume an attitude which would rescue them from those battles and intrigues the gods were always having. Therefore, these savior religions arose, which saved the people from the gods in themselves. They were then planetary gods; it was the astrological influence, the continuous fear of *heimarmene*,[5] all that compulsion of the bad stars. The soul was burdened with the influence of the bad stars; that was the so-called handwriting which was imprinted on the soul when it descended to earth through the spheres of the planets. And that had to be washed off by a savior; people had to be saved from the inexorable law of the old gods. The old gods were not exactly destroyed by Christianity: they died before Christ came. Therefore Augustus was obliged to regress to old Latin rites and ceremonies in order to do something toward restoring the old religion which was already giving out. It simply became obsolete, and then already people were filled with what the gods had been before. The gods became integrated in them.

For as soon as you cannot call an affect by a certain name – for instance, Cupid – it is in yourself. If you cannot say it is somewhere in space, in the planet Mars perhaps, it must be in yourself, and cannot be anywhere else. That causes a psychological disorder. We are apparently pretty far from these old facts because we don't realize the power of the archetypes; and we don't realize the mentality of a time when there were many gods, don't know what it would be like to be surrounded by divine, superior, demoniacal powers. We have the poetic conception, but that is nothing like the reality. So we don't know what it means to have lived in a time when these old gods descended upon man, when they became subjective factors, immediate magic.

From: "8 June 1932," *Visions II*

That individual relationship to the stars is a thought as old as mankind. The primitives believed that the falling stars were really souls descending from heaven to embody themselves in human bodies. They also believed that man was a fiery spark. Even those much quoted central Australian aborigines believe that. They are like paleolithic men, they have not yet invented clothes, they never hunt animals for their furs because they never thought of it, in spite of the fact that at times, towards morning, the temperature descends below zero; then they stand round fires and wait until the sun comes back to life. Now these people believe that the soul of man consists of a little fiery spark, and when such a spark – they are very swift and cunning – is flying about and happens to enter the womb of a woman, she immediately becomes pregnant. These fiery sparks, which they called by the Swiss-sounding expression *maiaurli*, are supposed to be the souls of ancestors and to live in particular rocks or trees, and any woman who passes must use special charms in order to ward off the *maiaurli* that jump out to impregnate her – they are always looking for a womb to enter. There was a similar idea in certain Gnostic systems: they thought that the soul was a fiery spark which fell down into the sea, or the creative womb, and then became a human soul, building a body round itself. It is a very interesting idea.

Later on, the stars were identified with the gods, who were supposed to be like human beings although at the same time they were stars; the planets Jupiter, Venus, Mercury, and so on were gods but they were also planets. That they could be both comes from the fact that those old gods were temperaments or constituents in the character of human beings. For instance, Mars personifies rage, a martial temperament is the warlike temperament, and in a horoscope Mars means a martial constituent. And a jovial temperament is like an exceedingly blue sky, like Jove benevolently smiling, and Jove – or Jupiter – in an important position in a horoscope indicates a jovial character. Venus means love or certain aspects of sex. Mercury is intellect. And Saturn personifies gloom and all those manifestations which originate in the state of gloom or cause gloom; the Tempter and the Purifier are two of Saturn's titles.

Now these character constituents in fairly primitive man are very often autonomous – a person's temperament may be autonomous, for instance. He may be pathologically jovial, jovial to such an extent that it is no longer a virtue but a vice. Or he may be good in a most vicious way, so good that he destroys himself and everyone round him; being a little too good is most dangerous for one's surroundings. And it is the same with the so-called malefic planets, Mars and Saturn. You see, the personification of those planets comes from the projection of such autonomous complexes and therefore they have been called gods. When a woman says: "But I feel so and so about the matter," it is most decisive, as you know, so one could call it a god. As a man says: "It is not according to my principle." I say: "Damn your principle, the situation is so-and-so." But his principle is a god to him, he would die rather than give up his most foolish principle, and this is simply based upon a fact of temperament, a deep-rooted emotional factor. Those temperamental qualities were quite rightly called gods and therefore projected. So here also is a link between man and the stars, his laws are found to be identical with the stars.

NOTES

1 [Here the astrological symbols which Jung put in by hand are missing in the file and cannot be restored. – EDITORS.]
2 The primitive assertion that the individual has a plurality of souls is in agreement with our findings. Cf. Tylor, *Primitive Culture*, I, pp. 391ff.; Schultze, *Psychologie der Naturvölker*, p. 268; Crawley, *The Idea of the Soul*, pp. 235ff; and Frazer, *Taboo and the Perils of the Soul*, pp. 27 and 80, and *Balder the Beautiful*, II, pp. 221ff.
3 Cf. *Psychology and Alchemy*, figs. 27, 57, 257.
4 Ibid., fig. 149. [KLG: This passage is noteworthy for, among other things, Jung coining the term *planetary archetype*.]
5 *Heimarmene*: destiny in the Poimandres vision.

Part II

Astrological symbolism in Jung's writings

INTRODUCTION

The three chapters that comprise this section illustrate how astrology was one of the rich symbolic systems from which Jung would draw in his amplifications of psychological material, whether personal or collective. "Amplificatory interpretation," writes Murray Stein, "as a therapeutic technique serves to save, or to restore, meaning and to ground individual experience in archetypal patterns."[1] Connecting the personal and archetypal is essential in meaning-making and in personal myth because then the individual is connected to the river of life that extends beyond the personal into what is both deeply human and transpersonal at the same time.

Chapter 4 is a collection of many passages from Jung's writings that display the analogical richness of astrological symbolism in his thought, illustrating his amplificatory process, which was in service to opening up or deepening the topic at hand. Since astrology was not a subject that Jung took up in the same in-depth way as alchemy, the reader will encounter pockets of insight organized around certain symbols rather than a comprehensive and equal exploration of zodiacal symbols or the planets. It may be noted that Jung almost exclusively focused on the traditional planets known to antiquity; therefore, there is no material related to what are called the "transpersonal" or collective planets: Uranus, Neptune, and Pluto. This chapter may be best engaged by dipping in and out, like a bird hovering over the surface of the sea waiting for her catch. Jung's insights are distinct and episodic, not systematized.

The astrological parallels to psychology come in succinct phrases. Jung wrote, "The psychic life-force, the libido, symbolizes itself in the sun or personifies itself in figures of heroes with solar attributes."[2] As in this example, in the mythological nature of the psyche, the goddesses and gods, heroes, dramatic plots, and themes are metaphors of the psyche's activity. Myths are metaphoric descriptions of the psyche's processes and reveal the unconscious. So we can turn to myth, literature, and art in order to access and better understand the psyche and our inner processes. The relevance of mytho-astrological research in psychological astrology is based on this primary principle of Jung's psychology.

Chapter 5 contains Jung's writing on the ancient Stoic idea of *heimarmene*, "the dependence of character and destiny on certain moments in time,"[3] which was understood to be illustrated by one's horoscope. One could be freed from *heimarmene*, which Jung called an "inborn bill of debt to fate,"[4] by journeying through the planetary houses as illustrated in alchemical texts. In psychological terms this journey can be understood as a widening of consciousness, which is what occurs in the process of individuation.

Chapter 6, on astrology and medicine, is devoted to Jung's interest in the ideas of Paracelsus, the sixteenth-century Swiss physician, alchemist, astrologer, and natural philosopher. For Paracelsus, astrology was a source of critical knowledge for the physician, for without this knowledge one was not able to interpret the inner heaven or "star of the body"[5] correctly and thus effect healing for the patient. Jung writes,

> There can be no doubt that Paracelsus was influenced by the Hermetic idea of "heaven above, heaven below." In his conception of the inner heaven he glimpsed an eternal primordial image, which was implanted in him and in all men, and recurs at all times and places. "In every human being," he says, "there is a special heaven, whole and unbroken."[6]

Safron Rossi

NOTES

1 Stein, *Jung's Treatment of Christianity*, p. 154.
2 Jung, *Symbols of Transformation* (*CW* 5), p. 202, par. 297.
3 Jung, "Introduction to the Religious and Psychological Problems of Alchemy" (1944), in *Psychology and Alchemy* (*CW* 12), p. 34, par. 40.
4 Jung, *Mysterium Coniunctionis* (*CW* 14), p. 225, par. 299.
5 Jung, "Paracelsus the Physician" (1942), in *Spirit in Man, Art and Literature* (*CW* 15), p. 16, par. 22.
6 Ibid., pp. 21–22, par. 31.

BIBLIOGRAPHY

Jung, Carl Gustav. "Introduction to the Religious and Psychological Problems of Alchemy." 1944. In *Psychology and Alchemy*, 1–37. 2nd Edition. Vol. 12 of *The Collected Works of C. G. Jung*. Translated by R.F.C. Hull. Princeton, NJ: Princeton University Press, 1968.

———. *Mysterium Coniunctionis*. 2nd Edition. 1955–1956. Vol. 14 of *The Collected Works of C. G. Jung*. Translated by R.F.C. Hull. Princeton: Princeton University Press, 1989.

———. "Paracelsus the Physician." 1941. In *The Spirit in Man, Art, and Literature*, 13–30. Vol. 15 of *The Collected Works of C. G. Jung*. Translated by R.F.C. Hull. Reprint, Princeton, NJ: Princeton University Press, 1966/1971.

———. *Symbols of Transformation*. 2nd Edition. Vol. 5 of *The Collected Works of C. G. Jung*. Translated by R.F.C. Hull. Princeton, NJ: Princeton University Press, 1967.

Stein, Murray. *Jung's Treatment of Christianity*. Wilmette, IL: Chiron Publications, 1986.

4 Planetary and zodiacal symbolism

THE SIGNS OF THE ZODIAC

From: "The Fish in Alchemy" (1951) (*CW* 9ii), par. 230

230 The zodia are important determinants in the horoscope, modifying the influence of the planets that have moved into them, or, even if there are no planets, giving the individual houses a special character. In the present instance the Fishes would characterize the ascendent, the moment of the world's birth.[1]

From: "9 October 1929," *Dream Analysis*

. . . The way of the individual . . . is symbolized by the serpentine way of the sun through the Zodiac, and the Zodiacal serpent is Christ, who said "I am the way."[2] He is the serpent, so in the early Christian church he is the sun, and the signs of the Zodiac, the apostles, are the twelve months of the year.

From: "11 December 1929," *Dream Analysis*

Christ is represented as a great serpent who carries twelve signs on his back, meaning the twelve signs of the zodiac and also the twelve apostles. He says, "I am the vine, ye are the branches."[3] He is the zodiacal serpent and they are the manifestations of the months.

From: "27 November 1929," *Dream Analysis*

This is the way the signs go:

Aquarius	Five thousand years ago, 3000 B.C. when the sun was in winter, there were floods of rain. Aquarius walked about pouring his water out right and left.
Pisces	Then the fish swam in the floods.
Aries	The little ram, the time of little shoots and buds.
Taurus	The Bull, the great push of nature.

Gemini The fertility of man. One seldom does better than twins.

Cancer A drawback, the summer solstice. The crab walking backward when the sun descends again.

Leo After the first inkling of solstice it dawns on man that the sun will really be going, from the 22nd of July till the 21st of August, just when all is most glowing.

Virgo When man is roaring like a lion there is nothing better to tame him than a virgin. She will cut the hair of the lion and make it short, like Samson and Delilah. It is not nice, the whole symbolism is somewhat obscene. But at that time of the year, the 15th of September in the Egyptian calendar, the left eye of the goddess is prepared to receive the god Ra, who is to walk into it.[4] The eye is a womb symbol. The female element takes the lead. The god enters the womb of darkness, Yang is under Yin. Woman is on top.

Libra The balance after the virgin has done her job.

Scorpion The fatal self-sacrifice of the sun. The sun gets cornered by the virgin and when the forces are equal (Libra), the sun commits suicide, and then comes a clear descent into the mother. There is a legend that when the scorpion is surrounded by fire it kills itself.

Sagittarius The death of the sun. Death is a sort of river or gap. There is a life beyond, but one is here on this bank of the river and cannot get there. Then comes the legend of the centaur, a good archer, who with his bow can send an arrow across. It is a means of communication. The archer Sagittarius with the arrow of intuition foresees new birth out of the unconscious. This is the advent season, when ghosts begin to walk again, when the unconscious begins to manifest itself.

Capricorn The goat-fish. (This was the imperial sign on the coat-of-arms of Augustus Caesar.) After the dead man contained in the sea, the next sign is this goat-fish. He is half fish and half goat, meaning that at first, as the fish, he is deep down in the sea, out of sight in the unconscious. Then he rises to the surface and climbs to the highest peaks and valleys. This is the sun, the promise of the new year, so some astrologers call the time after Christmas the "Promise of the Year." It is the time of the birth of Mithras, the birth of Christ, the birth of the new light, the whole hope of the coming year. People born then have strong hearts. They are ambitious, but they have to work hard to achieve their ends.

But the new year has to be generated. The sun generates the year in Aquarius. Aquarius pours out the waters of fecundity. He is also shown as a phallic god like Priapus. After the generating water the Fishes come again, and so on around.

This is how the Zodiac came into existence. It is really a seasonal cycle with particular qualities of climate – winter, spring, summer, autumn, qualified by the fantasies and metaphorical imagination of the human mind. And so man has called the stars that are synchronous with the seasons by names expressing the qualities of each particular season. The active principle is obviously the time and not at all the stars, they are merely incidental. If, at the time when astrology came into conscious existence, other constellations had been in the heavens, we would have had different groups of stars but they would have been called a lion or a man carrying a water-jug just the same. They are not at all like their names, even the most striking constellations. It is a tremendous strain for the imagination.

From: "A Study in the Process of Individuation" (1934/50) (*CW* 9i), pars. 604–607

Dr. Jung is discussing the symbolism of one mandala from a series created by a patient.

604 In Picture 10, begun in Zurich but only completed when Miss X again visited her motherland, we find the same division as before into above and below. The "soul-flower"[5] in the centre is the same, but it is surrounded on all sides by a dark blue night sky, in which we see the four phases of the moon, the new moon coinciding with the world of darkness below. The three birds have become two. Their plumage has darkened, but on the other

Figure 4.1 Mandala painting

Source: Reproduced from Jung's *Collected Works*, Vol. 9i.

hand the goat has turned into two semi-human creatures with horns and light faces, and only two of the four snakes remain. A notable innovation is the appearance of two *crabs* in the lower, chthonic hemisphere that also represents the body. The crab has essentially the same meaning as the astrological sign Cancer.[6] Unfortunately Miss X gave no context here. In such cases it is usually worth investigating what use has been made in the past of the object in question. In earlier, prescientific ages hardly any distinction was drawn between long-tailed crabs (*Macrura*, crayfish) and short-tailed crabs (*Brachyura*). As a zodiacal sign Cancer signifies *resurrection*, because the crab sheds its shell.[7] The ancients had in mind chiefly *Pagurus bernhardus*, the hermit crab. It hides in its shell and cannot be attacked. Therefore it signifies *caution* and *foresight, knowledge of coming events*.[8] It "depends on the moon, and waxes with it."[9] It is worth noting that the crab appears just in the mandala in which we see the phases of the moon for the first time. Astrologically, Cancer is the house of the moon. Because of its backwards and sideways movement, it plays the role of an unlucky animal in superstition and colloquial speech ("crabbed," "catch a crab," etc.). Since ancient times cancer (*καρκίνος*) has been the name for a malignant tumour of the glands. Cancer is the zodiacal sign in which the sun begins to retreat, when the days grow shorter. Pseudo-Kallisthenes relates that crabs dragged Alexander's ships down into the sea.[10] "Karkinos" was the name of the crab that bit Heracles in the foot in his fight with the Lernaean monster. In gratitude, Hera set her accomplice among the stars.[11]

605 In astrology, Cancer is a feminine and watery sign,[12] and the summer solstice takes place in it. In the *melothesiae*[13] it is correlated with the *breast*. It rules over the *Western sea.* In Propertius it makes a sinister appearance: "Octipedis Cancri terga sinistra time" (Fear thou the ill-omened back of the eight-footed crab).[14] De Gubernatis says: "The crab . . . causes now the death of the solar hero and now that of the monster."[15] The *Panchatantra* (V, 2) relates how a crab, which the mother gave to her son as apotropaic magic, saved his life by killing a black snake.[16] As De Gubernatis thinks, the crab stands now for the sun and now for the moon,[17] according to whether it goes forwards or backwards.

606 Miss X was born in the first degrees of Cancer (actually about 3°). She knew her horoscope and was well aware of the significance of the moment of birth; that is, she realized that the degree of the rising sign (the ascendent) conditions the individuality of the horoscope. Since she obviously guessed the horoscope's affinity with the mandala, she introduced her individual sign into the painting that was meant to express her psychic self.[18]

607 The essential conclusion to be drawn from Picture 10 is that the dualities which run through it are always inwardly balanced, so that they lose their sharpness and incompatibility. As Multatuli says: "Nothing is quite true, and even that is not quite true." But this loss of strength is counterbalanced by the unity of the centre, where the lamp shines, sending out coloured rays to the eight points of the compass.[19]

From: "4 February 1931," *Visions I*

Dr. Jung: That story exactly expresses what the primitives think about hair, so here it would be a symbol which contains a lot of mana. The same meaning is also to be found in the story of Samson and Delilah: when she cuts his hair, he loses all his strength. The name Samson comes from *Shemsh* which means sun-man or little sun, after the old Canaanite god Shemsh; so curtailing the rays of the sun means weakening the sun. There is an astrological interpretation of Delilah as the sign of Virgo, in which the sun loses its power, Virgo being followed by the autumnal equinox when the sun is definitely becoming weaker; the sun then loses its hair, its rays. So the hair is understood to be an emanation of the head, having to do with the mind and the most spiritual as well as magical forces.

From: "2 December 1931," *Visions I*

Dr. Jung: Ah, you mean the *taurabolia*. Yes, that is right. And there is an old astrological connection between the bull and the mother. The syncretistic cults of that era were based very largely upon astrological facts. On the Mithraic altar-stones, for instance, are the sun and the moon and the signs of the zodiac, it is evident that they are meant as astrological symbols. In the Christian cult it was more hidden, but the philosophical systems of the time were filled with astrological connotations. The bull in astrology is an earthly sign, it is the *domicilium Veneris*.[20] The cult of Attis belongs to the great group of mother cults, Attis is very much the son of the Great Mother; so the bull is very much connected with the cult of the Magna Mater.

From: "The Swiss Line in the European Spectrum" (1928) (*CW* 10), par. 914

914 Our loveliest mountain, which dominates Switzerland far and wide, is called the Jungfrau – the "Virgin." The Virgin Mary is the female patron saint of the Swiss. Of her Tertullian says: ". . . that virgin earth, not yet watered by the rains," and Augustine: "Truth has arisen from the earth, because Christ is born of a virgin." These are living reminders that the virgin mother is the earth. From olden times the astrological sign for Switzerland was either Virgo or Taurus; both are earth-signs, a sure indication that the earthy character of the Swiss had not escaped the old astrologers. From the earth-boundness of the Swiss come all their bad as well as their good qualities: their down-to-earthness, their limited outlook, their non-spirituality, their parsimony, stolidity, stubbornness, dislike of foreigners, mistrustfulness, as well as that awful *Schwizerdütsch* and their refusal to be bothered, or to put it in political terms, their neutrality.

From: "To Karl Schmid, 25 February 1958," *Letters II*

Sitting in the central mussel-shell, we [the Swiss] are the "sons of the mother." Hence the old astrological tradition says that our zodiacal sign is Virgo (♍). However, there is no unanimity on this score, since the other version says that our sign is Taurus (♉). It is a virile, creative sign, but *earthly* like Virgo. This ancient psychological insight expresses the fact that what is enclosed in the mother is a germinating seed that will one day burst through. . . . The stolidity, inaccessibility, obstinacy, and whatever else of the kind the Swiss are accused of are all marks of the feminine element Virgo. The union of ♂ and ♀ alludes to the *principium individuationis* as a supreme union of opposites . . .[21]

From: "A Study in the Process of Individuation" (1934/50) (*CW* 9i), par. 552

552 I would hazard that we have to do here with a *tetrameria* (as in Greek alchemy), a transformation process divided into four stages[22] of three parts each, analogous to the twelve transformations of the zodiac and its division into four. As not infrequently happens, the number 12 would then have a not merely individual significance (as the patient's birth number, for instance), but a time-conditioned one too, since the present aeon of the Fishes is drawing to its end and is at the same time the twelfth house of the zodiac.[23]

From: *Symbols of Transformation* (1912/52) (*CW* 5), pars. 423–425, 662

423 Horses also signify fire and light, like the fiery horses of Helios. Hector's horses were called Xanthos (yellow, glaring), Podargos (swift-footed), Lampos (shining), and Aithon (burning). Siegfried leaps over the wall of fire on the thunder-horse Grani, who was sired by Sleipnir and was the only one capable of taking the fiery hedge.[24] There is a distinct fire symbolism in the mystic quadriga mentioned by Dio Chrysostom:[25] the highest god always drives his chariot round in a circle. The chariot is drawn by four horses, and the outside horse moves very quickly. He has a shining coat, bearing on it the signs of the zodiac and the constellations.[26] The second horse goes more slowly and is illuminated on one side only. The third horse is slower still, and the fourth horse runs round himself. Once, however, the outside horse set the mane of the second horse on fire with his fiery breath, and the third horse drenched the fourth with streams of sweat. Then the horses dissolve and merge with the substance of the strongest and most fiery, which now becomes the charioteer. The horses represent the four elements. The catastrophe signifies world conflagration and the deluge, after which the division of God into Many ceases, and the divine One is restored.[27] There can be no doubt that the quadriga is meant as an astronomical symbol of Time. We saw in Part I that the Stoic conception of fate is a fire-symbol, so it is a logical continuation of this idea when the closely related conception of time exhibits the same libido symbolism.

424 The Brihadaranyaka Upanishad says:

> Dawn is the head of the sacrificial horse, the sun his eye, the wind his breath, the universal fire his open mouth. The year is the body of the

> sacrificial horse. The sky is his back, the air his belly, the earth the under-part of his belly. The poles are his flanks, the intermediate poles his ribs, the seasons his limbs, the months and half-months his joints, days and nights his feet, the stars his bones, the clouds his flesh. Sand is the food in his stomach, rivers are his entrails. His liver and lungs are the mountains; plants and trees, his hair. The rising sun is his forepart, the setting sun his hindpart. . . . The ocean is his kinsman, the sea his cradle.[28]

425 Here the horse is undoubtedly conceived as a time-symbol, besides being the whole world. In the Mithraic religion we meet with a strange god, Aion (pl. XLIV), also called Chronos or *deus leontocephalus* because he is conventionally represented as a lion-headed human figure. He stands in a rigid attitude, wrapped in the coils of a serpent whose head juts forward over the head of the lion. In each hand he holds a key, on his breast is a thunderbolt, on his back are the four wings of the wind, and on his body are the signs of the zodiac. His attributes are a cock and implements. In the Carolingian Utrecht Psalter, which was based on classical models, Aion is shown as a naked man bearing in his hand a snake.[29] As the name indicates, he is a time-symbol, and is composed entirely of libido-images. The lion, the zodiacal sign for the torrid heat of summer,[30] is the symbol of *concupiscentia effrenata*, "frenzied desire." ("My soul roars with the voice of a hungry lion," says Mechthild of Magdeburg.) In the Mithraic mysteries the snake is often shown as the antagonist of the lion, in accordance with the myth of the sun's fight with the dragon. In the Egyptian Book of the Dead, Tum is addressed as a tom-cat, because in that form he fought the Apophis-serpent. To be "entwined" or embraced is the same as to be "devoured," which as we saw means entering into the mother's womb. Time is thus defined by the rising and setting sun, by the death and renewal of libido, the dawning and extinction of consciousness. The attribute of the cock again points to time, and the implements to creation through time (Bergson's "durée créatrice"). Oromazdes (Ahura-Mazda) and Ahriman came into being through *Zrwan akarana*, "infinitely long duration." So time, this empty and purely formal concept, is expressed in the mysteries through transformations of the creative force, libido, just as time in physics is identical with the flow of the energic process. Macrobius remarks: "By the lion's head the present time is indicated . . . because its condition is strong and fervent."[31] Philo Judaeus evidently knows better:

> Time is regarded as a god by evil men who wish to hide the Essential Being. . . . Vicious men think that Time is the cause of the world, but the wise and good think it is God.[32]

662 There is a similar instinct-sacrificing symbolism in the Mithraic religion, where the essential portions of the mystery consisted in the catching and subduing of the bull. A parallel figure to Mithras is the Original Man, Gayomart. He was created together with his ox, and the two lived in a state of bliss for six thousand years. But when the world entered the aeon of Libra (the seventh

zodiacal sign), the evil principle broke loose. In astrology, Libra is known as the "Positive House" of Venus, so the evil principle came under the dominion of the goddess of love, who personifies the erotic aspect of the mother. Since this aspect, as we have seen, is psychologically extremely dangerous, the classical catastrophe threatened to overtake the son. As a result of this constellation, Gayomart and his ox died only thirty years later. (The trials of Zarathustra also lasted for thirty years.) Fifty-five species of grain and twelve kinds of healing plants came from the dead ox. His seed entered into the moon for purification, but the seed of Gayomart entered into the sun. This seems to suggest that the bull has a hidden feminine significance. Gosh or Drvashpa was the bull's soul and it was worshipped as a female divinity. At first she was so faint-hearted that she refused to become the goddess of cattle until, as a consolation, the coming of Zarathustra was announced to her. This has its parallel in the Purana where the earth received the promise of Krishna's coming.[33] Like Ardvisura, the goddess of love, Gosh rides in a chariot. So the bull-anima appears to be decidedly feminine. In astrology Taurus, too, is a House of Venus. The myth of Gayomart repeats in modified form the primitive "closed circle" of a self-reproducing masculine and feminine divinity.

SUN SYMBOLISM

From*: "7 June 1933," *Visions II

> "A great heat went through me and when I lifted my foot I saw marked upon the sole, a Chinese dragon twined upon a cross, and above the cross the head of a lion."

DR. JUNG: Yes, the bristling mane of the lion symbolizes the rays of the sun, like the hair of Samson. And the lion astrologically is the *domicilium solis*,[34] it is the sign between the 21st of July and the 24th of August, when the sun is at its greatest power. So this lion can stand for this sun but in the particular aspect of the lion. For the sun, or whatever the sun means, can be symbolized in many different ways; if by the lion, it would mean power of a special kind, in the form of a powerful animal, not of a powerful man. The sun is also symbolized by the face of Moses, with the horns meaning radiation, therefore they would be the horns of power. And his face radiated such light when he came down from Sinai that only when it was veiled could the people gaze upon it; that would be the sun in the form of enlightened man. Also the sun is symbolized by the crown of Helios, the sun god, the radiation or the crown of sun rays which the old Caesars used to wear; one sees it chiefly on Roman coins. There the sun would express the human mind or understanding, or the human spirit, it would be a specifically human quality. But here the sun is in the form of the animal. How do you explain that?

MR. ALLEMANN: It is a symbol of fierce impulsive energy. Sekhmet represented the heat of the sun, and she also had a lion's head.

DR. JUNG: Yes, those of you who have been in Luxor remember that great statue of the goddess Sekhmet. It is made of the most beautiful black basalt, and she has the head of a lioness. She personified the terrible destructive power of Ra, or the sun at its height, at the hottest time of the year.

From: *Symbols of Transformation* (1912/52) (*CW* 5), pars. 140–141, 148, 163

140 Symeon, the "New Theologian" (970–1040), says:

> My tongue lacks words, and what happens in me my spirit sees clearly but does not explain. It sees the Invisible, that emptiness of all forms, simple throughout, not complex, and in extent infinite. For it sees no beginning, and it sees no end, and is entirely unconscious of any middle, and does not know what to call that which it sees. Something complete appears, it seems to me, not indeed with the thing itself, but through a kind of *participation*. For you enkindle fire from fire, and you receive the whole fire; but this thing remains undiminished and undivided as before. Similarly, that which is imparted separates itself from the first, and spreads like something corporeal into many lights. But this is something spiritual, immeasurable, indivisible, and inexhaustible. For it is not separated when it becomes many, but remains undivided, and is in me, and rises in my poor heart like a sun or circular disc of the sun, like light, for it is a light.[35]

141 That the thing perceived as an inner light, as the sun of the other world, is an emotional component of the psyche, is clear from Symeon's words:

> And questing after it, my spirit sought to comprehend the splendour it had seen, but found it not as a creature and could not get away from created things, that it might embrace that uncreated and uncomprehended splendour. Nevertheless it wandered everywhere and strove to behold it. It searched through the air, it wandered over the heavens, it crossed the abysses, it searched, so it seemed, to the ends of the world.[36] But in all that it found nothing, for all was created. And I lamented and was sorrowful, and my heart burned, and I lived as one distraught in mind. But it came as it was wont, and descending like a luminous cloud, seemed to envelop my whole head, so that I cried out dismayed. But flying away again it left me alone. And when I wearily sought it, I realized suddenly that it was within me, and in the midst of my heart it shone like the light of a spherical sun.[37]

148 Amenophis IV achieved, by his reforms, a psychologically valuable work of interpretation. He united all the bull,[38] ram,[39] crocodile,[40] and pile-dwelling[41] gods into the sun-disc, and made it clear that their various attributes were compatible with those of the sun.[42] A similar fate overtook Hellenic and Roman

polytheism as a result of the syncretistic strivings of later centuries. An excellent illustration of this is in the beautiful prayer of Lucius to the Queen of Heaven (the moon):

> Queen of heaven, whether thou be named Ceres, bountiful mother of earthly fruits, or heavenly Venus, or Phoebus' sister, or Proserpina, who strikest terror with midnight ululations . . . . thou that with soft feminine brightness dost illume the walls of all cities . . .[43]

163 Not a few traces of sun-worship are preserved in ecclesiastical art,[44] for instance the nimbus round the head of Christ, and the haloes of the saints. Numerous fire- and light-symbols are attributed to the saints in Christian legend.[45] The twelve apostles, for example, were likened to the twelve signs of the zodiac and were therefore represented each with a star over his head.[46] No wonder the heathen, as Tertullian reports, took the sun for the God of the Christians! "Some, in a more human and probable way, believe the Sun to be our god."[47] Among the Manichees the sun actually was God. One of the most remarkable records of this period, an amalgam of pagan-Asiatic, Hellenistic, and Christian beliefs, is the, *'ΕξηΥησις περι τϖν εν Περσιδι πραχθεντων*,[48] a book of fables which affords deep insight into syncretistic symbolism. There we find the following magical dedication: *Διι 'Ηλιω θεϖ μεΥαλω βασιλει 'Ιησον*.[49] In certain parts of Armenia, Christians still pray to the rising sun, that it may "let its foot rest on the face of the worshipper."[50]

Figure 4.2 Serpent representing the orbit of the moon

Source: Reproduced from Jung's *Collected Works*, Vol. 5.

From: *Symbols of Transformation* (1912/52) (*CW* 5), par. 176

176 Before I enter upon the contents of this second part, it seems necessary to cast a backward glance over the singular train of thought which the analysis of the poem "The Moth to the Sun" has revealed. Although this poem is very different from the preceding "Hymn of Creation," closer investigation of the longing for the sun has led us into a realm of mythological ideas that are closely related to those considered in the first poem: the Creator God, whose dual nature was plainly apparent in the case of Job, has now taken on an astromythological, or rather an astrological, character. He has become the sun, and thus finds a natural expression that transcends his moral division into a Heavenly Father and his counterpart the devil. The sun, as Renan has observed, is the only truly "rational" image of God, whether we adopt the standpoint of the primitive savage or of modern science. In either case the sun is the father-god from whom all living things draw life; he is the fructifier and creator, the source of energy for our world. The discord into which the human soul has fallen can be harmoniously resolved through the sun as a natural object which knows no inner conflict. The sun is not only beneficial, but also destructive; hence the zodiacal sign for August heat is the ravaging lion which Samson[51] slew in order to rid the parched earth of its torment. Yet it is in the nature of the sun to scorch, and its scorching power seems natural to man. It shines equally on the just and the unjust, and allows useful creatures to flourish as well as the harmful. Therefore the sun is perfectly suited to represent the visible God of this world, i.e., the creative power of our own soul, which we call libido, and whose nature it is to bring forth the useful and the harmful, the good and the bad. That this comparison is not just a matter of words can be seen from the teachings of the mystics: when they descend into the depths of their own being they find "in their heart" the image of the sun, they find their own life-force which they call the "sun" for a legitimate and, I would say, a *physical* reason, because our source of energy and life actually is the sun. Our physiological life, regarded as an energy process, is entirely solar. The peculiar nature of this solar energy as inwardly perceived by the mystic is made clear in Indian mythology. The following passages, referring to Rudra,[52] are taken from the Shvetashvatara Upanishad:

> There is one Rudra only, they do not allow a second, who rules all the worlds by his powers. Behind all creatures he stands, the Protector; having created them, he gathers all beings together at the end of time.
>
> He has eyes on all sides, faces on all sides, arms on all sides, feet on all sides. He is the one God who created heaven and earth, forging all things together with his hands and wings.
>
> You who are the source and origin of the gods, the ruler of all, Rudra, the great seer, who of old gave birth to the Golden Seed – give us enlightenment![53]

SUN AND MOON SYMBOLISM

From: *Symbols of Transformation* (1912/52) (*CW* 5), pars. 290–299

290 The symbol for that portion of the zodiac in which the sun re-enters the yearly cycle at the time of the winter solstice is Capricorn, originally known as the "Goat-Fish" (αἰγόχερως, "goat-horned"): the sun mounts like a goat to the tops of the highest mountains, and then plunges into the depths of the sea like a fish. The fish in dreams occasionally signifies the unborn child,[54] because the child before its birth lives in the water like a fish; similarly, when the sun sinks into the sea, it becomes child and fish at once. The fish is therefore a symbol of renewal and rebirth.

291 The journey of Moses with his servant Joshua is a life-journey (it lasted eighty years). They grow old together and lose the life-force, i.e., the fish, which "in wondrous wise took its way to the sea" (setting of the sun). When the two notice their loss, they discover at the place where the source life is found (where the dead fish revived and sprang into the sea) Khidr wrapped in his mantle,[55] sitting on the ground. In another version he was sitting on an island in sea, "in the wettest place on earth," which means that he had just been born from the maternal depths. Where the fish vanished Khidr, the Verdant One, was born as a "son of the watery deep," his head veiled, proclaiming divine wisdom, like the Babylonian Oannes-Ea, who was represented in fish form and daily came out of the sea as a fish to teach the people wisdom.[56]

292 Oannes' name was brought into connection with John's. With the rising of the reborn sun the fish that dwelt in darkness, surrounded by all the terrors of night and death,[57] becomes the shining, fiery day-star. This gives the words of John the Baptist a special significance (Matthew 3:11):

> I indeed baptize you with water unto repentance; but he that cometh after me is mightier than I . . . he shall baptize you with the Holy Ghost, and with fire.

293 Following Vollers, we may compare Khidr and Elias (or Moses and his servant Joshua) with Gilgamesh and his brother Eabani (Enkidu). Gilgamesh wanders through the world, driven by fear and longing, to find immortality. His journey takes him across the sea to the wise Utnapishtim (Noah), who knows how to cross the waters of death. There Gilgamesh has to dive down to the bottom of the sea for the magical herb that is to lead him back to the land of men. On the return journey he is accompanied by an immortal mariner, who, banished by the curse of Utnapishtim, has been forbidden to return to the land of the blessed. But when Gilgamesh arrives home, a serpent steals the magic herb from him (i.e., the fish slips back into the sea). Because of the loss of the magic herb, Gilgamesh's journey has been in vain; instead he comes back in the company of an immortal, whose fate we cannot learn from the fragments of the epic. Jensen[58] believes that this banished immortal is the prototype of Ahasuerus.

294 Once again we meet the motif of the Dioscuri: mortal and immortal, the setting and rising sun. The Mithraic bull-sacrifice is often represented as flanked by the two dadophors, Gautes and Cautopates, one with a raised and the other with a lowered torch. They form a pair of brothers whose characters are revealed by the symbolic position of the torches. Cumont not unjustly connects them with the sepulchral Erotes, who as genies with inverted torches have a traditional meaning. One would stand for death, the other for life. There are certain points of resemblance between the Mithraic sacrifice (where the bull in the centre is flanked on either side by dadophors[59]) and the Christian sacrifice of the lamb (or ram). The Crucified is traditionally flanked by two thieves, one of whom ascends to paradise while the other descends to hell.[60] The Semitic gods were often flanked by two *paredroi*; for instance, the Baal of Edessa was accompanied by Aziz and Monimos (Baal being astrologically interpreted as the sun, and Aziz and Monimos as Mars and Mercury). According to the Babylonian view, the gods are grouped into triads. Thus the two thieves somehow go together with Christ. The two dadophors are, as Cumont has shown, offshoots[61] from the main figure of Mithras, who was supposed to have a secret triadic character. Dionysius the Areopagite reports that the magicians held a feast in honour of τοϋ τρι-πλασίου Μίθρον[62] (the threefold Mithras).[63]

295 As Cumont observes,[64] Cautes and Cautopates sometimes carry in their hands the head of a bull and of a scorpion respectively. Taurus and Scorpio are equinoctial signs,[65] and this is a clear indication that the sacrifice was primarily connected with the sun cycle: the rising sun that sacrifices itself at the summer solstice, and the setting sun. Since it was not easy to represent sunrise and sunset in the sacrificial drama, this idea had to be shown outside it.

296 We have already pointed out that the Dioscuri represent a similar idea in somewhat different form: one sun is mortal, the other immortal. As this whole solar mythology is psychology projected into the heavens, the underlying idea could probably be paraphrased thus: just as man consists of a mortal and an immortal part, so the sun is a pair of brothers, one of whom is mortal, the other immortal. Man is mortal, yet there are exceptions who are immortal, or there is something immortal in us. Thus the gods, or figures like Khidr and the Comte de Saint-Germain, are our immortal part which continues intangibly to exist. The sun comparison tells us over and over again that the dynamic of the gods is psychic energy. This is our immortality, the link through which man feels inextinguishably one with the continuity of all life.[66] The life of the psyche is the life of mankind. Welling up from the depths of the unconscious, its springs gush forth from the root of the whole human race, since the individual is, biologically speaking, only a twig broken off from the mother and transplanted.

297 The psychic life-force, the libido, symbolizes itself in the sun[67] or personifies itself in figures of heroes with solar attributes. At the same time it expresses itself through phallic symbols. Both possibilities are found on a late Babylonian gem from Lajard's collection. In the middle stands an androgynous deity. On the masculine side there is a snake with a sun halo round its head; on the

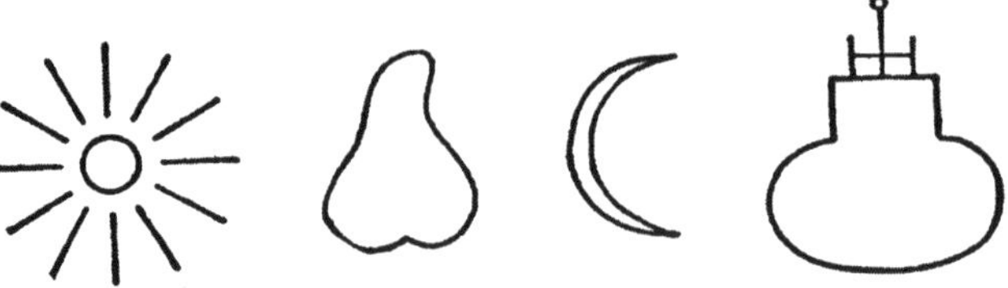

Figure 4.3 Roman symbols
Source: Reproduced from Jung's *Collected Works*, Vol. 5.

feminine side another snake with a sickle moon above it. This picture has a symbolic sexual nuance: on the masculine side there is a lozenge, a favourite symbol of the female genitals, and on the feminine side a wheel without its rim. The spokes are thickened at the ends into knobs, which, like the fingers we mentioned earlier, have a phallic meaning. It seems to be a phallic wheel such as was not unknown in antiquity. There are obscene gems on which Cupid is shown turning a wheel consisting entirely of phalli.[68] As to what the sun signifies, I discovered in the collection of antiquities at Verona a late Roman inscription with the following symbols.[69]

298 The symbolism is plain: sun = phallus, moon = vessel (uterus). This interpretation is confirmed by another monument from the same collection. The symbols are the same, except that the vessel[70] has been replaced by the figure of a woman. Certain symbols on coins can probably be interpreted in a similar manner. In Lajards *Recherches sur la culte de Vénus* there is a coin from Perga, showing Artemis as a conical stone flanked by a masculine figure (alleged to be the deity Men) and a female figure (alleged to be Artemis). Men (otherwise called Lunus) appears on an Attic bas-relief with a spear, flanked by Pan with a club, and a female figure.[71] From this it is clear that sexuality as well as the sun can be used to symbolize the libido.

299 One further point deserves mention here. The dadophor Cautopates is often represented with a cock[72] and pine-cones. These are the attributes of the Phrygian god Men, whose cult was very widespread. He was shown with the pileus[73] (or "Phrygian cap") and pine-cones, riding on the cock, and also in the form of a boy, just as the dadophors were boyish figures. (This latter characteristic relates both them and Men to the Cabiri and Dactyls.) Now Men has affinities with Attis, the son and lover of Cybele. In Imperial times Men and Attis merged into one. Attis also wears the pileus like Men, Mithras, and the dadophors. As the son and lover of his mother he raises the incest problem. Incest leads logically to ritual castration in the Attis-Cybele cult; for according to legend the hero, driven mad by his mother, mutilates himself. I must refrain from going into this question more deeply at present, as I would prefer to discuss the incest problem at the end of this book. Here I would only point out that the incest motif is bound to arise, because when the regressing libido is introverted for internal or external reasons it always reactivates the

parental imagos and thus apparently re-establishes the infantile relationship. But this relationship cannot be re-established, because the libido is an adult libido which is already bound to sexuality and inevitably imports an incompatible, incestuous character into the reactivated relationship to the parents.[74] It is this sexual character that now gives rise to the incest symbolism. Since incest must be avoided at all costs, the result is either the death of the son lover

Figure 4.4 Androgynous divinity

Source: Reproduced from Jung's *Collected Works*, Vol. 5.

Figure 4.5 Cybele and her son-lover

Source: Reproduced from Jung's *Collected Works*, Vol. 5.

or his self-castration as punishment for the incest he has committed, or else the sacrifice of instinctuality, and especially of sexuality, as a means of preventing or expiating the incestuous longing. Sex being one of the most obvious examples of instinctuality, it is sex which is liable to be most affected by these sacrificial measures, i.e., through abstinence. The heroes are usually wanderers,[75] and wandering is a symbol of longing,[76] of the restless urge which never finds its object, of nostalgia for the lost mother. The sun comparison can easily be taken in this sense: the heroes are like the wandering sun, from which it is concluded that the myth of the hero is a solar myth. It seems to us, rather, that he is first and foremost a self-representation of the longing of the unconscious, of its unquenched and unquenchable desire for the light of consciousness. But consciousness, continually in danger of being led astray by its own light and of becoming a rootless will o' the wisp, longs for the healing power of nature, for the deep wells of being and for unconscious communion with life in all its countless forms.

VENUS AND MARS SYMBOLISM

From: "Synchronicity: An Acausal Connecting Principle" (1952) (*CW* 8), par. 879

879 . . . The relation of Mars to Venus can reveal a love relation, but a marriage is not always a love relation and a love relation is not always a marriage.

From: "The Psychology of the Transference" (1946) (*CW* 16), pars. 506–518

506 A remarkable contribution to the role of feminine psychology in alchemy is furnished by the letter which the English theologian and alchemist, John Pordage,[77] wrote to his *soror mystica* Jane Leade. In it[78] he gives her spiritual instruction concerning the *opus*:

> 507 This sacred furnace, this *Balneum Mariae*, this glass phial, this secret furnace, is the place, the matrix or womb, and the centre from which the divine Tincture flows forth from its source and origin. Of the place or abode where the Tincture has its home and dwelling I need not remind you, nor name its name, but I exhort you only to knock at the foundation. Solomon tells us in his Song that its inner dwelling is not far from the navel, which resembles a round goblet filled with the sacred liquor of the pure Tincture.[79] You know the fire of the philosophers, it was the key they kept concealed. . . . The fire is the love-fire, the life that flows forth from the Divine Venus, or the Love of God; the fire of Mars is too choleric, too sharp, and too fierce, so that it would dry up and burn the *materia*: wherefore the love-fire of Venus alone has the qualities of the right true fire.
>
> 508 This true philosophy will teach you how you should know yourself, and if you know yourself rightly, you will also know the pure nature; for the pure

nature is in yourself. And when you know the pure nature which is your true selfhood, freed from all wicked, sinful selfishness, then also you will know God, for the Godhead is concealed and wrapped in the pure nature like a kernel in the nutshell. . . . The true philosophy will teach you who is the father and who is the mother of this magical child. . . . The father of this child is Mars, he is the fiery life which proceeds from Mars as the father's quality. His mother is Venus, who is the gentle love-fire proceeding from the son's quality. Here then, in the qualities and forms of nature, you see male and female, man and wife, bride and bridegroom, the first marriage or wedding of Galilee, which is celebrated between Mars and Venus when they return from their fallen state. Mars, or the husband, must become a godly man, otherwise the pure Venus will take him neither into the conjugal nor into the sacred marriage bed. Venus must become a pure virgin, a virginal wife, otherwise the wrathful jealous Mars in his wrath-fire will not wed with her nor live with her in union; but instead of agreement and harmony, there will be naught but strife, jealousy, discord, and enmity among the qualities of nature. . . .

509 Accordingly, if you think to become a learned artist, look with earnestness to the union of your own Mars and Venus, that the nuptial knot be rightly tied and the marriage between them well and truly consummated. You must see to it that they lie together in the bed of their union and live in sweet harmony; then the virgin Venus will bring forth her pearl, her water-spirit, in you, to soften the fiery spirit of Mars, and the wrathful fire of Mars will sink quite willingly, in mildness and love, into the love-fire of Venus, and thus both qualities, *as fire and water*, will mingle together, agree, and flow into one another; and from their agreement and union there will proceed the first conception of the magical birth which we call Tincture, the love-fire Tincture. Now although the Tincture is conceived in the womb of your humanity and is awakened to life, yet there is still a great danger, and it is to be feared that, because it is still in the body or womb, it may yet be spoiled by neglect before it be brought in due season into the light. On this account you must look round for a good nurse, who will watch it in its childhood and will tend it properly: and such must be your own pure heart and your own virginal will. . . .

510 This child, this tincturing life, must be assayed, proved, and tried in the qualities of nature; and here again great anxiety and danger will arise, seeing that it must suffer the damage of temptation in the body and womb, and you may thus lose the birth. For the delicate Tincture, this tender child of life, must descend into the forms and qualities of nature, that it may suffer and endure temptation and overcome it; it must needs descend into the Divine Darkness, into the darkness of Saturn, wherein no light of life is to be seen: there it must be held captive, and be bound with the chains of darkness, and must live from the food which the prickly Mercurius will give it to eat, which to the Divine Tincture of life is naught but dust and ashes, poison and gall, fire and brimstone. It must enter into the fierce wrathful Mars, by whom (as happened to Jonah in the belly of hell) it is

swallowed, and must experience the curse of God's wrath; also it must be tempted by Lucifer and the million devils who dwell in the quality of the wrathful fire. And here the divine artist in this philosophical work will see the first colour, where the Tincture appears in its blackness, and it is the blackest black; the learned philosophers call it their black crow, or their black raven, or again their blessed and blissful black; for in the darkness of this black is hidden the light of lights in the quality of Saturn; and in this poison and gall there is hidden in Mercurius the most precious medicament against the poison, namely the life of life. And the blessed Tincture is hidden in the fury or wrath and curse of Mars.

511 Now it seems to the artist that all his work is lost. What has become of the Tincture? Here is nothing that is apparent, that can be perceived, recognized, or tasted, but darkness, most painful death, a hellish fearful fire, nothing but the wrath and curse of God; yet he does not see that the Tincture of Life is in this putrefaction or dissolution and destruction, that there is light in this darkness, life in this death, love in this fury and wrath, and in this poison the highest and most precious Tincture and medicament against all poison and sickness.

512 The old philosophers named this work or labour their descension, their cineration, their pulverization, their death, their putrefaction of the *materia* of the stone, their corruption, their *caput mortuum*. You must not despise this blackness, or black colour, but persevere in it in patience, in suffering, and in silence, until its forty days of temptation are over, until the days of its tribulations are completed, when the seed of life shall waken to life, shall rise up, sublimate or glorify itself, transform itself into whiteness, purify and sanctify itself, give itself the redness, in other words, transfigure and fix its shape. When the work is brought thus far, it is an easy work: for the learned philosophers have said that the making of the stone is then woman's work and child's play. Therefore, if the human will is given over and left, and becomes patient and still and as a dead nothing, the Tincture will do and effect everything in us and for us, if we can keep our thoughts, movements, and imaginations still, or can leave off and rest. But how difficult, hard, and bitter this work appears to the human will, before it can be brought to this shape, so that it remains still and calm even though all the fire be let loose in its sight, and all manner of temptations assail it!

513 Here, as you see, there is great danger, and the Tincture of life can easily be spoiled and the fruit wasted in the womb, when it is thus surrounded on all sides and assailed by so many devils and so many tempting essences. But if it can withstand and overcome this fiery trial and sore temptation, and win the victory: then you will see the beginning of its resurrection from hell, death, and the mortal grave, appearing first in the quality of Venus; and then the Tincture of life will itself burst forth mightily from the prison of the dark Saturn, through the hell of the poisonous Mercurius, and through the curse and direful death of God's wrath that burns and flames in Mars, and the gentle love-fire of the Venus quality will gain the upper hand, and the love-fire Tincture will be preferred in the government and

have supreme command. And then the gentleness and love-fire of Divine Venus will reign as lord and king in and over all qualities.

514 Nevertheless there is still another danger that the work of the stone may yet miscarry. Therefore the artist must wait until he sees the Tincture covered over with its other colour, as with the whitest white, which he may expect to see after long patience and stillness, and which truly appears when the Tincture rises up in the lunar quality: illustrious Luna imparts a beautiful white to the Tincture, the most perfect white hue and a brilliant splendour. And thus is the darkness transformed into light, and death into life. And this brilliant whiteness awakens joy and hope in the heart of the artist, that the work has gone so well and fallen out so happily. For now the white colour reveals to the enlightened eye of the soul cleanliness, innocence, holiness, simplicity, heavenly-mindedness, and righteousness, and with these the Tincture is henceforth clothed over and over as with a garment. She is radiant as the moon, beautiful as the dawn. Now the divine virginity of the tincturing life shines forth, and no spot or wrinkle nor any other blemish is to be seen.

515 The old masters were wont to call this work their white swan, their albification, or making white, their sublimation, their distillation, their circulation, their purification, their separation, their sanctification, and their resurrection, because the Tincture is made white like a shining silver. It is sublimed or exalted and transfigured by reason of its many descents into Saturn, Mercurius, and Mars, and by its many ascents into Venus and Luna. This is the distillation, the *Balneum Mariae:* because the Tincture is purified in the qualities of nature through the many distillations of the water, blood, and heavenly dew of the Divine Virgin Sophia, and, through the manifold circulation in and out of the forms and qualities of nature, is made white and pure, like brilliantly polished silver. And all uncleanliness of the blackness, all death, hell, curse, wrath, and all poison which rise up out of the qualities of Saturn, Mercury, and Mars are separated and depart, wherefore they call it their separation, and when the Tincture attains its whiteness and brilliance in Venus and Luna they call it their sanctification, their purification and making white. They call it their resurrection, because the white rises up out of the black, and the divine virginity and purity out of the poison of Mercurius and out of the red fiery rage and wrath of Mars. . . .

516 Now is the stone shaped, the elixir of life prepared, the lovechild or the child of love born, the new birth completed, and the work made whole and perfect. Farewell! fall, hell, curse, death, dragon, beast, and serpent! Good night! mortality, fear, sorrow, and misery! For now redemption, salvation, and recovery of everything that was lost will again come to pass within and without, for now you have the great secret and mystery of the whole world; you have the Pearl of Love; you have the unchangeable eternal essence of Divine Joy from which all healing virtue and all multiplying power come, from which there actively proceeds the active power of the Holy Ghost. You have the seed of the woman who has trampled on the head of the serpent. You have the seed of the virgin and the blood of the virgin in one essence and quality.

> 517 O wonder of wonders! You have the tincturing Tincture, the pearl of the virgin, which has three essences or qualities in one; it has body, soul, and spirit, it has fire, light, and joy, it has the Father's quality, it has the Son's quality, and has also the Holy Ghost's quality, even all these three, in one fixed and eternal essence and being. This is the Son of the Virgin, this is her first-born, this is the noble hero, the trampler of the serpent, and he who casts the dragon under his feet and tramples upon him. . . . For now the Man of Paradise is become clear as a transparent glass, in which the Divine Sun shines through and through, like gold that is wholly bright, pure, and clear, without blemish or spot. The soul is henceforth a most substantial seraphic angel, she can make herself doctor, theologian, astrologer, divine magician, she can make herself whatsoever she will, and do and have whatsoever she will: for all qualities have but one will in agreement and harmony. And this same one will is God's eternal infallible will; and from henceforth the Divine Man is in his own nature become one with God.[80]

518 This hymn-like myth of love, virgin, mother, and child sounds extremely feminine, but in reality it is an archetypal conception sprung from the masculine unconscious, where the Virgin Sophia corresponds to the anima (in the psychological sense).[81] As is shown by the symbolism and by the not very clear distinction between her and the son, she is also the "paradisal" or "divine" being, i.e., the self. The fact that these ideas and figures were still mystical for Pordage and more or less undifferentiated is explained by the emotional nature of the experiences which he himself describes.[82] Experiences of this kind leave little room for critical understanding. They do, however, throw light on the processes hidden behind the alchemical symbolism and pave the way for the discoveries of modern medical psychology. Unfortunately we possess no original treatises that can with any certainty be ascribed to a woman author. Consequently we do not know what kind of alchemical symbolism a woman's view would have produced. Nevertheless, modern medical practice tells us that the feminine unconscious produces a symbolism which, by and large, is compensatory to the masculine. In that case, to use Pordage's terms, the leitmotiv would not be gentle Venus but fiery Mars, not Sophia but Hecate, Demeter, and Persephone, or the matriarchal Kali of southern India in her brighter and darker aspects.[83]

MANDALAS, BIRTH CHARTS, AND THE SELF

From: "Individual Dream Symbolism in Relation to Alchemy" (1936) (*CW* 12), par. 314

314 As to the interpretation [of a mandala] based on comparative historical material, we are in a more favourable position, at least as regards the general aspects of this figure. We have at our disposal, firstly, the whole mandala symbolism of three continents, and secondly, the specific time symbolism of the mandala as this developed under the influence of astrology, particularly in the West. The

horoscope [see Figure 4.6] is itself a mandala (a clock) with a dark centre, and leftward *circumambulatio* with "houses" and planetary phases. The mandalas of ecclesiastical art, particularly those on the floor before the high altar or beneath the transept, make frequent use of zodiacal beasts or the yearly seasons.

Figure 4.6 Horoscope, showing the houses, zodiac, and planets

Source: Woodcut by Erhard Schoen for the nativity calendar of Leonhard Reymann (1515); reproduced from Jung's *Collected Works*, vol. 12.

From: "The Tavistock Lectures: Lecture V" (1935) (*CW* 18), pars. 409–412

409 This structure is called in Sanskrit a mandala. The word means a circle, particularly a magic circle. In the East, you find the mandala not only as the ground-plan of temples, but as pictures in the temples, or drawn for the day of certain religious festivals. In the very centre of the mandala there is the god, or the symbol of divine energy, the diamond thunderbolt. Round this innermost circle is a cloister with four gates. Then comes a garden, and round this there is another circle which is the outer circumference.

410 The symbol of the mandala has exactly this meaning of a holy place, a *temenos*, to protect the centre. And it is a symbol which is one of the most important motifs in the objectivation of unconscious images.[84] It is a means of protecting the centre of the personality from being drawn out and from being influenced from outside.

411 This picture by Dr. Bennet's patient is an attempt to draw such a mandala. It has a centre, and it contains all his psychic elements, and the vase would be the magic circle, the temenos, round which he has to do the *circumambulatio*. Attention is thus directed towards the centre, and at the same time all the disparate elements come under observation and an attempt is made to unify them. . . .

412 In this picture he makes an attempt at symmetry. . . . A most remarkable thing is that he also gathers in the stars. That means that the cosmos, his world, is collected into the picture. It is an allusion to the unconscious astrology which is in our bones, though we are unaware of it.

From: "On Resurrection" (1954) (*CW* 18), par. 1573

1573 As roundness signifies completeness or perfection, it also expresses rotation (the rolling movement) or progress on an endless circular way, an identity with the sun and the stars (hence the beautiful confession in the "Mithraic Liturgy"; *εγώ είμι σύμπλανος υμϊν άστήρ* ("I am a Star following his way like you"). The realization of the self also means a re-establishment of Man as the microcosm, i.e., man's cosmic relatedness. Such realizations are frequently accompanied by synchronistic events. (The prophetic experience of vocation belongs to this category.)

From: "Transformation Symbolism in the Mass" (1940/54) (*CW* 11), par. 418

418 Since olden times the circle with a centre has been a symbol for the Deity, illustrating the wholeness of God incarnate: the single point in the centre and the series of points constituting the circumference. Ritual circumambulation often bases itself quite consciously on the cosmic picture of the starry heavens revolving, on the "dance of the stars," an idea that is still preserved in the

comparison of the twelve disciples with the zodiacal constellations, as also in the depictions of the zodiac that are sometimes found in churches, in front of the altar on the roof of the nave.

From: "A Psychological Approach to the Dogma of the Trinity" (1942/48) (*CW* 11), par. 246

246 As compared with the trinitarian thinking of Plato, ancient Greek philosophy favoured thinking of a quaternary type. In Pythagoras, the great role was played not by three but by four; the Pythagorean oath, for instance, says that the tetraktys "contains the roots of eternal nature."[85] The Pythagorean school was dominated by the idea that the soul was a square and not a triangle. The origin of these ideas lies far back in the dark pre-history of Greek thought. The quaternity is an archetype of almost universal significance. It forms the logical basis for any whole judgment. If one wishes to pass such a judgment, it must have this fourfold aspect. For instance, if you want to describe the horizon as a whole, you name the four quarters of heaven. . . . There are always four elements, four prime qualities, four colours, four castes, four ways of spiritual development, etc. So, too, there are four aspects of psychological orientation, beyond which nothing fundamental remains to be said. In order to orient ourselves, we must have a function which ascertains that something is there (sensation); a second function which establishes *what* it is (thinking); a third function which states whether it suits us or not, whether we wish to accept it or not (feeling); and a fourth function which indicates where it came from and where it is going (intuition). When this has been done, there is nothing more to say.

From: "The Personification of the Opposites" (1955/56) (*CW* 14), pars. 260–262

260 The Red Sea appears in a very peculiar manner in the "Tractatus Aristotelis ad Alexandrum Magnum," where a recipe says:

> Take the serpent, and place it in the chariot with four wheels, and let it be turned about on the earth until it is immersed in the depths of the sea, and nothing more is visible but the blackest dead sea. And there let the chariot with the wheels remain, until so many fumes rise up from the serpent that the whole surface [*planities*] becomes dry, and by desiccation sandy and black. All that is the earth which is no earth, but a stone lacking all weight. . . . [And when the fumes are precipitated in the form of rain,] you should bring the chariot from the water to dry land, and then you have placed the four wheels upon the chariot, and will obtain the result if you will advance further to the Red Sea, running without running, moving without motion [*currens sine cursu, movens sine motu*].[86]

261 This curious text requires a little elucidation. The serpent is the prima materia, the Serpens Hermetis, "which he [Hermes] sent to King Antiochus,

that he might do battle with thee [Alexander] and thine army."[87] The serpent is placed "in the chariot of its vessel and is led hither and thither by the fourfold rotation of the natures, but it should be securely enclosed." The wheels are the "wheels of the elements." The vessel or vehicle is the "spherical tomb" of the serpent.[88] The fourfold rotation of the natures corresponds to the ancient tetrameria of the opus (its division into four parts), i.e., transformation through the four elements, from earth to fire. This symbolism describes in abbreviated form the essentials of the opus: the serpent of Hermes or the Agathodaimon, the Nous that animates the cold part of nature – that is, the unconscious – is enclosed in the spherical vessel of diaphanous glass which, on the alchemical view, represents the world and the soul.[89] The psychologist would see it rather as the psychic reflection of the world, namely, *consciousness* of the world and the psyche.[90] The transformation corresponds to the psychic process of assimilation and integration by means of the transcendent function.[91] This function unites the pairs of opposites, which, as alchemy shows, are arranged in a quaternio when they represent a totality. The totality appears in quaternary form only when it is not just an unconscious fact but a conscious and differentiated totality; for instance, when the horizon is thought of not simply as a circle that can be divided into any number of parts but as consisting of four clearly defined points. Accordingly, one's given personality could be represented by a continuous circle, whereas the conscious personality would be a circle divided up in a definite way, and this generally turns out to be a quaternity. The quaternity of basic functions of consciousness meets this requirement. It is therefore only to be expected that the chariot should have four wheels,[92] to correspond with the four elements or natures. The chariot as a spherical vessel and as consciousness rests on the four elements or basic functions,[93] just as the floating island where Apollo was born, Delos, rested on the four supports which Poseidon made for it. The wheels, naturally, are on the outside of the chariot and are its motor organs, just as the functions of consciousness facilitate the relation of the psyche to its environment. It must, however, be stressed that what we today call the schema of functions is archetypally prefigured by one of the oldest patterns of order known to man, namely the quaternity, which always represents a consciously reflected and differentiated totality. Quite apart from its almost universal incidence it also appears spontaneously in dreams as an expression of the total personality. The "chariot of Aristotle" can be understood in this sense as a symbol of the self.

262 The recipe goes on to say that this symbolic vehicle should be immersed in the sea of the unconscious for the purpose of heating and incubation,[94] corresponding to the state of *tapas*,[95] incubation by means of "self-heating." By this is obviously meant a state of introversion in which the unconscious content is brooded over and digested. During this operation all relations with the outside world are broken off; the feelers of perception and intuition, discrimination and valuation are withdrawn. The four wheels are "placed upon the chariot": outside everything is quiet and still, but deep inside the psyche the wheels go

on turning, performing those cyclic evolutions which bring the mandala of the total personality,[96] the ground-plan of the self, closer to consciousness.

From: "To Dr. H., 30 August 1951," *Letters II*

In consequence of the predominance of the archetype the personality that is "gripped" is in direct contact with the *mundus archetypus*,[97] and his life or biography is only a brief episode in the eternal course of things or in the eternal revolution of "divine" images. That which is eternally present appears in the temporal order as a succession.

NOTES

1 This interpretation accords with modern astrological speculations.
2 John 14:6.
3 John 15:5.
4 "It [the first day in autumn] is the day on which 'the goddess Nehmit completes her work, so that the god Osiris may enter the left eye.'" – Heinrich Brugsch, *Religion und Mythologie der alten Aegypter* (Leipzig, 1885), pp. 281ff, quoted in *Symbols of Transformation*, par. 408 (as in 1912 edn.).
5 153 Cf. Rahner, "Die seelenheilende Blume."
6 Cf. Bouché-Leclercq, *L'Astrologie grecque*, p. 136: Cancer = "crabe ou écrevisse." The constellation was usually represented as a tailless crab.
7 "The crab is wont to change with the changing seasons; casting off its old shell, it puts on a new and fresh one." This, says Picinelli, is an "emblema" of the resurrection of the dead, and cites Ephesians 4:23: ". . . be renewed in the spirit of your minds" (RSV). (*Mondo simbolico*, Lib. VI, No. 45.)
8 Foreseeing the flooding of the Nile, the crabs (like the tortoises and crocodiles) bring their eggs in safety to a higher place. "They foresee the future in their mind long before it comes," Caussin, *Polyhistor symbolicus* (1618), p. 442.
9 Masenius, *Speculum imaginum veritatis occultae* (1714), cap. LXVII, 30, p. 768.
10 De Gubernatis, *Zoological Mythology*, II, p. 355.
11 Roscher, *Lexikon*, II, col. 959, s.v. "Karkinos." The same motif occurs in a dream described in *Two Essays on Analytical Psychology*, pars. 80ff.
12 In Egypt, the heliacal rising of Cancer indicates the beginning of the annual flooding of the Nile and hence the beginning of the year. Bouché-Leclercq, p. 137.
13 [Cf. "Psychology and Religion," p. 67, n. 5. – EDITORS.]
14 Propertius, trans, by Butler, p. 275.
15 De Gubernatis, II, p. 356.
16 *The Panchatantra Reconstructed*, ed. by Edgerton, II, pp. 403f. Cf. also Hoffmann-Krayer et al., *Handwörterbuch des Deutschen Aberglaubens*, V, col. 448, s.v. "Krebs."
17 De Gubernatis, II, p. 356.
18 Her horoscope shows four earth signs but no air sign. The danger coming from the animus is reflected in: ☽ □ ☿.
19 Cf. the Buddhist conception of the "eight points of the compass" in the *Amitāyur-dhyāna Sūtra*; cf. "The Psychology of Eastern Meditation," pp. 560ff.
20 [SR: *domicilium Veneris* translates as house of Venus. Venus rules Taurus, the sign of the bull.]
21 [KLG: The birth chart for Switzerland (12 September 1848, 12:55 pm, Bern) places the Sun in Virgo in an opposition to Saturn. Saturn is also opposite Mercury, Venus, and Mars. The Sun-Saturn opposition has strong associations with a number of the

traits listed by Jung ("stolidity, inaccessibility, obstinacy"). As Jung notes, there is also a Venus-Mars conjunction. Mars is associated with the masculine principle and traits such as aggression, assertion, and force; Venus is associated with the feminine principle and traits such as pleasure, romance, beauty, and harmony. See "Nation: Switzerland 1848," www.astro.com/astro-databank/Nation:_Switzerland_1848 (accessed 2 December 2016).]

22 *Psychology and Alchemy*, index, s.v. "quartering."

23 [KLG: Astrologers usually distinguish between signs and houses. Signs are derived from the division of the year into twelve; houses are derived from the division of a day into twelve. Pisces is the twelfth sign of the zodiac and has a symbolic connection with the twelfth house. Both are "ruled" by Neptune (modern ruler) and Jupiter (ancient ruler).]

24 Schwartz, p. 141.

25 *Opera*, XXXVI, 6. Cited in Cumont, *Mysteries of Mithra*, p. 25.

26 This is a special motif which must have something typical about it. A schizophrenic patient ("The Psychology of Dementia Praecox," par. 290) declared that her horses had "half-moons" under their skins "like little curls." The *I Ching* is supposed to have been brought to China by a horse that had the magic signs (the "river map") on his coat. The skin of the Egyptian sky-goddess, the heavenly cow, is dotted with stars. (Cf. fig. 25.) The Mithraic Aion bears the signs of the zodiac on his skin (cf. pl. XLIV).

27 This is the result of a world catastrophe. In mythology, too, the blossoming and withering of the tree of life denotes the turning point, the beginning of a new age.

28 Br. Up., 1, i, trans, by Hume, p. 73, modified.

29 Cumont, *Textes*, I, p. 76.

30 Therefore the lion was killed by Samson, who afterwards harvested honey from the carcass. Summer's end is autumn's plenty. The legend of Samson is a parallel of the Mithraic sacrifice. Cf. Steinthal, "Die Sage von Simson," pp. 129ff.

31 *Saturnaliorum Libri VII*, I, 20, 15, in *Opera*, II, p. 189. ("Leonis capite monstratur praesens tempus – quia conditio ejus . . . valida fervensque est.")

32 In *Genesim*, I, 100, in *Opera omnia*, VI, p. 338. Cited in Cumont, *Textes*, I, p. 82.

33 Spiegel, *Eränische Altertumskunde*, II, p. 76.

34 [SR: *domicilium solis* translates as house of the sun. The sun rules Leo, the sign of the lion.]

35 "Love-songs to God," in Buber, p. 40. There is a related symbolism in Carlyle ("Heroes and Hero Worship," p. 280): "The great fact of Existence is great to him. Fly as he will, he cannot get out of the awful presence of this Reality. His mind is so made; he is great by that, first of all. Fearful and wonderful, real as Life, real as Death, is this Universe to him. Though all men should forget its truth, and walk in a vain show, he cannot. *At all moments the Flame-image glares in upon him.*" One could take any amount of examples from literature. For instance, S. Friedlander says, in *Jugend* (1910), p. 823: "Her longing demands only the purest from the beloved. Like the sun, she burns to ashes with the flame of her immense vitality anything that does not desire to be light. This sun-like eye of love," etc.

36 This image contains the psychological root of the "heavenly wanderings of the soul," an idea that is very old. It is an image of the wandering sun, which from its rising to its setting travels over the world. This comparison has been indelibly imprinted on man's imagination, as is clear from the poem "Grief" of Mathilde von Wesendonck (1828–1902):

> The sun, every evening weeping.
> Reddens its beautiful eyes for you;
> When early death seizes you,
> Bathing in the mirror of the sea.
>
> Still in its old splendour
> The glory rises from the dark world;

> You awaken anew in the morning
> Like a proud conqueror.
>
> Ah, why then should I lament,
> When my heart, so heavy, sees you?
> Must the sun itself despair?
> Must the sun set?
>
> And does death alone bear life?
> Do griefs alone give joys?
> O, how grateful I am that
> Such pains have given me nature!

There is another parallel in a poem by Ricarda Huch (1864–1947);

> As the earth, separating from the sun,
> Withdraws in quick flight into the stormy night,
> Starring the naked body with cold snow,
> Deafened, it takes away the summer joy.
> And sinking deeper in the shadows of winter,
> Suddenly draws close to that which it flees,
> Sees itself warmly embraced with rosy light
> Leaning against the lost consort.
> Thus I went, suffering the punishment of exile,
> Away from your countenance, into the ancient place.
> Unprotected, turning to the desolate north,
> Always retreating deeper into the sleep of death;
> And then would I awake on your heart,
> Blinded by the splendour of the dawn.
>
> [Both poems as trans.
> in the Hinkle edn. (1916).]

The heavenly journey is a special instance of the journeys of the hero, a motif that was continued as the *peregrinatio* in alchemy. The earliest appearance of this motif is probably the heavenly journey of Plato (?) in the Harranite treatise "Platonis liber quanorum" (*Theatrum chemicum*, V, p. 145). See also my *Psychology and Alchemy*, par. 457.

37 Buber, p. 45.
38 The Apis-bull as manifestation of Ptah.
39 Amon.
40 Sobk of the Fayum.
41 The god of Dedu, in the Delta, who was worshipped as a wooden post.
42 This reformation as initiated with a great deal of fanaticism but soon collapsed.
43 [SR: See original essay for illustration of "The life-giving Sun: Amenophis IV on his throne." Relief, Egypt.]
44 The pictures in the catacombs likewise contain a good deal of sun symbolism. For instance there is a swastika (sun-wheel) on the robe of Fossor Diogenes in the cemetery of Peter and Marcellinus. The symbols of the rising sun – bull and ram – are found in the Orpheus frescoes in the cemetery of Domitilla; also the ram and peacock (a sun-symbol like the phoenix) on an epitaph in the Callistus catacomb.
45 Numerous examples in Görres, *Die Christliche Mystik*.
46 Le Blant, *Sarcophages de la Gaule*. In the Homilies of Clement of Rome (*Homil.* II, 23, cited in Cumont, *Textes*, I, p. 356) we read: *τϖ κυριω ΥεΥσνασιν δωδεκα ἀπόστολοι τϖν του ηλίου δωδεκα μηνϖν φεροντες τὸν ἀριθμὸν* (The Lord had twelve apostles, bearing the number of the twelve months of the sun) (trans. by Roberts and Donaldson, p. 42). This image evidently refers to the sun's course through the zodiac. The course of the sun (like the course of the moon in Assyria; cf. fig. 10) was represented as a

snake carrying the signs of the zodiac on its back (like the *Deus leontocephalus* of the Mithraic mysteries; cf. Pl/ XLIV). This view is supported by a passage from a Vatican Codex edited by Cumont (190, 13th cent., p. 229; in Textes, I, p. 35): *Τότε ό πάνσοφος δημιουργός äκρω νευματι εκινησε τον μεγαν δράκοντα συν τω κεκοσμημενω στεφάνω, λεγω δη τὰ ιβ' ζωδια, βαστάζοντα επι του νωτου αυτου* (Then the all-wise Demiurge, by his highest command, set in motion the great dragon with the spangled crown, I mean the twelve signs of the zodiac which are borne on his back). In the Manichaean system, the symbol of the snake, and actually the snake on the tree of Paradise, was attributed to Christ. Cf. John 3:14: "And as Moses lifted up the serpent in the wilderness, so must the Son of man be lifted up" (Pl. IX*b*.).

47 *Apologia* 16: "Alii humanius et verisimilius Solem credunt deum nostrum."

48 "Report on the Happenings in Persia," from an 11th-cent. MS. in Munich: Wirth, ed., *Aus orientalischen Chroniken*, p. 151.

49 "To the great God Zeus Helios, King Jesus" (p. 166, § 22).

50 Abeghian, *Der armenische Volksglaube*, p. 43.

51 Samson as a sun-god. See Steinthal, "Die Sage von Simson." The killing of the lion, like the Mithraic bull-sacrifice, is an anticipation of the god's self-sacrifice.

52 Rudra, properly – as father of the Maruts (winds) – a wind- or storm-god, appears here as the sole creator-god, as the text shows. The role of creator and fertilizer naturally falls to him as a wind-god. Cf. my comments on Anaxagoras in pars. 67 and 76, above.

53 Trans. of this and the following passages (Shvet. Up. 3. 2–4; 7, 8, 11; 12–15) based on Hume, *The Thirteen Principal Upanishads*, pp. 399–401; and Max Muller, *The Upanishads*, II, pp. 244ff.

54 This interpretation is still a bit mythological; to be more accurate, the fish signifies an autonomous content of the unconscious. Manu had a fish with horns. Christ was a fish, like *Ἰχθύς*, son of the Syrophoenician Derceto. Joshua ben Nun was called "son of the fish." The "two-horned" (Dhulqarnein = Alexander) turns up in the legend of Khidr. (Cf. pl. xx*a*.)

55 The wrapping signifies invisibility, hence to be a "spirit." That is why the neophytes were veiled in the mysteries. (Cf. pl. Iv*b*.) Children born with a caul over their heads are supposed to be particularly fortunate.

56 The Etruscan Tages, the boy who sprang from the freshly ploughed furrow, was also a teacher of wisdom. In the Litaolane myth of the Basuto (Frobenius, p. 105), we are told how a monster devoured all human beings and left only one woman alive, who gave birth to a son, the hero, in a cowshed (instead of a cave). Before she could prepare a bed of straw for the infant, he was already grown up and spoke "words of wisdom." The rapid growth of the hero, a recurrent motif, seems to indicate that the birth and apparent childhood of the hero are extraordinary because his birth is really a rebirth, for which reason he is able to adapt so quickly to his heroic role. For a more detailed interpretation of the Khidr legend, see my paper "Concerning Rebirth," pars. 240ff. [SR: See original essay for illustration of a priest with a fish-mask, representing Oannes. Relief, Nimrud.]

57 Cf. Ra's fight with the night serpent.

58 *Gilgamesch-Epos*, I, p. 50. When revising this book, I left the above account, which is based mainly on Jensen, in its original form, though certain details could have been supplemented by the results of recent research. I refer the reader to Heidel, *The Gilgamesh Epic and Old Testament Parallels*; Schott, *Das Gilgamesch-Epos*; Speiser's version in Pritchard, ed., *Ancient Near Eastern Texts*; and especially to Thompson's remarkable trans., *The Epic of Gilgamish.*

59 [SR: Mithraic gods of light.]

60 The difference between this and the Mithraic sacrifice is significant. The dadophors are harmless gods of light who take no part in the sacrifice. The Christian scene is much more dramatic. The inner relation of the dadophors to Mithras, of which I will speak later, suggests that there was a similar relation between Christ and the two thieves.

61 For instance, there is the following dedication on a monument. "D[eo] Ifnvicto] M[ithrae] Cautopati." One finds that "Deo Mithrae Caute" or "Deo Mithrae Cautopati" is interchangeable with "Deo Invicto Mithrae" or "Deo Invicto," or simply "Invicto." Sometimes the dadophors are equipped with knife and bow, the attributes of Mithras. From this we can conclude that the three figures represent three different states, as it were, of a single person. Cf. Cumont, *Textes*, I, pp. 208f.

62 Ibid., p. 208f.

63 The triadic symbolism is discussed in my "A Psychological Approach to the Dogma of the Trinity," pars. 172ff.

64 *Textes*, I, p. 210.

65 For the period from 4300 to 2150 B.C. So, although these signs had long been superseded, they were preserved in the cults until well into the Christian era.

66 The Shvetashvatara Upanished (4, 6ff.) uses the following parable to describe the individual and the universal soul, the personal and transpersonal atman:

> Behold, upon the selfsame tree.
> Two birds, fast-bound companions, sit.
> This one enjoys the ripened fruit,
> The other looks, but does not eat.
>
> On such a tree my spirit crouched,
> Deluded by its powerlessness,
> Till seeing with joy how great its Lord,
> It found from sorrow swift release. . . .
>
> Hymns, sacrifices, Vedic lore,
> Past, future, all by him are taught.
> The Maya-Maker thinks the world
> In which by Maya we are caught.
>
> (Trans, based on Hume, pp. 403f.)

67 Among the elements composing man, the Mithraic liturgy lays particular stress on fire as the divine element, describing it as *το εις εμην κρασιν θεοδώρητον* (the divine gift in my composition). Dieterich, *Mithrasliturgie*, p. 58.

68 An illustration of the periodicity or rhythm expressed in sexuality.

69 Reproduced not from a photograph, but from a drawing I myself made.

70 In a myth of the Bakairi Indians, of Brazil, a woman appears who sprang from a corn mortar. A Zulu myth tells a woman to catch a drop of blood in a pot, then close the pot, put it aside for eight months, and open it again in the ninth month. She follows this advice, opens the pot in the ninth month, and finds a child inside it. (Frobenius, I, p. 237.)

71 Roscher, *Lexikon*, II, 2733/4, s.v. "Men."

72 A well-known sun-animal.

73 Like Mithras and the dadophors.

74 This explanation is not satisfactory, because I found it impossible to go into the archetypal incest problem and all its complications here. I have dealt with it at some length in my "Psychology of the Transference."

75 Like Gilgamesh, Dionysus, Heracles, Mithras, etc.

76 Cf. Graf, *Richard Wagner inn Fliegenden Holländer*.

77 John Pordage (1607–1681) studied theology and medicine in Oxford. He was a disciple of Jakob Boehme and a follower of his alchemical theosophy. He became an accomplished alchemist and astrologer. One of the chief figures in his mystical philosophy is Sophia. ("She is my divine, eternal, essential self-sufficiency. She is my wheel within my wheel," etc. – Pordage's *Sophia*, p. 21.)

78 The letter is printed in Roth-Scholz, *Deutsches Theatrum chemicum*, I, pp. 557–97. The first German edition of this "Philosophisches Send-Schreiben vom Stein der Weissheit"

seems to have been published in Amsterdam in 1698. [The letter was evidently written in English, since the German version in Roth-Scholz, 1728–1732, is stated to be "aus dem Englischen übersetzet." But no English edition or MS. can be traced at the British Museum, the Library of Congress, or any of the other important British and American libraries. Pordage's name does not occur among the alumni at Oxford. – EDITORS.]

79 One of the favourite allusions to the Song of Songs 7:2: "Thy navel is like a round goblet, which wanteth not liquor." Cf. also *Aurora consurgens*, I, Ch. XII.

80 The concluding passages are very reminiscent of the teachings of the "secta liberi spiritus," which were propagated as early as the 13th century by the Béguines and Beghards.

81 Hence Pordage's view is more or less in agreement with woman's conscious psychology, but not with her unconscious psychology.

82 Pordage, *Sophia*, Ch. I.

83 There is a modern work that gives an excellent account of the feminine world of symbols: Esther Harding's *Woman's Mysteries*.

84 [Cf. "Commentary on *The Secret of the Golden Flower*" (*CW*, vol. 13) and "Concerning Mandala Symbolism" (*CW*, vol. 9, 1) – EDITORS.]

85 The four *ριςωματα* of Empedocles.

86 The rest of the title is: "olim conscriptus et a quodam Christiano Philosopho collectus" (Written of old and gathered together by a certain Christian Philosopher). *Theatr. chem.*, V, pp. 880ff.

87 Here the author adds (p. 886): "It is better to take pleasure in the opus than in riches or in works of virtuosity (*virtuoso labore*)." The rare "virtuosus" is equivalent to the Greek ἐνάρετος.

88 Ibid., p. 885.

89 In his sermon on the "vessel of beaten gold" (Ecclesiasticus 50 : 9) Meister Eckhart says: "I have spoken a word which could be spoken of Saint Augustine or of any virtuous soul, such being likened to a golden vessel, massive and firm, adorned with every precious stone." Cf. Evans, I, p. 50.

90 Not only the vessel must be round, but the "fimarium" it is heated in. The "fimarium" is made of *fimus equinus* (horse-dung). *Theatr. chem.*, V, p. 887.

91 Cf. *Psychological Types*, def. 29 and par. 828, and "The Transcendent Function."

92 Cf. *Psychology and Alchemy*, par. 469.

93 Cf. *Two Essays on Analytical Psychology*, par. 367.

94 Cf. the heating and incubation of the Philosophers in the triple glass-house at the bottom of the sea in the Arisleus Vision. (Ruska, "Die Vision des Arisleus," *Historische Studien und Skizzen zu Natur- und Heilwissenschaft*, pp. 22 IÏ.; cf. the "Psychology of the Transference," par. 455 and n. 22.)

95 *Tapas* is a technical term, meaning "self-incubation" ("brooding") in the *dhyana* state.

96 For the psychology of the mandala see my "Commentary on *The Secret of the Golden Flower*," pars. 31ff., *Psychology and Alchemy*, pars, 122ff., "A Study in the Process of Individuation," and "Concerning Mandala Symbolism."

97 The archetypal, potential world as underlying pattern of the actual world. In the psychological sense, the collective unconscious. CF. *Mysterium*, CW 14, par. 761.

5 Fate, *heimarmene*, and ascent through the planetary spheres

From: "Introduction to the Religious and Psychological Problems of Alchemy" (1944) (*CW* 12), par. 40

40 Our understanding of these deeper layers of the psyche [the collective unconscious] is helped not only by a knowledge of primitive psychology and mythology, but to an even greater extent by some familiarity with the history of our modern consciousness and the stages immediately preceding it. On the one hand it is a child of the Church; on the other of science, in whose beginnings very much lies hid that the Church was unable to accept – that is to say, remnants of the classical spirit and the classical feeling for nature which could not be exterminated and eventually found refuge in the natural philosophy of the Middle Ages. As the "spiritus metallorum" and the astrological components of destiny the old gods of the planets lasted out many a Christian century.[1] Whereas in the Church the increasing differentiation of ritual and dogma alienated consciousness from its natural roots in the unconscious, alchemy and astrology were ceaselessly engaged in preserving the bridge to nature, i.e., to the unconscious psyche, from decay. Astrology led the conscious mind back again and again to the knowledge of Heimarmene, that is, the dependence of character and destiny on certain moments in time . . .

From: "The Personification of the Opposites" (1955/56) (*CW* 14), pars. 297–300, 303, 306, 308–309

297 Returning now to Michael Maier's journey to the seven mouths of the Nile, which signify the seven planets, we bring to this theme a deepened understanding of what the alchemists meant by ascent and descent. It was the freeing of the soul from the shackles of darkness, or unconsciousness; its ascent to heaven, the widening of consciousness; and finally its return to earth, to hard reality, in the form of the tincture or healing drink, endowed with the powers of the Above. What this means psychologically could be seen very clearly from the *Hypnerotomachia*[2] were its meaning not overlaid by a mass of ornate detail. It should therefore be pointed out that the whole first part of the book is a description of the dreamer's ascent to a world of gods and

heroes, of his initiation into a Venus mystery, followed by the illumination and semi-apotheosis of Poliphilo and his Polia. In the second, smaller part this leads to disenchantment and the cooling off of the lovers, culminating in the knowledge that it was all only a dream. It is a descent to earth, to the reality of daily life, and it is not altogether clear whether the hero managed to "preserve in secret the nature of the heavenly centre which he acquired by the ascent."[3] One rather doubts it. Nevertheless, his exciting adventure has left us a psychological document which is a perfect example of the course and the symbolism of the individuation process. The spirit, if not the language, of alchemy breathes through it and sheds light even on the darkest enigmas and riddles of the Masters.[4]

298 Maier's journey through the planetary houses begins with Saturn, who is the coldest, heaviest, and most distant of the planets, the maleficus and abode of evil, the mysterious and sinister Senex (Old Man), and from there he ascends to the region of the sun, to look for the Boy Mercurius, the longed-for and long-sought goal of the adept. It is an ascent ever nearer to the sun, from darkness and cold to light and warmth, from old age to youth, from death to rebirth. But he has to go back along the way he came, for Mercurius is not to be found in the region of the sun but at the point from which he originally started. This sounds very psychological, and in fact life never goes forward except at the place where it has come to a standstill.[5] The sought-for Mercurius is the *spiritus vegetativus*, a living spirit, whose nature it is to run through all the houses of the planets, i.e., the entire Zodiac. We could just as well say through the entire horoscope, or, since the horoscope is the chronometric equivalent of individual character, through all the characterological components of the personality. Individual character is, on the old view, the curse or blessing which the gods bestowed on the child at its birth in the form of favourable or unfavourable astrological aspects. The horoscope is like the "chirographum," the "handwriting of the ordinances against us . . . which Christ blotted out; and he took it out of the way, nailing it to his cross. And after having disarmed the principalities and powers he made a show of them openly, and triumphed over them."[6]

299 This very ancient idea of what we might call an inborn bill of debt to fate is the Western version of a prenatal karma. It is the archons, the seven rulers of the planets, who imprint its fate upon the soul. Thus Priscillian (d. *c.* 385) says that the soul, on its descent to birth, passes through "certain circles" where it is made captive by evil powers, "and in accordance with the will of the victorious prince is forced into divers bodies, and his handwriting inscribed upon it."[7] Presumably this means that the soul is imprinted with the influences of the various planetary spheres. The descent of the soul through the planetary houses corresponds to its passage through the gates of the planets as described by Origen: the first gate is of lead and is correlated with Saturn,[8] from which it is clear that Maier is following an old tradition.[9] His peregrinatio chymica repeats the old "heavenly journey of the soul," an idea which seems to have been developed more particularly in Persia.

300 I shall not go more closely here into the transitus through the planetary houses;[10] it is sufficient to know that Michael Maier, like Mercurius, passes through them on his mystic journey.[11]

303 He can find Mercurius only through the rite of ascent and descent, the "circular distillation," beginning with the black lead, with the darkness, coldness, and malignity of the malefic Saturn; then ascending through the other planets to the fiery Sol, where the gold is heated in the hottest fire and cleansed of all impurities; and finally returning to Saturn, where this time he meets Mercurius and receives some useful teachings from him. Saturn has here changed from a star of ill omen into a "domus barbae" (House of the Beard), where the "wisest of all," Thrice-Greatest Hermes, imparts wisdom.[12]

306 The sequence of colours coincides by and large with the sequence of the planets. Grey and black correspond to Saturn[13] and the evil world; they symbolize the beginning in darkness, in the melancholy, fear, wickedness, and wretchedness of ordinary human life. It is Maier from whom the saying comes about the "noble substance which moves from lord to lord, in the beginning whereof is wretchedness with vinegar."[14] By "lord" he means the archon and ruler of the planetary house. He adds: "And so it will fare with me." The darkness and blackness can be interpreted psychologically as man's confusion and lostness; that state which nowadays results in an anamnesis, a thorough examination of all those contents which are the cause of the problematical situation, or at any rate its expression.

308 Astrologically, as we have said, this process corresponds to an ascent through the planets from the dark, cold, distant Saturn to the sun. To the alchemists the connection between individual temperament and the positions of the planets was self-evident, for these elementary astrological considerations were the common property of any educated person in the Middle Ages as well as in antiquity. The ascent through the planetary spheres therefore meant something like a shedding of the characterological qualities indicated by the horoscope, a retrogressive liberation from the character imprinted by the archons. The conscious or unconscious model for such an ascent was the Gnostic redeemer, who either deceives the archons by guile or breaks their power by force. A similar motif is the release from the "bill of debt to fate." The men of late antiquity in particular felt their psychic situation to be fatally dependent on the compulsion of the stars, Heimarmene, a feeling which may be compared with that inspired by the modern theory of heredity, or rather by the pessimistic use of it. A similar demoralization sets in in many neuroses when the patient takes the psychic factors producing the symptoms as though they were unalterable facts which it is useless to resist. The journey through the planetary houses, like the crossing of the great halls in the Egyptian underworld, therefore signifies the overcoming of a psychic obstacle, or of an autonomous complex, suitably represented by a planetary god or demon. Anyone who has passed through all the spheres is free from compulsion; he has won the crown of victory and become like a god.

309 In our psychological language today we express ourselves more modestly: the journey through the planetary houses boils down to becoming conscious of the good and the bad qualities in our character, and the apotheosis means no more than maximum consciousness, which amounts to maximal freedom of the will. This goal cannot be better represented than by the alchemical symbol of the *μεσουράνισμα ἡλί.ον* (position of the sun at noon) in Zosimos.[15] But at the zenith the descent begins. The mystic traveller goes back to the Nile mouth from which he started. He repeats, as it were, the descent of the soul which had led in the first place to the imprinting of the "chirographum." He retraces his steps through the planetary houses until he comes back to the dark Saturn. This means that the soul, which was imprinted with a horoscopic character at the time of its descent into birth, conscious now of its godlikeness, beards the archons in their lairs and carries the light undisguised down into the darkness of the world.

From: "Adam and Eve" (1955/56) (*CW* 14), pars. 576, 578–579

576 The seven archons correspond to the seven planets and represent so many spheres with doors which the celebrant has to pass through on his ascent. . . . The old world-picture, with the earth as the centre of the universe, consisted of various "heavens" – spherical layers or spheres – arranged concentrically round the centre and named after the planets. The outermost planetary sphere or archon was Saturn. Outside this would be the sphere of the fixed stars . . .

578 In the introduction to his diagram Celsus reports on the idea, found among the Persians and in the Mithraic mysteries, of a stairway with seven doors and an eighth door at the top. The first door was Saturn and was correlated with lead, and so on. The seventh door was gold and signified the sun. The colours are also mentioned.[16] The stairway represents the "passage of the soul" (*animae transitus*). The eighth door corresponds to the sphere of the fixed stars.

579 The archetype of the seven appears again in the division of the week and the naming of its days, and in the musical octave, where the last note is always the beginning of a new cycle.

From: "The Components of the Coniunctio" (1955/56) (*CW* 14), pars. 5–6

5 The arrangement of the opposites in a quaternity is shown in an interesting illustration in Stolcenberg's *Viridarium chymicum*,[17] which can also be found in the *Philosophia reformata* of Mylius.[18] The goddesses represent the four seasons of the sun in the circle of the Zodiac (Aries, Cancer, Libra, Capricorn) and at the same time the four degrees of heating,[19] as well as the four elements "combined" around the circular table.[20] The synthesis of the elements is effected by means of the circular movement in time (*circulatio, rota*) of the sun through the houses of the Zodiac. As I have shown elsewhere,[21] the aim of the *circulatio* is the production (or rather, reproduction) of the Original Man,

who was a sphere. Perhaps I may mention in this connection a remarkable quotation from Ostanes in Abu'l-Qasim, describing the intermediate position between two pairs of opposites constituting a quaternio:

> Ostanes said, Save me, O my God, for I stand between two exalted brilliancies known for their wickedness, and between two dim lights; each of them has reached me and I know not how to save myself from them. And it was said to me, Go up to Agathodaimon the Great and ask aid of him, and know that there is in thee somewhat of his nature, which will never be corrupted. . . . And when I ascended into the air he said to me, Take the child of the bird which is mixed with redness and spread for the gold its bed which comes forth from the glass, and place it in its vessel whence it has no power to come out except when thou desirest, and leave it until its moistness has departed.[22]

6 The quaternio in this case evidently consists of the two *malefici*, Mars and Saturn (Mars is the ruler of Aries, Saturn of Capricorn); the two "dim lights" would then be feminine ones, the moon (ruler of Cancer) and Venus (ruler of Libra). The opposites between which Ostanes stands are thus masculine/feminine on the one hand and good/evil on the other. The way he speaks of the four luminaries – he does not know how to save himself from them – suggests that he is subject to Heimarmene, the compulsion of the stars; that is, to a transconscious factor beyond the reach of the human will. Apart from this compulsion, the injurious effect of the four planets is due to the fact that each of them exerts its specific influence on man and makes him a diversity of persons, whereas he should be *one*.[23] It is presumably Hermes who points out to Ostanes that something incorruptible is in his nature which he shares with the Agathodaimon,[24] something divine, obviously the germ of unity. This germ is the gold, the *aurum philosophorum*,[25] the bird of Hermes or the son of the bird, who is the same as the *filius philosophorum*.[26] He must be enclosed in the *vas Hermeticum* and heated until the "moistness" that still clings to him has departed, i.e., the *humidum radicale* (radical moisture), the prima materia, which is the original chaos and the sea (the unconscious). Some kind of coming to consciousness seems indicated. We know that the synthesis of the four was one of the main preoccupations of alchemy, as was, though to a lesser degree, the synthesis of the seven (metals, for instance). Thus in the same text Hermes says to the Sun:

> . . . I cause to come out to thee the spirits of thy brethren [the planets], O Sun, and I make them for thee a crown the like of which was never seen; and I cause thee and them to be within me, and I will make thy kingdom vigorous.[27]

This refers to the synthesis of the planets or metals with the sun, to form a crown which will be "within" Hermes. The crown signifies the kingly totality; it stands for unity and is not subject to Heimarmene. This reminds us of the seven- or twelve-rayed crown of light which the Agathodaimon serpent wears on Gnostic gems,[28] and also of the crown of Wisdom in the *Aurora Consurgens*.[29]

NOTES

1 Paracelsus still speaks of the "gods" enthroned in the *mysterium magnum* (*Philosophia and Athenienses*, p. 403), and so does the 18th-cent. treatise of Abraham Eleazar, *Uraltes chymisches Werk*, which was influenced by Paracelsus.
2 Colonna, *Hypnerotomachia Poliphili* (1499).
3 Dorn, "Phys. Trismeg.," *Theatr. chem*, I, p. 409.
4 For a thorough psychological analysis of the text see Fierz-David, *The Dream of Poliphilo*, pp. 578.
5 A psychological statement which, like all such, only becomes entirely true when it can be reversed.
6 Colossians 2 : 14f. (AV, mod.).
7 Orosius, *Ad Aurelium Augustinum commonitorium* (CSEL., XVIII, p. 153).
8 *Contra Celsum*, VI, 22 (trans. by Chadwick), p. 334. (Migne, P.G., vol. 9, col. 1324).
9 Usually the series seems to begin with Saturn. Cf. Bousset, "Die Himmelsreise der Seele."
10 The interested reader is referred to Cumont, *Textes et Monuments relatifs aux Mysteres de Mithra*, I, pp. 36ff.; Bousset, "Himmelsreise"; and Reitzenstein, "Himmelswanderung und Drachenkampf."
11 Cf. the journey motif in *Psychology and Alchemy*, pars. 304f., 457 and n. 75. Concerning Mercurius see the *puer-senex* motif in Curtius, *European Literature and the Latin Middle Ages*, pp. 98ff.
12 "Therefore I am called Hermes Trismegistos, as having three parts of the Philosophy of the whole world." "Tabula smaragdina," *De alchemia* (1541), cap. 12. "Domus barbae" comes from Arab *al-birba*, "pyramid," where Hermes was said to be buried.
13 "In the first place Saturn reigns in the *nigredo*." *Symb. aur. mensae*, p. 156.
14 Ibid., p. 568.
15 Berthelot, *Alch. grecs*, III, v bis (text vol., p. 118).
16 "For these two metals recall the colours of the sun and moon." (Cf. *Contra Celum*, p. 334.)
17 [SR: See essay in *CW* 14, fig. XLII.]
18 Mylius 1622, p. 117.
19 Mylius, p. 118. The fourth degree is the *coniunctio*, which would thus correspond to Capricorn.
20 Mylius remarks (p. 115): ". . . equality arises . . . from the four incompatibles mutually partaking in nature." A similar ancient idea seems to be that of the ἡλιακή τραπςα (solar table) in the Orphic mysteries. Cf. Proclus, *Commentaries on the Timaeus of Plato*, trans., by Taylor, II, p. 378: "And Orpheus knew indeed of the Crater of Bacchus, but he also establishes many others about the solar table." Cf. also Herodotus, *The Histories*, III, 17–18 (trans, by de Selincourt, p. 181), and Pausanias, *Description of Greece*, VI, 26, 2 (trans. by Jones, III, pp. 156ff.).
21 Cf. *Psychology and Alchemy*, index, s.v. "rotundum," "sphere," "wheel," and especially (par. 469, n. 110) the wheel with twelve buckets for raising souls in the *Acta Archelai*.
22 Holmyard, *Kitāb al-'ilm al-muktasab*, p. 38.
23 The idea of uniting the Many into One is found not only in alchemy but also in Origen, *In Libr. I Reg.* [*1 Sam.*] *Hom.*, I, 4 (Migne, *P.G.*, vol. 12, col. 998): "*There was one man*. We, who are still sinners, cannot obtain this title of praise, for each of us is not one but many. . . . See how he who thinks himself one is not one, but to have as many personalities as he has moods, as also the Scripture says: A fool is changed as the moon." In another homily, *In Ezech.*, 9, 1 (Migne, *P.G.*, col. 732) he says: "Where there are sins, there is multitude . . . but where virtue is, there is singleness, there is union." Cf. *Porphyry the Philosopher to His Wife Marcella*, trans., by Zimmern, p. 61: "If thou wouldst practise to ascend into thyself, collecting together all the powers which the body hath scattered and broken up into a multitude of parts

unlike their former unity . . ." Likewise the Gospel of Philip (cited from Epiphanius, *Panarium*, XXVI, 13): "I have taken knowledge (saith the soul) of myself, and have gathered myself together out of every quarter and have not begotten (sown) children unto the Ruler, but have rooted out his roots and gathered together the members that were scattered abroad. And I know thee who thou art, for I (she saith) am of them that are from above." (James, *The Apocryphal New Testament*, p. 12.) Cf. also *Panarium*, XXVI, 3: "I am thou, and thou art I, and wherever thou art, there I am, and I am scattered in all things, and from wherever thou wilt thou canst gather me, but in gathering me thou gatherest together thyself." The inner multiplicity of man reflects his microcosmic nature, which contains within it the stars and their (astrological) influences. Thus Origen (*In Lev. Hom.*, V, 2; Migne, *P.G.*, vol. 12, cols. 449–50) says: "Understand that thou hast within thyself herds of cattle . . . flocks of sheep and flocks of goats. . . . Understand that the fowls of the air are also within thee. Marvel not if we say that these are within thee, but understand that thou thyself art another world in little, and hast within thee the sun and the moon, and also the stars. . . . Thou seest that thou hast all those things which the world hath." And Dorn ("De tenebris contra naturam," *Theatr. chem.* I, p. 533) says: "To the four less perfect planets in the heavens there correspond the four elements in our body, that is, earth to Saturn, water to Mercury [instead of the moon, see above], air to Venus, and fire to Mars. Of these it is built up, and it is weak on account of the imperfection of the parts. And so let a tree be planted from them, whose root is ascribed to Saturn," etc., meaning the philosophical tree, symbol of the developmental process that results in the unity of the filius Philosophorum, or lapis. Cf. my "The Philosophical Tree," par. 409.

24 The *ἀγαθὸs δαίμων* is a snakelike, chthonic fertility daemon akin to the "genius" of the hero. In Egypt as well it was a snakelike daemon giving life and healing power. In the Berlin Magic Papyrus it is the *ἀγαθὸs γεωργός* who fertilizes the earth. On Gnostic gems it appears together with Enoch, Enoch being an early parallel of Hermes. The Sabaeans who transmitted the Agathodaimon to the Middle Ages as the *πνεῦμα πάρεδρον* (familiar spirit) of the magical procedure, identified it with Hermes and Orpheus. (Chwolsohn, *Die Ssabier*, II, p. 624.) Olympiodorus (Berthelot, *Alch. grecs*, II, iv, 18) mentions it as the "more secret angel" (*μυστικώτερον ἄγγελον*), as the uroboros or "heaven," on which account it later became a synonym for Mercurius.

25 Cf. the Indian teachings concerning *hiranyagarbha*, "golden germ," and *purusha*. Also "The Psychology of Eastern Meditation," pars. 917f.

26 Cf. *υλη της ὀρνιθογονίας* (the matter of the generation of the bird) in Zosimos (Berthelot, III, xliv, 1).

27 Holmyard, p. 37.

28 Cf. *Psychology and Alchemy*, figs. 203–5.

29 von Franz, pp. 53f. Cf. also Goodenough, "The Crown of Victory. . . ." Senior (*De chemia*, p. 41) calls the *terra alba foliata* "the crown of victory." In *Heliodori carmina*, v. 252 (ed. by Goldschmidt, p. 57) the soul, on returning to the body, brings it a νικητικύν στέμμα, "wreath of victory." In the Cabala the highest Sefira (like the lowest) is called Kether, the Crown. In Christian allegory the crown signifies Christ's humanity: Rabanus Maurus, *Allegoriae in Sacram Scripturam* (Migne, *P.L.*, vol. 112, col. 909). In the Acts of John, §109 (James, *Apocryphal New Testament*, p. 268) Christ is called the diadem.

6 Astrology and medicine

From: "Paracelsus as a Spiritual Phenomenon" (1942) (*CW* 13), par. 154

154 ... There was no form of manticism and magic that Paracelsus did not practise himself or recommend to others. Dabbling in these arts – no matter how enlightened one thinks one is – is not without its psychological dangers. Magic was and still is a source of fascination. At the time of Paracelsus, certainly, the world teemed with marvels; everyone was conscious of the immediate presence of the dark forces of nature. Astronomy and astrology were not yet separated. Kepler still cast horoscopes. Instead of chemistry there was only alchemy. Amulets, talismans, spells for healing wounds and diseases were taken as a matter of course.

From: "Paracelsus the Physician" (1942) (*CW* 15), pars. 22, 29–38

22 ... [Paracelsus] was mainly interested in the cosmic correlations, such as he found in the astrological tradition. His doctrine of the "star in the body" was a favourite idea of his, and it occurs everywhere in his writings. True to the conception of man as a microcosm, he located the "firmament" in man's body and called it the "astrum" or "Sydus." It was an endosomatic heaven, whose constellations did not coincide with the astronomical heaven but originated with the individual's nativity, the "ascendant" or horoscope.

29 The physician had to be not only an alchemist but also an astrologer,[1] for a second source of knowledge was the "firmament." In his *Labyrinthus medicorum* Paracelsus says that the stars in heaven must be "coupled together," and that the physician must "extract the judgment of the firmament from them."[2] Lacking this art of astrological interpretation, the physician is but a "pseudomedicus." The firmament is not merely the cosmic heaven, but a body which is a part or content of the human body. "Where the body is, there will the eagles gather. And where the medicine is, there do the physicians gather."[3] The firmamental body is the corporeal equivalent of the astrological heaven.[4] And since the astrological constellation makes a diagnosis possible, it also

indicates the therapy. In this sense the firmament may be said to contain the "medicine." The physicians gather round the firmamental body like eagles round a carcass because, as Paracelsus says in a not very savoury comparison, "the carcass of the natural light" lies in the firmament. In other words, the *corpus sydereum* is the source of illumination by the *lumen naturae*, the "natural light," which plays the greatest possible role not only in the writings of Paracelsus but in the whole of his thought. This intuitive conception is, in my opinion, an achievement of the utmost historical importance, for which no one should grudge Paracelsus undying fame. It had a great influence on his contemporaries and an even greater one on the mystic thinkers who came afterwards, but its significance for philosophy in general and for the theory of knowledge in particular still lies dormant. Its full development is reserved for the future.

30 The physician should learn to know this inner heaven. "For if he knows heaven only externally, he remains an astronomer and an astrologer; but if he establishes its order in man, then he knows two heavens. Now these two give the physician knowledge of the part which the upper sphere influences. This [part?] must be present without infirmity in the physician in order that he may know the *Caudam Draconis* in man, and know the *Arietem* and *Axem Polarem*, and his *Lineam Meridionalem*, his Orient and his Occident." "From the external we learn to know the internal." "Thus there is in man a firmament as in heaven, but not of one piece; there are two. For the hand that divided light from darkness, and the hand that made heaven and earth, has done likewise in the microcosm below, having taken from above and enclosed within man's skin everything that heaven contains. For that reason the external heaven is a guide to the heaven within. Who, then, will be a physician who does not know the external heaven? For we live in this same heaven and it lies before our eyes, whereas the heaven within us is not before the eyes but behind them, and therefore we cannot see it. For who can see through the skin? No one."[5]

31 We are involuntarily reminded of Kant's "starry heaven above me" and "moral law within me" – that "categorical imperative" which, psychologically speaking, took the place of the Heimarmene (compulsion of the stars) of the Stoics. There can be no doubt that Paracelsus was influenced by the Hermetic idea of "heaven above, heaven below."[6] In his conception of the inner heaven he glimpsed an eternal primordial image, which was implanted in him and in all men, and recurs at all times and places. "In every human being," he says, "there is a special heaven, whole and unbroken."[7] "For a child which is being conceived already has its heaven." "As the great heaven stands, so it is imprinted at birth."[8] Man has "his Father in heaven and also in the air, he is a child that is made and born from the air and from the firmament." There is a "linea lactea" in heaven and in us. "The galaxa goes through the belly."[9] The poles and the zodiac are likewise in the human body. "It is necessary," he says, "that a physician should recognize the ascendants, the conjunctions, the exaltations, etc., of the planets, and that he understand and know all the constellations. And if he knows these things externally in the Father, it follows that he

will know them in man, even though the number of men is so very great, and where to find heaven with its concordance in everyone, where health, where sickness, where beginning, where end, where death. For heaven is man and man is heaven, and all men are one heaven, and heaven is only one man."[10] The "Father in heaven" is the starry heaven itself. Heaven is the *homo maximus*, and the *corpus sydereum* is the representative of the *homo maximus* in the individual. "Now man was not born of man, for the first man had no progenitor, but was created. From created matter there grew the *Limbus*, and from the *Limbus* man was created and man has remained of the *Limbus*. And since he has remained so, he must be apprehended through the Father and not from himself, because he is enclosed in the skin (and no one can see through this and the workings within him are not visible). For the external heaven and the heaven within him are one, but in two parts. Even as Father and Son are two [aspects of one Godhead], so there is one Anatomy [which has two aspects]. Whoever knows the one, will also know the other."[11]

32 The heavenly Father, the *homo maximus*, can also fall sick, and this enables the physician to make his human diagnoses and prognoses. Heaven, says Paracelsus, is its own physician, "as the dog of its wounds." But man is not. Therefore he must "seek the locus of all sickness and health in the Father, and be mindful that this organ is of Mars, this of Venus, this of Luna," etc.[12] This evidently means that the physician has to diagnose sickness and health from the condition of the Father, or heaven. The stars are important aetiological factors. "Now all infection starts in the stars, and from the stars it follows afterwards in man. That is to say, if heaven is for it, then it begins in man. Now heaven does not enter into man – we should not talk nonsense on that account – but the stars in man, as ordered by God's hand, copy what heaven starts and brings to birth externally, and therefore it follows in man. It is like the sun shining through a glass and the moon giving light on the earth: but this does not injure a man, corrupting his body and causing diseases. For no more than the sun itself comes down to the earth do the stars enter a man, and their rays give a man nothing. The *Corpora* must do that and not the rays, and these are the *Corpora Microcosmi Astrali*, which gives the nature of the Father."[13] The *Corpora Astrali* are the same as the aforementioned *corpus sydereum* or *astrale*. Elsewhere Paracelsus says that "diseases come from the Father"[14] and not from man, just as the woodworm does not come from the wood.

33 The *astrum* in man is important not only for diagnosis and prognosis, but also for therapy. "From this emerges the reason why heaven is unfavourable to you and will not guide your medicine, so that you accomplish nothing: heaven must guide it for you. And the art lies, therefore, in that very place [i.e., heaven]. Say not that Melissa is good for the womb, or Marjoram for the head: so speak the ignorant. Such matters lie in Venus and in Luna, and if you wish them to have the effect you claim, you must have a favourable heaven or there will be no effect. Therein lies the error that has become

prevalent in medicine: Just hand out remedies, if they work, they work. Any peasant lad can engage in such practices, it takes no Avicenna or Galen."[15] When the physician has brought the *corpus astrale*, that is, the physiological Saturn (spleen) or Jupiter (liver), into the right connection with heaven, then, says Paracelsus, he is "on the right road." "And he should know, accordingly, how to make the Astral Mars and the physical Mars [the *corpus astrale*] subservient to one another, and how to conjugate and unite them. For this is the core which no physician from the first until myself has bit into. Thus it is understood that the medicine must be prepared in the stars and become firmamental. For the upper stars bring sickness and death, and also make well. Now if anything is to be done, it cannot be done without the *Astra*. And if it is to be done with the *Astra*, then the preparation should be completed at the same time as the medicine is being made and prepared by heaven."[16] The physician must "recognize the kind of medicine according to the stars and that, therefore, there are *Astra* both above and below. And since medicine can do nothing without heaven, it must be guided by heaven." This means that the astral influence must direct the alchemical procedure and the preparation of arcane remedies. "The course of heaven teaches the course and regimen of the fire in the Athanar.[17] For the virtue which lies in the sapphire comes from heaven by means of solution and coagulation and fixation."[18] Of the practical use of medicines Paracelsus says: "Medicine is in the will of the stars and is guided and directed by the stars. What belongs to the brain is directed to the brain by Luna; what belongs to the spleen is directed to the spleen by Saturn; what belongs to the heart is directed to the heart by Sol; and similarly to the kidneys by Venus, to the liver by Jupiter, to the bile by Mars. And not only is this so with these [organs], but with all the others which cannot be mentioned here."[19]

34 The names of diseases should likewise be correlated with astrology, and so should anatomy, which for Paracelsus meant nothing less than the astro-physiological structure of man, a "concordance with the machine of the world," and nothing at all resembling what Vesalius understood by it. It was not enough to cut open the body, "like a peasant looking at a psalter."[20] For him anatomy meant something like analysis. Accordingly he says: "Magic is the *Anatomia Medicinae*. Magic divides up the corpora of medicine."[21] But anatomy was also a kind of re-remembering of the original knowledge inborn in man, which is revealed to him by the *lumen naturae*. In his *Labyrinthus medicorum* he says: "How much labour and toil did the Mille Artifex[22] need to wrest this Anatomy from out the memory of man, to make him forget this noble art and lead him into vain imaginings and other mischief wherein there is no art, and which consume his time on earth unprofitably! For he who knows nothing loves nothing . . . but he who understands loves, observes, sees."[23]

35 With regard to the names of diseases, Paracelsus thought they should be chosen according to the zodiac and the planets, e.g., *Morbus leonis, sagittarii,*

martis, etc. But he himself seldom adhered to this rule. Very often he forgot how he had called something and then invented a new name for it – which, incidentally, only adds to our difficulties in trying to understand his writings.

36 We see, therefore, that for Paracelsus aetiology, diagnosis, prognosis, therapy, nosology, pharmacology, pharmaceutics, and – last but not least – the daily hazards of medical practice were all directly related to astrology. Thus he admonished his colleagues: "You should see to it, all you physicians, that you know the cause of fortune and misfortune: until you can do this, keep away from medicine."[24] This could mean that if the indications elicited from the patient's horoscope were unfavourable, the doctor had an opportunity to make himself scarce – a very welcome one in those robust times, as we also know from the career of the great Dr. Cardan.

37 But not content with being an alchemist and astrologer, the physician had also to be a philosopher. What did Paracelsus mean by "philosophy"? Philosophy, as he understood it, had nothing whatever to do with our conception of the matter. For him it was something "occult," as we would say. We must not forget that Paracelsus was an alchemist through and through, and that the "natural philosophy" he practised had far less to do with thinking than with *experience*. In the alchemical tradition "philosophia," "sapientia," and "scientia" were essentially the same. Although they were treated as abstract ideas, they were in some strange way imagined as being quasi-material, or at least as being contained in matter,[25] and were designated accordingly. Hence they appeared in the form of quicksilver or Mercurius, lead or Saturn, gold or *aurum non vulgi*, salt or *sal sapientiae*, water or *aqua permanens*, etc. These substances were arcana, and like them philosophy too was an arcanum. In practice, this meant that philosophy was as it were concealed in matter and could also be found there.[26] We are obviously dealing with psychological projections, that is, with a primitive state of mind still very much in evidence at the time of Paracelsus, the chief symptom of which is the unconscious identity of subject and object.

38 These preparatory remarks may help us to understand Paracelsus's question: "What is nature other than philosophy?"[27] "Philosophy" was in man and outside him. It was like a mirror, and this mirror consisted of the four elements, for in the elements the microcosm was reflected.[28] The microcosm could be known from its "mother,"[29] i.e., elemental "matter." There were really two "philosophies," relating respectively to the lower and higher spheres. The lower philosophy had to do with minerals, the higher with the *Astra*.[30] By this he meant astronomy, from which we can see how thin was the dividing line between philosophy and "Scientia." This is made very clear when we are told that philosophy was concerned with earth and water, astronomy with air and fire.[31] Like philosophy, Scientia was inborn in all creatures; thus the pear-tree produced pears only by virtue of its Scientia. Scientia was an "influence" hidden in nature, and one needed "magic" in order to reveal this arcanum. "All else is vain delusion and madness,

from which are begotten the fantasts." The gift of Scientia had to be "raised alchemically to the highest pitch,"[32] that is to say it had to be distilled, sublimated, and subtilized like a chemical substance. If the "Scientiae of nature" are not in the physician, "you will only hem and haw and know nothing for certain but the babbling of your mouth."[33]

NOTES

1 Paracelsus makes no real distinction between astronomy and astrology.
2 Ch. II (Huser, I), p. 267.
3 Ibid.
4 *Paragranum*, p. 50: "As in the heavens so also in the body the stars float free, pure, and have an invisible influence, like the arcana."
5 Ibid., p. 52.
6 Paracelsus certainly knew the "Tabula smaragdina," the classical authority of medieval alchemy, and the text: "What is below is like what is above. What is above is like what is below. Thus is the miracle of the One accomplished."
7 *Paragranum*, p. 56.
8 Ibid., p. 57.
9 P. 48. Cf. the description in "De elite astrali," *Fragmenta ad Paramirum* (Huser, I, p. 132): "The heavens are a spirit and a vapour in which we live just like a bird in time. Not only the stars or the moon etc. constitute the heavens, but also there are stars in us, and these which are in us and which we do not see constitute the heavens also . . . the firmament is twofold, that of the heavens and that of the bodies, and these latter agree with each other, and not the body with the firmament . . . man's strength comes from the upper firmament and all his power lies in it. As the former may be weak or strong, so, too, is the firmament in the body . . ."
10 *Paragranum*, p. 56.
11 Ibid., p. 55.
12 Ibid., p. 60.
13 Ibid., p. 54.
14 Ibid., p. 48.
15 Ibid., p. 73.
16 Ibid., p. 72.
17 Alchemical furnace.
18 *Paragranum*, p. 77.
19 Ibid., p. 73.
20 *Lab. med.*, ch. IV (Huser, I), p. 270.
21 Ibid., ch. IX, p. 277.
22 The devil.
23 *Lab. med.*, ch. IX, p. 278.
24 *Paragranum*, p. 67.
25 Hence the alchemists' strange but characteristic use of language, as for instance: "That body is the place of the science, gathering it together," etc. (Mylius, *Philosophia reformata*, p. 123.)
26 The "Liber quartorum" (10th cent.) speaks of the *extraction of thought*. The relevant passage runs: "Those seated by the river Euphrates are the Chaldaeans, who are skilled in the stars and in judging them, and they were the first to accomplish the extraction of thought." These inhabitants of the banks of the Euphrates were probably the Sabaeans or Harranites, to whose learned activities we owe the transmission of a great many scientific treatises of Alexandrian origin. Here, as in Paracelsus, alchemical transformation

is connected with the influence of the stars. The same passage says: "They who sit by the banks of the Euphrates convert gross bodies into a simple appearance, with the help of the movement of the higher bodies" (*Theatrum chemicum*, 1622, V, p. 144). Compare the "extraction of thought" with the Paracelsan saying that the Archasius "attracts science and prudence." See infra, par. 39.

27 *Paragranum*, p. 26.
28 Ibid., p. 27.
29 Ibid., pp. 28, 29.
30 Ibid., pp. 13, 33.
31 Ibid., p. 47.
32 *Lab. med.*, ch. VI (Huser, I), p. 273.
33 Ibid.

Part III

Astrological ages

INTRODUCTION

The worldview that periods of time or aeons are ruled by certain principles that are related to the divine order of the cosmos and the gods is a universal idea present in many cultures and religious traditions. The idea of astrological ages, or Platonic months, is one such idea from the Western tradition originating in ancient Greece. It is based on the image of the twelve signs of the zodiac with their constellations forming a belt around the Earth through which the sun appears to journey from our earthbound, geocentric perspective. The completion of a full cycle of the sun through the zodiac, called a Great or Platonic Year, takes approximately 26,000 years.

An astrological age is one twelfth of the Great Year, corresponding with the one zodiacal sign, therefore lasting approximately 2,200 years. It is calculated by assessing which zodiacal constellation hosts the sun at the time of the spring equinox in the northern hemisphere (20 March). That the sign in which the spring point falls changes is due to what is called the precession of the equinoxes. The Earth's wobble on its axis causes the location of the sun to change zodiac signs at the spring point. Thus, for the last 2,200 years the sun has been in the constellation of Pisces on the spring equinox point – hence this period is called the Age of Pisces. As the sun's position at the spring equinox moves into the next preceding sign of the zodiac, the age shifts to that of Aquarius.[1] We are currently in a period of great transition wherein the ruling principles are shifting.

Jung's interest in the astrological ages and the symbolic significance of the precession of the equinoxes has to do with the archetypal perspective that it affords to larger cycles of the collective. What he and others identified is how the religious symbolism of an era coincides with that of the astrological sign. As Alice O. Howell puts it, the zodiac in its Platonic cycle can be understood as

> a marvellously slow moving clock that seems to describe the evolution of the Collective Unconscious, since each of these ages has an uncanny way of bringing forth a new spiritual movement or religion that by an odd synchronicity or coincidence uses in its method and symbols the very characteristics and symbols of the astrological constellation that it reflects.[2]

Jung's interest in the astrological ages provided him with a symbolic perspective on the shifting values and perspectives of the Christian era and modern life. The chapters that comprise this part of the book are taken mostly from *Aion*, Jung's later-life work that focused on the psychology of Christianity and the Christ-symbol. While this figure symbolized the collective consciousness of the early Christian era, and represents the self and the movement to psychic completion, Jung argues that the Christ-symbol only does so partially because of Christ's one-sided goodness and perfection: "The self is best represented by symbols that unite the opposites, while the Christ-symbol represents only one side, the other being shown by his enemy, the Antichrist or Satan."[3] The astrological Age of Pisces, which is symbolized by the two fishes in the Pisces glyph, provided Jung with an archetypal ground for his views on the psychology of Christianity and the problem of the opposites when there is a splitting between good and evil. Jung wrote, "A synchronicity exists between the life of Christ and the objective astronomical event, the entrance of the spring equinox into the sign of Pisces. Christ is therefore the 'Fish' . . . and comes forth as the ruler of the new aeon."[4] The resulting psychological task for modern individuation becomes the overcoming of this opposition. This is symbolized by the coming Age of Aquarius whose zodiac sign is a human figure who pours water from a vase.

Astrological amplification helped Jung establish and deepen his psychological insights on the archetypal background to historical events. His interest in the synchronicity or coincidence between the religious ideas that grip the collective unconscious during the ruling astrological age and the insights afforded through astrological symbolism is illustrated in the following chapters.

Chapter 7 gathers together Jung's varied articulations about the astrological ages in general, with some concluding thoughts as to the character of the approaching Age of Aquarius. Where the problem of opposites was symbolized in the two fishes of Pisces, so the Age of Aquarius brings a human figure who unites the opposites.

Chapters 8, 9, and 10 are taken from *Aion* and deal with the symbolism of Pisces, which Jung often called "the sign of the fishes," and its connections to the Christ-symbol and the age of Christianity. These three chapters focus on the historical and symbolic significance of the sign of the fishes in order to amplify and give a meaningful orientation to the problem of the opposites inherent in the psychology of Christianity. In this vein Jung makes use of the astrological prophecies of Nostradamus, a sixteenth-century French physician who predicted major world events in his work *The Prophecies* (1555).

Safron Rossi

NOTES

1 The topic of the precession of the equinoxes and the astrological ages is explained with succinct clarity by Howell, *Jungian Symbolism in Astrology*.

2 Howell, *Jungian Symbolism in Astrology*, 23.

3 Stein, *Jung's Treatment of Christianity*, 148. See Jung, "Christ, A Symbol of the Self," in *Aion* (*CW* 9ii).
4 Jung, *Memories, Dreams, Reflections*, 220–221.

BIBLIOGRAPHY

Howell, Alice O. *Jungian Symbolism in Astrology*. Wheaton, IL: Quest Books, 1987.

Jung, Carl Gustav. *Aion*. Vol. 9, part II of *The Collected Works of C. G. Jung*. 2nd Edition. Translated by R. F. C. Hull. Princeton, NJ: Princeton University Press, 1951.

———. *Memories, Dreams, Reflections*. Edited by Aniela Jaffé. Translated by Richard Winston and Clara Winston. New York: Vintage Books, 1989.

Stein, Murray. *Jung's Treatment of Christianity*. Wilmette, IL: Chiron Publications, 1986.

7 The symbolic significance of the precession

ASTROLOGICAL AGES AND CULTURAL TRANSITION

From: "Liber Secundus: The Magician," *The Red Book*: *Liber Novus* (1913), p. 394

Salvation is the resolution of the task. The task is to give birth to the old in a new time. The soul of humanity is like the great wheel of the zodiac that rolls along the way. Everything that comes up in a constant movement from below to the heights was already there. There is no part of the wheel that does not come around again.

From: "A Study in the Process of Individuation" (1934/50) (*CW* 9i), par. 551

551 . . . There exist universal ideas of world periods, critical transitions, gods and half gods who personify the aeons. The unconscious naturally does not produce its images from conscious reflections, but from the worldwide propensity of the human system to form such conceptions as the world periods of the Parsees, the yugas and avatars of Hinduism, and the Platonic months of astrology with their bull and ram deities and the "great" Fish of the Christian era.[1]

From: "The Meaning of Psychology for Modern Man" (1933/34) (*CW* 10), par. 293

293 Thus, the sickness of dissociation in our world is at the same time a process of recovery, or rather, the climax of a period of pregnancy which heralds the throes of birth. A time of dissociation such as prevailed during the Roman Empire is simultaneously an age of rebirth. Not without reason do we date our era from the age of Augustus, for that epoch saw the birth of the symbolical figure of Christ, who was invoked by the early Christians as the Fish, the Ruler of the aeon of Pisces which had just begun.[2] He became the ruling spirit of the next two thousand years. Like the teacher of wisdom in Babylonian legend, Oannes, he rose up from the sea, from the primeval darkness, and brought a world-period to an end.

From: "Flying Saucers: A Modern Myth" (1958) (*CW* 10), pars. 589–590

589 As we know from ancient Egyptian history, they are manifestations of psychic changes which always appear at the end of one Platonic month and at the beginning of another. Apparently they are changes in the constellation of psychic dominants, of the archetypes, or "gods" as they used to be called, which bring about, or accompany, long-lasting transformations of the collective psyche. This transformation started in the historical era and left its traces first in the passing of the aeon of Taurus into that of Aries, and then of Aries into Pisces, whose beginning coincides with the rise of Christianity. We are now nearing that great change which may be expected when the spring-point enters Aquarius.

590 It would be frivolous of me to try to conceal from the reader that such reflections are not only exceedingly unpopular but even come perilously close to those turbid fantasies which becloud the minds of world-reformers and other interpreters of "signs and potents." But I must take the risk, even if it means putting my hard-won reputation for truthfulness, reliability, and capacity for scientific judgment in jeopardy. I can assure my readers that I do not do this with a light heart. I am, to be quite frank, concerned for all those who are caught unprepared by the events in question and disconcerted by their incomprehensible nature. Since, as far as I know, no one has yet felt moved to examine and set forth the possible psychic consequences of this foreseeable astrological change, I deem it my duty to do what I can in this respect. I undertake this thankless task in the expectation that my chisel will make no impression on the hard stone it encounters.

From: "To Pater Lucas Menz, O.S.B., 22 February 1955," *Letters II*

Now once again we are in a time of decay and transition, as around 2000 B.C., when the Old Kingdom of Egypt collapsed, and at the beginning of the Christian era, when the New Kingdom finally came to an end and with it classical Greece. The vernal equinox is moving out of the sign of Pisces into the sign of Aquarius, just as it did out of Taurus (the old bull gods) into Aries (the sacrificed lamb) into Pisces (*Ἰχθύς*). . . . 1500 years ago . . . [when] the seeds of a new culture germinating in the decay were bedded in the new spirit of Christianity. Our apocalyptic epoch likewise contains the seeds of a different unprecedented, and still inconceivable future which could be bedded in the Christian spirit if only this would renew itself, as happened with the seeds that sprouted from the decay of classical culture.

From: "Scrutinies," *The Red Book*: *Liber Novus* (1914), p. 543

The time has come when each must do his own work of redemption. Mankind has grown older and a new month has begun.[3]

FROM THE AGE OF ARIES TO THE AGE OF AQUARIUS

From: "The Work," *Memories, Dreams, Reflections* (1963), pp. 220–221

In *Aion* I embarked upon a cycle of problems that needed to be dealt with separately. I had attempted to explain how the appearance of Christ coincided with the beginning of a new aeon, the age of the Fishes. A synchronicity exists between the life of Christ and the objective astronomical event, the entrance of the spring equinox into the sign of Pisces. Christ is therefore the "Fish" (just as Hammurabi before him was the "Ram"), and comes forth as the ruler of the new aeon. This led to the problem of synchronicity, which I discussed in my paper "Synchronicity: An Acausal Connecting Principle."[4]

From: "17 May 1933," *Visions II*

DR. JUNG: . . . In that highly differentiated religious form Christianity, the primitive *is* the sacrifice. That is the thing which has to be killed, to be offered up to the God; in other words, it is given back to the unconscious, because the gods are the overpowering factors of the unconscious. So they offer the primitive man that is in everybody to the unconscious; he has to be killed for the sake of the existence of the higher form. Therefore also the astrological signs which characterize certain months of the Platonic year are represented in the Christian cult as the sacrificial animals. The sacrificed lamb referred to the earlier age of Aries, the Ram; and the sacrifice of the bull represented the age before that, the Age of the Bull, which was from about 4300 to 2200 B.C. There was the same idea in the fish meal of the early Christian; the astrological sign is two fishes, and the communion was then not celebrated in the present form with wine and bread, it was a meal of fish. The Christians were called fishes as well as lambs and they wore rings with the little fish or fishes engraved upon them. The Pope's ring contains a gem on which is carved the miraculous draught of fishes, symbolizing the shepherd – or the fisher – that draws the flock into the church. This fish meal was by no means Christian only; it occurred in other cults of those early days when Christianity was just one of a number of mystery cults.

From: "22 June 1932," *Visions II*

DR. JUNG: Do you know the symbology of Christ's crucifixion? When did the crucifixion take place?

MRS. CROWLEY: At the spring point.

DR. JUNG: Yes, in the neighborhood of the vernal equinox, the sacrifice of the lamb takes place. Now the lamb is really Aries, the little ram; the Greek word for lamb is *tó arníon*, and that comes from the root word *arēn* meaning the ram, so the *arníon* is the little lamb that was sacrificed at the spring point of the year, between 100 and 150 B.C., when Aries came to an end. When the sun changed from the month of the Ram into the month of the Fishes, the lamb was sacrificed. Therefore Christ was called *Ichthys*, the fish. Now the sacrifice of the spring point, the time of the vernal equinox, is symbolic, it is the time of the cross. What is the vernal cross?

DR. OTT: It is the time when the ecliptic crosses the equator.

DR. JUNG: Exactly, the spring point is just when the ecliptic crosses the equator. That concept was already known to the old Babylonians; therefore the idea of the cross has often been associated with this astronomical feature. The idea is rather too abstract, it is not quite satisfactory, yet when one realizes how much astrology went into the early symbology, one can hardly doubt it, it is most probable. Like the relationship of John the Baptist to Christ. John the Baptist was born six months before Christ, which would be the time of the summer increase, and John says of Christ: "He must grow but I must decrease." So when the sun is in the summer solstice it must decrease, but when it is in the winter solstice, when Christ was born, it must increase. That shows how much of astronomy and astrology has gone into these legends. The cross, then, is the vernal sacrifice. And of what did the vernal sacrifice consist in antiquity?

DR. OTT: It was the time of the Passover.

DR. JUNG: Yes, and there were other parallels. It was particularly this *sacrifice des primeurs*, the first fruits of the field, the first vegetables, the first lambs and the other young animals, and so on. And the firstborn son, Christ the son of God, is also sacrificed at the time of the vernal equinox. This idea of youth being sacrificed was called in Rome the *ver sacrum*, the sacred spring. What does it symbolize? Why should youth be sacrificed then? Or why should it be sacrificed at all?

MRS. CROWLEY: It is still connected with the astrological situation.

DR. JUNG: That was projected. The sacrifices took place much earlier than the astrological projection.

DR. OTT: Was it not a guarantee of the future, a sort of propitiatory sacrifice?

DR. JUNG: Yes, you could say the best things of the future were sacrificed in order to propitiate the gods of the future, to ensure a fertile continuation of the year.

From: "8 June 1932," *Visions II*

DR. JUNG: I have something rather extraordinary to show you today. This is not a map of America or Europe, it is a map of a part of the sky, of certain zodiacal signs. We have come to this problem through the remark which Dr. Curtius made in our last seminar about the astrological implication in the symbolism of the Pegasus. The patient was lifted up to the sky by a white winged horse, they flew among the stars till they came to the white city in the clouds, and there she found that other woman who was crucified, lying on the ground on a black cross. And she saw that her breast was pierced by a spear and that there was a star on the other end of the spear,

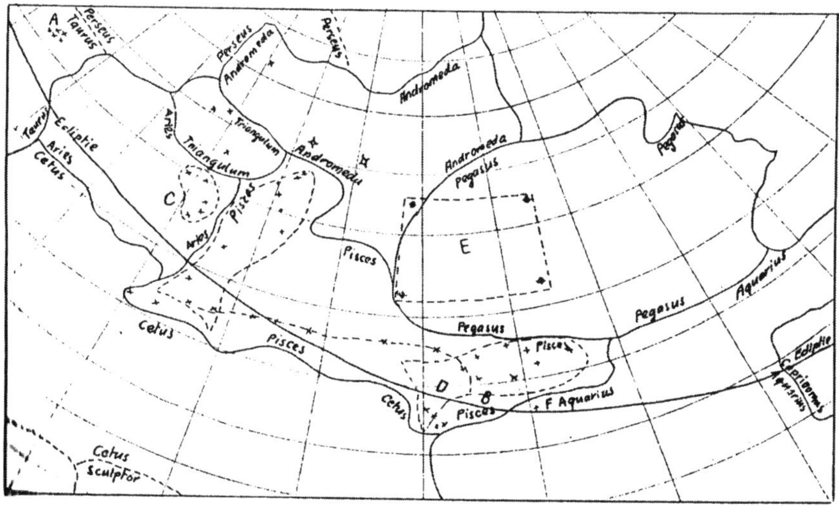

Figure 7.1 Zodiacal map

Source: Reproduced from Jung's *Visions*.

so that the picture looks, you remember, as if a shaft of light were descending from the star and piercing her heart. Then standing as if in the air behind the cross, rather ghostlike, was that white winged horse, the Pegasus. Dr. Curtius asked whether this had not to do with astrology. Now we have no definite indication from the text, nor do I know from the patient herself directly, whether she had any consciousness of such relation. As far as I know, if she had any knowledge at all of astrology it would be very superficial, enough perhaps to give little information about the structure of a horoscope – it would be necessary to know about the sun and the moon, the planets, and the signs of the zodiac – but not enough to give her any idea of the other constellations and their meanings.

The series of the zodiacal signs consist of the belt of constellations from the sky, which is characterized as marking the passage of the sun. But besides these constellations there are others which are just as mythological as the zodiacal signs; besides Aries and Taurus and Aquarius and Pisces, for instance, there are the Corona Borealis, the Ursa Major, the Pisces Austrinus, and many more, which play apparently very little role in modern astrology, though originally they had a certain meaning. For as the zodiacal symbolism was not written in the stars, but originated in the human unconscious and was projected to the sky, so naturally all the other constellations in the heavens have been produced and characterized by projections of unconscious contents. Therefore if there is any kind of psychological mythology in the zodiac – and apparently there is – we must assume that the other constellations also contain psychological meaning. It might turn out, however, that the human unconscious is to be found written only in the constellations of the northern hemisphere and not in the southern hemisphere. From what may one recognize that possibility? What is the characteristic of the southern constellations?

MRS. BAYNES: I think they don't lend themselves so readily to these pictures.

DR. JUNG: Human imagination can do a lot, but it is perfectly true that the southern constellations are far less impressive; one is really disappointed when one sees them. The famous Southern Cross, for instance, is a pretty poor invention. But of course that would be no reason why people should not make projections into them. As a matter of fact they have names, but they are by no means mythological, they are chiefly technical, nautical technics or terms. There is a compass, for instance, and a microscope, entirely modern designations invented by seamen who compared to these constellations to certain instruments they used or knew about. Apparently there is absolutely no mythology in the southern sky, which comes from the fact that all the civilizations which have influenced us have arisen in the northern hemisphere. Though if we knew about Peruvian astronomy, for instance – which probably existed – no doubt we would discover kind of mythological terminology similar to ours.

This map shows a part of the belt of the zodiac. You see here are constellations above and below, taking the north as above, the region of the polar star. We have the field of constellations above reaching down to the zodiac, and below, they approach the horizon and slowly die away below the horizon line. The ecliptic is the way of the precession of the equinoxes, and upon that line is the so-called spring point, namely, the point where the sun rises on the 21st of March, where spring begins. And that point, in the year 2200 B.C., was near the Pleiades – which is a group of stars here (A) – and then each year it receded. It is a sort of regression. The sun always moves to the west, and Aries would be the first spring month, from the 21st of March to the 21st of April. Then from the 21st of April to the 21st of May comes Taurus, the Bull. But the spring point is receding every year by fifty-five seconds; so in 1000 B.C. the spring point was above Aries, the Ram, and in 100 B.C. the spring point was in zero Aries. So in 2100 years the spring point receded for thirty degrees through the sign of Aries, and then entered the area which is designated as Pisces. Usually one finds two Fishes as the zodiacal symbol, but this is a map of the real constellation, and you can see the group of stars which forms the first Fish into which the spring point entered. By comparing it with the meridians leading to the zenith, you can see that this Fish is vertical, the head towards the northern point. Then there is a series of stars called the ribbon or the *commissura*, leading to a second Fish which is horizontal. The spring point has now advance through that sign, and our actual position is about here (B); it is still moving along in the field of the Fishes, it goes parallel to the second Fish, in its immediate vicinity but not exactly through it.

Now astrology suggests that anyone born under Aries, or in the age that is characterized by Aries, has some intellectual quality, a sprouting intelligence;

if his rising sign is in Aries, he will have a certain kind of temperamental intellect consisting chiefly of a sort of intensity, and impulsiveness, which does not last very long. There are always intellectual interests, yet, because it is a spring sign, they are of short duration, like the little shoots of grass in early spring. Now, why it should be just intellect must be taken for granted, that is what astrology says. Whether it is so or not does not matter, that is something else.

Then, anyone born under Fishes is easily influenced or overcome by certain atmospheric influences or currents, or by surrounding human influences; it is as if such people were always swimming in a sort of current. There are also most contradictory things about the Fishes. Instead of the astronomical position where one Fish is horizontal, in the astrological sign written in the symbolic form, one Fish is upright and the other upside down, and the *commissura* in between. Of course the conventional sign is like this ♓ but the original sign is as I have drawn it, so there is a peculiar kind of contrast. There is also a contrasting movement in the sign of Cancer, which is like this: ♋ with a rather irrational sort of spring in between the two. It is characteristic of everyone who is influenced by the Fishes that they are moved by paradoxical contradictory currents.

Now, the world month is the twelfth part of the so-called platonic year, which lasts twenty-six thousand years and which is based upon the movement of the spring point, or the precession of the equinoxes. In other words the movement of the spring point takes twenty-six thousand years to go around and return – only in twenty-six thousand years is that point reached again. Each sign of the zodiac is a twelfth part of that platonic year, and one month lasts about two thousand one hundred and fifty years, sometimes more and sometimes less. The idea that the epoch characterized by Aries would be a time in which the intellect developed is to a certain extent historically true. In the age between 2200 and 100 B.C. human civilization and the human intellect advanced tremendously. We know little of the time before – the age of Taurus – but it seems to have been chiefly a period in which the arts and crafts, and politics and strategy developed, which comes from the fact that everything influenced by Taurus is supposed to be artistic

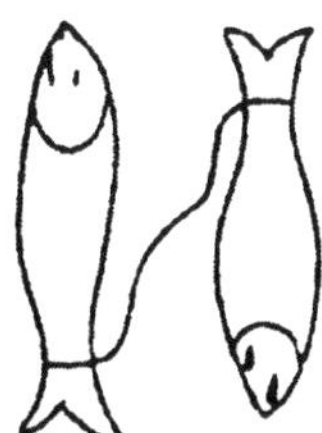

Figure 7.2 Constellation of Pisces

Source: Reproduced from Jung's *Visions*.

and of a very earthly nature, because Taurus is in the *Domicilium Veneris*,[5] which makes everything beautiful. That time was characterized by earthly beauty and power, empire, great conquests, etc., all of the chthonic nature. But Aries was of a different quality; it is quite true that the intellect developed then, it was an age of great philosophical development. Great philosophy, and the Vedic philosophy – the Upanishads – and the great Chinese philosophy all arose at about that time. There was a group of particularly brilliant stars towards the end of Aries (C), between Alpha Aries and Beta Aries, and that would be exactly the time between 600 and 400 B.C. which is characterized by the great schools of Athens, such as the school of Pythagoras and the Greek philosophers down to Plato; and in China, by Lao-tze and Confucius, down to Chuang-tze. It was the time of the greatest unfolding of the human mind before our era.

I have already told you of the two Fishes, and how Christ was called Ichthys, the Fish, and about the antichrist, the antithesis of Christ; also the chronology, the fact that the middle of the *commissura* corresponds to the year 1500 and the great schism occurred, the dissociation of the universal Catholic Church. That was the end of the old Christianity and the beginning of Protestantism. And then here (D) would be about 1720, the time of Diderot and the French Enlightenment, when Christianity became the object of criticism for the first time since the beginning of our time reckoning. The French Revolution followed, the liberation of human reason, and after that the exodus of science out of the church. Finally the complete reversal, the breaking away of a great part of the Eurasian continent, with the Russian Bolsheviks violently destroying Christianity, and the church is entirely deserted. All that fits in with astrological psychology, so there is something in astrology that holds water.

Now in studying the psychology of these projections we should pay attention to the neighboring fields, and there we shall see very interesting things. For if we give any weight to this projected psychology, we must assume that the surrounding constellations are not merely accidental, they probably have a psychological connection with each other, forming a sort of meaningful tissue; so it is worthwhile to study them from that point of view. I call your attention first to the constellations that are below, and that is a pretty simple affair. The big constellation is Cetus, the whale. The idea is that below the conscious sphere of man, which is given in the zodiacal signs, is an enormous whale. As you know, the whale plays a great role in mythology, it is the great whale dragon. One still finds the idea in Jewish cabalism, which is built upon very early premises, that a third of the sea is filled by one animal called the Leviathan, the enormous whale monster. The Japanese myth that the world is built upon the back of an enormous salamander is similar. And all the legends of heroes that overcome male dragons have probably to do with that huge monster. For we always have the feeling that the unconscious – often called the *sub*-conscious – is below the brain somewhere or below our feet, just as we think of hell as below. Since the two world months of Aries and the Fishes seem to have the character of consciousness above, it is quite possible that Cetus below represents the great monster of the unconscious, ever threatening to swallow the conscious world. People were beginning to follow all sorts of conscious pursuits, but there was always the fact of the monster that might swallow the whole world just coming into existence. And Cetus, the sign of that condition, the enormous danger of the unconscious, extends practically to the point where we are now.

We come now to the region above. We speak of things above, we mean, psychologically, a ruling principle, the eternal ideas above our heads, the good God above, the law, superior consciousness; all leading, or redeeming principles are thought of as being above. Therefore, people often object to the idea that the unconscious is below, under the feet; they insist that there is something unconscious above, a sort of superior unconscious. Of course to speak of the unconscious as under our feet is just a *façon de parler*,[6] whatever is above is equally in the sphere of the psychological unconscious, only in a different role. So we find above – up on the left of the map – the constellation of Perseus, the famous hero who killed the monster that was threatening Andromeda. He was one of the old heroes of Greece, like Heracles and Theseus; they belonged to the very remote hero ancestors. He was the son of Zeus and Danaë, and he was created by a miracle; Zeus could not get to that girl because she was walled into an iron room, so he had to come in through the roof as a golden shower of rain, and in that form he impregnated Danaë. This son Perseus overcame all sorts of horrors, the Graeae, for instance, those three horrible women of fate, who had only one eye and one tooth between them. Then he acquired a helmet which made him invisible like Siegfried, and a pair of winged soles and a diamond sickle like Hermes – all sorts of beautiful things. He also rode a marvellous horse, and he killed the Gorgon and got the head. Then comes the story of Andromeda, who was the daughter of the king and was destined to be a sacrifice to an awful sea monster. She was fastened naked to a rock and the monster was making for her, when Perseus came walking through the air on his winged soles, holding in his hand the Gorgon's head, and at the moment when the monster came out of the sea, Perseus confronted him with the head of Medusa, whereupon the monster became instantly transformed into stone. You see, Perseus is the hero who was invented to fight this enormous monster in the sea, that always threaten to swallow the king's beautiful daughter. The motif of the sacrifice of the most beautiful girl to the monster repeats itself very often in myths. What is this beautiful daughter?

MISS HANNAH: The Self.

DR. JUNG: Why should that be a beautiful girl? I am quite certain that *my* Self is not a beautiful girl. These were not fairy tales, they were really myths, they were sacred texts to be narrated for healing or magical purposes, and they were invented by medicine men, they are absolutely masculine. Andromeda is his anima, his soul, who was to be captured by the monster in the sea, just spirited away. By that fact, we know that the soul was always in the possession of the unconscious, even at a time when the intellect was beginning to develop; and only sacrifice could sever the connection and save mankind from its all-devouring and ever threatening power. It was necessary to invent a method of the hero to kill the monster, this formidable activity of the unconscious. So the sign of Perseus leads directly to the sign of Andromeda; the hero who overcomes the dragon liberates the soul from the curse of unconsciousness. Now the constellation of Andromeda is separated from the sphere of Aries by another little constellation, the so-called *triangulum*. What is the triangle in comparison with Perseus and Andromeda? It lies in the immediate vicinity, but a bit earlier than that group of stars which indicate the beginning of philosophy. You see, it is an abstract symbol; if a triangle occurred in a dream, you would interpret it as an abstract thought.

MR. ALLEMANN: It is an intellectual concept.

DR. JUNG: Yes, an intellectual concept here becomes the leading symbol. According to astrological reckoning, and about the year 1000 B.C. the intellect began to stir in man through the vicinity of the triangulum; abstract ideas appear, and philosophy ensues, projecting a sort of philosophical concept up into heaven as a guide. It is no longer Perseus, the mystical hero, doing great deeds and liberating mankind from the Leviathan in the sea; it is now philosophy, it is abstract human notions. But they receive their light from the particularly brilliant stars of Andromeda, and that belongs to the field of the anima. So one could say that wisdom was then influenced less by man – of course by men primarily, but chiefly through the anima. And there, out of the anima, appears the figure of Sophia that one finds in the Gnostic development of the anima, also in the second part of *Faust*. Moreover, as Aries would be under the masculine principle – the beginning of the intellectual predominance, of the abstract idea – the compensatory feminine principle then appears, and from that time on we have a world which is under the feminine principle. The age of the Fishes begins here, and that is influenced until the fifteenth or sixteenth centuries by the unconscious Virgo. Fishes also symbolize little children, and one sees that influence in the Christian symbolism, the little lambs as well as the Fishes. The Pope still wears a ring with the picture of the miraculous draft of fishes, meaning that he is pulling all the peoples of the earth into his net. But the ruling principle of that part of Fishes would be feminine, it was most certainly the church, *Ecclesia Mater*, or the Virgin Mother, the Heavenly Bride, etc., and that would last up to about the sixteenth century.

Then begins a new period of time which is usually calculated from the 30 Years' War, or the Reformation – with great justification because that was the age when the great discoveries of the world took place, when the vertical position of the Fish came to an end and the horizontal extension began. Until then the development of civilization was like a Gothic spire, our ancestors were all concentrated upon the narrow peninsula Europe, and beyond this very little of the world was known. Then the great voyages began, and the fact that the world was a globe is discovered. That had been known in Greek times already, but it was forgotten in the meantime. So an entirely new world was created. It was at last realized that the earth was not the center of the universe, but that it rotated around the sun. This was a great shock, which changed our whole outlook; it was really the birth of natural science.

Now here (E) we get under a new ruling principle which is no longer female, it is Pegasus, and as we had there a *triangulum*, we have here a *quadrangulum*, the square of Pegasus. That would be the sign which now rules this meridian; it would begin a bit before 1900 or now in 1932, so Pegasus is the ruling principle at this time. And people are now tremendously busy with squares as they were busy with the trinity before; all the old gods of India and Egypt and Greece were trinities. The interesting thing is that Pegasus is entirely symbolic, it is no longer a human principle, it is not a hero, nor is it a female principle, it is quite decidedly the animal principle. We would say that the horse was a libido symbol, representing the animal part of man, and by pulling himself up upon it, by riding it, it thus becomes winged and divine; it is not only an ordinary animal, it is a divine animal. So it would mean a time in which man discovers that the real guiding principle is the living libido, and that would be represented by a square. How the people of that time could ever imagine that Pegasus should be represented by a square is a miracle to me, but they actually did. Now why that square?

MRS. SIGG: It is the four functions.

DR. JUNG: One might say the four functions. It is simply the *tetraktys*, the number four, which is characterized by Pythagoras as the creative essence, or the process of the world, as it were. Now this four is peculiar; it might be a continuation of the three; Aries was an intellect intellectual age, and Pisces a decidedly feeling age, therefore Christianity is a feeling religion. But this is something else, it has a different influence, it appears in the time when the principle of the Fishes is reversed. After all the originally good and positive spiritual influences, beautiful feeling, comes the reverse feeling, the bitter bad feeling, the evil aspect, and then the square appears. If you take that as a psychological process in an individual, it would mean a feeling personality, a perfectly human, nice person who had always had very nice feelings, and then suddenly the change to bitter feelings, hostility, envy, all sorts of resentments. And that condition would amount to a sort of neurosis; people in such a condition are neurotic because they cannot understand how they could have lost their beautiful feeling values, the ideas they believed in, and how they could be so repulsive and disgusting. They become absolutely dissociated from themselves, they cannot accept themselves, and in such a neurosis the square would appear as a leading principle. That is merely a logical deduction; from all that we have been saying, one could prophesy that the square would appear as a most helpful symbol. As in the age when the conscious intellect of man was threatened by the monster in the sea, the hero who could cut off the Gorgon's head would come in very handy; for ordinary people could do nothing against that huge monster, they always had to sacrifice a soul to it, so a hero-redeemer was needed to be the helpful principle and the bitter struggle of mankind against the terrible danger of the unconscious. And so in a neurosis, where there was still the danger of the whale from below, the square would be most useful.

It is possible that our patient, in this symbol of Pegasus, might have really nosed up the astrological symbolism from her unconscious where all projections take their start. All these names and terms, descriptions, myths, originated in the unconscious; they are actually buried in us, and if anyone falls into such an archetypal situation he is apt to nose out this knowledge from below. Of course, there is no doubt about her knowing that the horse is Pegasus, but I am convinced that she never thought of it as an astrological constellation, nor that Pegasus would be the leading principle at about this time.

When you understand analysis as an honest attempt to overcome certain evils of our time, you are not astonished to find that one of the fundamental concepts of the system is the idea of half-divine and half-animal libido which is one in itself, and therefore the medicine for an age that is not one in itself, that is suffering from a tremendous dissociation. Also it is an age when the old triangle values, the Trinity idea, is being reversed, adding the fourth function to the three. The Trinity consists of God the Father, God the Son, and God the Holy Ghost; and the fourth is God the devil. That makes the square. You see, this whole astrological picture, this ensemble, is exactly like the tissue of the unconscious, like one of these fantasies, or a dream.

There is now only one thing to do, and that is to try to make out what will happen next. We are out of the second Fish and are just approaching the borderline between Pisces and the next sign. It will take us still about ten years to arrive there, and if we move a little farther on we come to a star (F) which is not very big but it seems to be particularly influential. This is the first star of Aquarius. Now Aquarius is the only human sign with the exception of Virgo. Gemini doesn't count because it refers only to children, but Aquarius and Virgo are adult human signs. Aquarius is a male sign, and it is not just a question of currents – he has caught the water in the two jugs and he says: "Now I am going to show what currents are." The water itself no longer moves, and if there are fishes in it, he has also caught the fishes; he carries the jugs and pours out the water himself. So he has acquired a certain superiority and it is an entirely human figure, above and below. The old Egyptian symbolic sign for water is this: ♒. The lower line is the heavy sticky atmosphere that covers the surface of the earth, and the line above is spiritual, it belongs to the high heavens. Aquarius represents the thing above as well as the thing below. Therefore in semiantique representations of Aquarius – there is one most interesting old illustration in a codex of the seventh or eighth century – he is shown as an ithyphallic figure, like a very primitive god of fertility.

MISS WOLFF: In medieval representations the sign of Aquarius often has a fish's tail.

DR. JUNG: Yes, like a mermaid, but that is rather exceptional. In the oldest representations it is always the man with the water jugs; he obviously has a double nature, but in one man.

DR. OTT: Could we not correlate here the idea of transition from the static to the energetic? We have had the three dimensions of space, and now we have added the concept of the fourth dimension, or time, which brings in the idea of energy.

DR. JUNG: That would all be contained. The idea of the fourth dimension is a wonderful myth of our time, it is of the same nature. Aquarius, then, is the sign of the man whose ideal is the union, the oneness, of animal and divine, and in the square the two things are brought together. And that fits in with our ideas perfectly, we have no argument against it.

Now below Aquarius we must expect something else, like that huge whale, as a basis or threat, whatever it may be. And coming out of Cetus the whale is a southern constellation, which is not visible with us and which is not a mythological concept. It is called the Sculptor, the artist who produces. On this map we can see only a corner of it, but it continues some distance to the right, and it is below the first half of Aquarius. Then comes the constellation Piscis Austrinus, the southern Fish. It is as if the age of the Fishes had sunk down into the unconscious when it vanished. One can speculate about that, it is a most interesting conception.

MRS. BAYNES: I think it is a horrible fate to have to regird ourselves for another Fish. I am so sick of Fishes.

DR. JUNG: The Whale has produced the Sculptor, and then comes the Piscis Austrinus, and after that Capricorn, half fish and half mountain goat. Now up to the present moment we had only the authority of Dr. Curtius for talking of the astrological implications of our symbolism. Yet there is something in both the text and the picture which also gives us a certain justification for establishing this connection between an individual fantasy and the world of stars.

DR. REICHSTEIN: The patient said in the text that she flew up into the sky on Pegasus, and in the picture also Pegasus is in the sky.

MRS. SAWYER: And the large brilliant star.

DR. JUNG: Yes, she is obviously somewhere in the neighborhood of the stars, so we are quite safe in assuming that the unconscious is indicating a situation in which human beings usually do not find themselves. Down here on the surface of the earth one is in the thick atmosphere, but a mythological horse could carry one much further up into the air than any aeroplane or zeppelin could. She is going up to the stratosphere like Professor Piccard, to an extra-mundane place, and abstract heavenly place, to the stars were there is a city that is foursquare. The city within the four walls is the star in itself, and in the middle of the city is the open square. So this is really an extra-mundane place where one could quite naturally encounter extra-mundane symbols. Moreover a star penetrates the woman's body, and we can take that quite naïvely as the leading star, the guiding principle – as one speaks of one star, one's fate, one's fortune, etc. It is obviously her individual star, and in this picture it is an influence which penetrates her heart, the center. This is such definite symbolism that we are quite safe in assuming that it is not only central in so far as her own personal psychology is concerned, it is also central in the cosmic sense, it is at the same time a universal human principle.

That individual relationship to the stars is a thought as old as mankind. The primitives believed that the falling stars were really souls descending from heaven to embody themselves in human bodies. They also believed that man was a fiery spark. Even those much quoted central Australian aborigines believe that. They are like paleolithic men, they have not yet invented clothes, they never hunt animals for their furs because they never thought of it, in spite of the fact that at times, towards morning, the temperature descends below zero; then they stand round fires and wait until the sun comes back to life. Now these people believe that the soul of man consists of a little fiery spark, and when such a spark – they are very swift and cunning – is flying about and happens to enter the womb of a woman, she immediately becomes pregnant. These fiery sparks, which they called by the Swiss-sounding expression *maiaurli*, are supposed to be the souls of ancestors and to live in particular rocks or trees, and any woman who passes must use special charms in order to ward off the *maiaurli* that jump out to impregnate her – they are always looking for a womb to enter. There was a similar idea in certain Gnostic systems: they thought that the soul was a fiery spark which fell down into the sea, where the creative womb, and then became a human soul, building a body round itself. It is a very interesting idea.

Later on, the stars were identified with the gods, who were supposed to be like human beings although at the same time they were stars; the planets Jupiter, Venus, Mercury, and so on were gods but they were also planets. That they could be both comes from the fact that those old gods were temperaments or constituents in the character of human beings. For instance, Mars personifies rage, a martial temperament is the warlike temperament, and in a horoscope Mars means a martial constituent. And a jovial temperament is like an exceedingly blue sky, like Jove benevolently smiling, and Jove – or Jupiter – in an important position in a horoscope indicates a jovial character. Venus means love or certain aspects of sex. Mercury is intellect. And Saturn personifies gloom and all those manifestations which originate in the state of gloom or cause gloom; the Tempter and the Purifier are two of Saturn's titles.

Now these character constituents in fairly primitive man are very often autonomous – a person's temperament may be autonomous, for instance. He may be pathologically jovial, jovial to such an extent that it is no longer a virtue but a vice. Or he may be good in a most vicious way, so good that he destroys himself and everyone around him; being a little too good is most dangerous for one surroundings. And it is the same with the so-called malefic planets, Mars and Saturn. You see, the personification of those planets comes from the projection of such autonomous complexes and therefore they have been called gods. When a woman says: "But I feel so and so about the matter," it is most decisive, as you know, so one could call it a god. As a man says: "It is not according to my principle." I say: "Damn your principle, the situation is so-and-so." But his principle is a god to him, he would die rather than give up his most foolish principle, and this is simply based upon a fact of temperament, the deep-rooted emotional factor. Those temperamental qualities were quite rightly called gods and therefore projected. So here also is a link between man and the stars, his laws are found to be identical with the stars.

From*: "14 June 1933," *Visions II

DR. JUNG: Here is a question by Miss Hannah: "You said last time that it was very questionable if there was any movement for the better in the world. What did you mean by better? I had thought that every platonic year the consciousness gained might be a little beyond the point reached by the era before. A spiral seems to make more sense than an endlessly repeated circle. Or does time lose its significance altogether in higher consciousness, so making the circle idea bearable?"

The first question is difficult to answer definitely as you can appreciate. There was a more or less temperamental remark – that it was rather questionable whether things would be better and better in every way. For what does one mean by "better"? If one calls it better when consciousness widens out and civilization increases, then I say we are moving towards an improved state of things, for it is very probable that civilization does increase with certain relapses from time to time. There have been cycles when things fall back into relative chaos, but then they picked up again. As a whole, if one compares the year 10,000 B.C. with the year 2000 A.D. one must say that there is a difference; things seem to be less primitive than they were then. And if one could compare, say, the year 5000 with 150,000 B.C. in central Europe, one would again mark a quite noticeable difference. So in that sense one could say things have become better. But in another sense that is most questionable. I don't know whether our life is happier than the life of the primitive man, whether life today is better than life in the Middle Ages . . .

It is quite different now, however; when one hears of shooting somewhere, one knows the next minute it may be right at one's door because the world has been thrown into a general conflagration. . . . Formerly we jumped when something fell down in our room, but now we jump when a pistol goes off 5000 miles away. So in those respects it is quite doubtful whether things have become better. But if one takes the increase of civilization, the widening out of consciousness, for the real goal of mankind, if one says it is bad when things are unconscious and better when they become conscious, then things have become better, and it *is* a spiral, as far as we can judge of humanity.

But don't forget that we have very limited knowledge, we don't know whether these three months of the platonic year are not a mere episode. Taurus, Aries, and the Fishes are the three spring months, and we don't know what will happen in two signs from now, in about 2300 years, when we reach the equivalent of the winter solstice, the turning point. Whether that whole episode of the widening out of consciousness will not be something quite different, whether it will not then be an involution of consciousness, we simply do not know. This problem is linked up with our attitude to human things in general, namely, the question whether we have to think of the earthly life that we know empirically as the only life possible, or whether there is another form of existence, whether the goal of all things living is fulfilled by their existence here, or whether this is merely a means to an end.

ASTROLOGICAL AGES AND CHRISTIAN SYMBOLISM

From: "24 June 1931," *Visions I*

DR: Jung (upon being presented with roses): Thank you very much. This is the day of roses by the way; it is the day of St. John the Baptist, who, for reasons unknown to me, is associated with the mystical rose. The Freemasons distribute roses on the day of St. John the Baptist because of that association. You see the astrological opposition is this:

John	Jesus
24 June	24 December

John was born under Cancer, which is the retrograde sign of the culmination of the sun, the longest day; and Jesus was born on the shortest day when the sun is increasing; therefore it was said that he must grow but John must decrease.

John Jesus

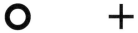

Now Jesus is characterized by the cross, and John by the rose, and the two together make this:

The interesting fact is that we here come to the inner tradition. On the one side is John, and on the other side is Jeshū ben Miriam – Jesus, the son of Mary – called the Deceiver according to the Book of John; here is the opposition between the cross and the rose.

From: "27 January 1932," *Visions I*

The antichrist legend was . . . a true expression of the spirit of that time. It was also expressed in the astrological symbolism, for that was the time of the beginning of the sign of the Fishes. According to the actual position of the astronomical constellation of the Fishes, one fish is upright in the other fish is horizontal, and between is the *commissura*, a sort of string from tail to tail. (Note that the vertical and horizontal lines indicate across.) The upright one would be the Christian fish

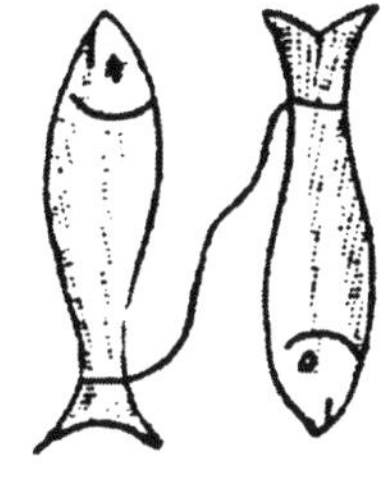

Figure 7.3 Pisces

Source: Reproduced from Jung's *Visions*.

in the horizontal one the anti-Christian fish. Therefore Christ was called *Ichthys*. He is the one rising to heaven, the head pointing to the summit, the Antichrist never leaves the earth, it is the ugliest man, the devil. So this Christian psychology belongs to the time of the fishes and we are still there, but our present psychology is nearing the head of the horizontal fish. In about 1940 we shall be approaching the first stars of the next sign, Aquarius. Of course there are no definite lines in the sky which would indicate the exact borderline but in 1940/1950 we shall be in the vicinity of Aquarius.

We shall be getting to that point in a time when we may expect another change, as in the time of the first fish. The second fish is not like the traditional astrological symbolism, heading in exactly the opposite direction; the Antichrist is not contradictory, it is only horizontal, and one cannot see why that horizontal fish should be so evil. It is only evil because it doesn't rise to heaven, it remains on the earth. That is the chthonic man. So the result has been that the redeeming symbol developed farther and farther away from the spiritual hero, and the humanity of man was emphasized. Therefore when the spring point was in the middle of the *commissura*, it was the year 1500, the time of the Renaissance followed by the Reformation. And we enter the tale of the horizontal fish in about 1720, when the French Enlightenment began, when Christianity was overthrown and the Goddess of Reason was enthroned in Paris instead. The dividing line is just in the middle of the *commissura*; from that time on we have the humanists and an entirely new point of view. It is as if the tremendous heights of the Gothic times were collapsing, sinking down to earth, and as if men were reaching *out*, instead of reaching up to heaven like the first fish. Energy was no longer heaped up, it extended horizontally; man then discovered the earth. That was the time of the great voyages and great discoveries, and the growth of natural science, when man became all-important.

Now we have developed so far on that line that there is nothing but man, even the heavens have become entirely depopulated. As a crazy patient once told me, "I have disinfected the whole heavens with chloride of mercury and I have not found a god there." You see, the man had been a doctor with a very good scientific education. That expresses it exactly; we have disinfected the heavens with mercury (the astrological sign for mind) and nothing has been found, so we are left entirely alone with the tremendous inflation; for since that time all those hierarchies of angels and archangels, with God himself, have entered man. I quoted last term a passage from Synesius, Bishop of Edessa, who really was half heathen, he certainly was not very Christian, and he was also a poet. He said that the *spiritus phantasticus*, which is really human imagination, can even enter divinity. And that is exactly what St. Paul says – that through thinking we can know God. But in that form it will have to sustain or to suffer the divine punishment, dismemberment – the human mind will be dismembered. This is of course a destructive process, the dismemberment of all that we've heaped up in the first fish, the whole spiritual point of view dismembered by that extraordinary horizontal extension, that following of the earth. Man has covered the Earth, and everything is subservient to him. But we are still under the influence of the first fish, and have not yet accepted the earth, we are like spirits hovering over the Earth and above ourselves.

And now we have to accept ourselves. The complete acceptance of man as he is would be the necessary conclusion of the age of the Fishes. Since man thinks himself divine and behaves as if he were divine, he shall eat himself, he shall become acquainted with himself. But it proves to be a hell of a shock when one becomes acquainted with oneself. A new book by Graf Keyserling[7] will appear very soon, in which he will show you how he, as a Christian spirit, met the impact of the earth, and how it got him. Nietzsche avoided it, he didn't dare look at the thing. That acceptance of man as he is, is the psychological, or, if you like to call it so, the spiritual or religious problem of today; that is exactly what we are up against now. But the vision goes on and says that when that happens, the serpent will take the place of the Redeemer on the cross. That means the antichrist. What would seem to us the principle of evil, will be the redeeming symbol. Then again the cycle will be completed, and we shall be as if back at the first century A.D. when they discovered that the serpent was really the Redeemer. You see, then something new may begin.

From: "A Psychological Approach to the Dogma of the Trinity" (1942/48) (*CW* 11), pars. 255, 257

255 Inasmuch as the devil was an angel created by God and "fell like lightning from heaven," he too is a divine "procession" that became Lord of this world. It is significant that the Gnostics thought of him sometimes as the imperfect demiurge and sometimes as the Saturnine archon, Ialdabaoth. Pictorial representations of this archon correspond in every detail with those of a diabolical demon. He symbolized the power of darkness from which Christ came to rescue humanity. The archons issued forth from the womb of the unfathomable abyss, i.e., from the same source that produced the Gnostic Christ.

257 . . . The idea of the Antichrist . . . was probably connected on the one hand with the astrological synchronicity of the dawning aeon of Pisces,[8] and on

the other hand with the increasing realization of the duality postulated by the Son, which in turn is prefigured in the fish symbol: ♓, showing two fishes, joined by a commissure, moving in opposite directions. It would be absurd to put any kind of causal construction on these events. Rather, it is a question of preconscious, prefigurative connections between the archetypes themselves, suggestions of which can be traced in other constellations as well and above all in the formation of myths.

From: "Answer to Job" (1952) (*CW* 11), par. 733

733 John anticipated the alchemists and Jakob Böhme; maybe he even sensed his own personal implication in the divine drama, since he anticipated the possibility of God's birth in man, which the alchemists, Meister Eckhart, and Angelus Silesius also intuited. He thus outlined the programme for the whole aeon of Pisces, with its dramatic enantiodromia, and its dark end which we have still to experience, and before whose – without exaggeration – truly apocalyptic possibilities mankind shudders. The four sinister horsemen, the threatening tumult of trumpets, and the brimming vials of wrath are still waiting; already the atom bomb hangs over us like the sword of Damocles, and behind that lurk the incomparably more terrible possibilities of chemical warfare, which would eclipse even the horrors described in the Apocalypse. *Luciferi vires accendit Aquarius acres* – "Aquarius sets aflame Lucifer's harsh forces." Could anyone in his right senses deny that John correctly foresaw at least some of the possible dangers which threaten our world in the final phase of the Christian aeon? He knew, also, that the fire in which the devil is tormented burns in the divine pleroma forever. God has a terrible double aspect: a sea of grace is met by a seething lake of fire, and the light of love glows with a fierce dark heat of which it is said "ardet non lucet" – it burns but gives no light. That is the eternal, as distinct from the temporal, gospel: *one can love God but must fear him.*

From: "Transformation Symbolism in the Mass" (1940/54) (*CW* 11), pars. 417–419

417 Paradox is a characteristic of the Gnostic writings. It does more justice to the *unknowable* than clarity can do, for uniformity of meaning robs the mystery of its darkness and sets it up as something that is *known*. That is a usurpation, and it leads the human intellect into hybris by pretending that it, the intellect, has got hold of the transcendent mystery by a cognitive act and has "grasped" it. The paradox therefore reflects a higher level of intellect and, by not forcibly representing the unknowable as known, gives a more faithful picture of the real state of affairs.

418 These antithetical predications show the amount of *reflection* that has gone into the hymn: it formulates the figure of our Lord in a series of paradoxes, as God and man, sacrificer and sacrificed. The latter formulation is important because the hymn was sung just before Jesus was arrested, that is, at about the

moment when the synoptic gospels speak of the Last Supper and John – among other things – of the parable of the vine. John, significantly enough, does not mention the Last Supper, and in the Acts of John its place is taken by the "round dance." But the round table, like the round dance, stands for synthesis and union. In the Last Supper this takes the form of participation in the body and blood of Christ, i.e., there is an ingestion and assimilation of the Lord, and in the round dance there is a circular circumambulation round the Lord as the central point. Despite the outward difference of the symbols, they have a common meaning: Christ is taken into the midst of the disciples. But, although the two rites have this common basic meaning, the outward difference between them should not be overlooked. The classical Eucharistic feast follows the synoptic gospels, whereas the one in the Acts of John follows the Johannine pattern. One could almost say that it expresses, in a form borrowed from some pagan mystery feast, a more immediate relationship of the congregation to Christ, after the manner of the Johannine parable: "I am the vine, ye are the branches. He that abideth in me, and I in him, the same bringeth forth much fruit" (John 15:5). This close relationship is represented by the circle and central point: the two parts are indispensable to each other and equivalent. Since olden times the circle with a centre has been a symbol for the Deity, illustrating the wholeness of God incarnate: the single point in the centre and the series of points constituting the circumference. Ritual circumambulation often bases itself quite consciously on the cosmic picture of the starry heavens revolving, on the "dance of the stars," an idea that is still preserved in the comparison of the twelve disciples with the zodiacal constellations, as also in the depictions of the zodiac that are sometimes found in churches, in front of the altar or on the roof of the nave. Some such picture may well have been at the back of the medieval ball-game of pelota that was played in church by the bishop and his clergy.

419 At all events, the aim and effect of the solemn round dance is to impress upon the mind the image of the circle and the centre and the relation of each point along the periphery to that centre.[9] Psychologically this arrangement is equivalent to a mandala and is thus a symbol of the self,[10] the point of reference not only of the individual ego but of all those who are of like mind or who are bound together by fate. The self is not an ego but a supraordinate totality embracing the conscious and the unconscious. But since the latter has no assignable limits and in its deeper layers is of a collective nature, it cannot be distinguished from that of another individual. As a result, it continually creates that ubiquitous *participation mystique* which is the unity of many, the *one* man in all men.

From: "Liber Secundus: The Magician," *The Red Book: Liber Novus* (1913), p. 405

I hold together what Christ has kept apart in himself and through his examples in others, since the more the one half of my being strives toward the good, the more the other half journeys to Hell.

When the month of the Twins has ended, the men said to their shadows: "You are I," since they had previously had their spirit around them as a second person. Thus the two became one, and through this collision the formidable broke out, precisely that spring of consciousness that one calls culture and which lasted until the time of Christ.[11] But the fish indicated the moment when what was united split, according to the eternal law of contrasts, into an underworld and upperworld. If the power of growth begins to cease, then the united falls into its opposites. Christ sent what is beneath to Hell, since it strives toward the good. That had to be. But the separated cannot remain separated forever. It will be united again and the month of the fish will soon be over.[12] We suspect and understand that growth needs both, and hence we keep good and evil close together. Because we know that too far into the good means the same as too far into evil, we keep them both together.[13]

From: "Contacts with Jung – Kenneth Lambert," *C. G. Jung Speaking* (1977), pp. 160–161

Then the symbolism became astrological. Jung stated that, at the birth of Christ, Saturn the maleficent god and Jupiter the beneficent god were so near to each other that they were almost one star, that is, the star of Bethlehem, when the new self, Christ, good and evil, was born. Jung then associated to this by telling two stories about people. A man told Jung about a Quaker who seemed a perfectly good man. So where was his shadow? Jung asked about his wife. Apparently she was perfect, too. His children? "Oh," said the inquirer, "one of them is a thief." In Jung's words, "He went out wagging his tail." The second story concerned a theologian without a shadow, but it turned out that his son was "getting into the way of forging checks." Jung's comment was, "The son assumes the father's shadow. His father was stealing, you see, from God his sins. The son was punished for the father's sins not rendered to God.

THE COMING AGE OF AQUARIUS

From: "On the Frontiers of Knowledge," *C. G. Jung Speaking* (1977), pp. 398–399

You speak of a change of eras, of a new Platonic month, of the passage into another sign of the zodiac.[14] *What do you mean by that, what reality do such constellations have?*

People don't like you to talk about that, you will get yourself laughed at. Nobody has read Plato – you haven't either. Yet he is one of those who has come closest to the truth. The influence of the constellations, the zodiac, they exist; you cannot explain why, it's a "Just-So Story," that proves itself by a thousand signs. But men always go from one extreme to the other, either they don't believe, or they are credulous, any knowledge or faith can be ridiculed on the basis of what small minds do with it. That's stupid and, above all, it's dangerous. The great astrological periods do exist. Taurus and Gemini were prehistoric periods, we don't know much about them. But

Aries the Ram is closer; Alexander the Great was one if its manifestations.[15] That was from 2000 B.C. to the beginning of the Christian era. With that era we came into the sign of the Fishes. It was not I who invented all the fish symbols there are in Christianity: the fisher of men, the *pisciculi christianorum*. Christianity has marked us deeply because it incarnates the symbols of the era so well. It goes wrong in so far as it believes itself to be the only truth; when what it is is one of the great expressions of truth in our time. To deny it would be to throw the baby out with the bathwater. What comes next? Aquarius, the Water-pourer, the falling of water from one place to another. And the little fish receiving the water from the pitcher of the Water-pourer, and whose principal star is Fomalhaut, which means the "fish's mouth." In our era the fish is the content; with the Water-pourer, he becomes the container. It's a very strange symbol. I don't dare interpret it. So far as one can tell, it is the image of a great man approaching. One finds, besides, a lot of things about this in the Bible itself: there are more things in the Bible than the theologians can admit.

It's a matter of experience that the symbolism changes from one sign to another, and there is the risk that this passage will be all the more difficult for the men of today and tomorrow because they no longer believe in it, no longer want to be conscious of it. Why when Pope Pius XII in one of his last discourses deplored that the world was no longer conscious enough of the presence of angels, he was saying to his faithful Catholics in Christian terms exactly what I am trying to say in terms of psychology to those who stand more chance of understanding this language than any other.

From: "At the Basel Psychology Club," *C. G. Jung Speaking* (1977), p. 375

At all events, it is highly probable that we are heading for an extremely critical time, which all of us may perhaps not experience – the peak of it, that is – because we are the end of the Pisces aeon and can certainly expect that with the transition to the new aeon of Aquarius, approximately 150–200 years from now, our distant descendants will experience all sorts of things. This atom bomb business, for instance, is terribly characteristic of Aquarius, whose ruler is Uranos, the Lord of unpredictable events.

From: "Doctors on Holiday on the Rigi – Esther Harding," *C. G. Jung Speaking* (1977), p. 173

Dr. Jung was, as he put it, "not quite pessimistic" about the inevitability of the destruction of our civilization. He found some indications – quite slight clues, to be sure – in the dreams of all sorts of people and in the particular way that certain things have happened, which suggest that this moment, with its upheaval and disorder, may be truly the transition to a new order, as we have all been hoping for so long. He said that the uprush of brutality, which he had observed so generally in dreams of Germans before the War, was giving way to constructive symbols of a new phase. One rather interesting astrological fact, he noted, is that the line of the ecliptic, at present traversing the second fish of the sign of Pisces, the fish of the Anti-Christ, does not pass through its head but below. This would mean that, according to the stars, the sinister forces of not reach their maximum, do not quite "come to a head." Of course he made no claim to be a prophet, but merely an observer of whatever indications there might be.

From: "Late Thoughts," *Memories, Dreams, Reflections* (1963), pp. 339–340

I do not imagine that in my reflections on the meaning of man and his myth I have uttered a final truth, but I think that this is what can be said at the end of our aeon of the Fishes, and perhaps must be said in view of the coming aeon of Aquarius (the Water Bearer), who has a human figure and is next to the sign of the Fishes. This is a *coniunctio oppositorum* composed of two fishes in reverse. The Water Bearer seems to represent the self. With a sovereign gesture he pours the contents of his jug into the mouth of *Piscis austrinus*,[16] which symbolizes a son, a still unconscious content. Out of this unconscious content will emerge, after the passage of another aeon of more than two thousand years, a future whose features are indicated by the symbol of Capricorn: an *aigokeros*, the monstrosity of the Goat-Fish,[17] symbolizing the mountains and the depths of the sea, a polarity made up of two undifferentiated animal elements which have grown together. This strange being could easily be the primordial image of a Creator-god confronting "man," the Anthropos. On this question there is a silence within me, as there is in the empirical data at my disposal – the products of the unconscious of other people with which I am acquainted, or historical documents. If insight does not come by itself, speculation is pointless. It makes sense only when we have objective data comparable to our material on the aeon of Aquarius.

NOTES

1 The "giant" fish of the Abercius inscription (c. A.D. 200). [Cf. *Aion*, par. 127, n. 4. – EDITORS.]
2 [Cf. *Aion*, passim – EDITORS.]
3 The reference is to the Platonic months. In Red Book, see note 273, p. 405.
4 In C. G. Jung and W. Pauli, *The Interpretation of Nature and the Psyche* (New York and London, 1954); also in *The Structure and Dynamics of the Psyche* (CW 8).
5 "The House of Venus," one of the twelve houses in the astrological zodiac.
6 *Façon de parler:* "way of speaking".
7 See 18 Feb. 1931, n. 4. *Sudamerikanische Meditationen* (Stuttgart, 1932), tr.
8 In antiquity, regard for astrology was nothing at all extraordinary. [Cf. "Synchronicity: An Acausal Connecting Principle," pars. 872ff., and *Aion*, pars. 127ff. – EDITORS.]
9 Another idea of the kind is that every human being is a ray of sunlight. This image occurs in the Spanish poet Jorge Guillen. *Cantico: Fe de Vida*, pp. 24–25 ("Más allá," VI):

> Where could I stray to, where?
> This point is my centre . . .
> With this earth and this ocean
> To rise to the infinite:
> One ray more of the sun.
> (Trans, by J. M. Cohen.)

10 Cf. *Aion*, Ch. IV.

11 The reference is to the astrological conception of the Platonic month, or aeon, of Pisces, which is based on the precession of the equinoxes. Each Platonic month consists of one zodiacal sign, and lasts approximately 2,300 years. Jung discusses the symbolism attached to this in *Aion* (1951, CW 6, ch. 6). He notes that around 7 BC there was a conjunction of Saturn and Jupiter, representing a union of extreme opposites, which would place the birth of Christ under Pisces. Pisces (Latin for "fishes") is known as the sign of the fish and is often represented by two fish swimming in opposite directions. On the Platonic months, see Alice Howell, *Jungian Synchronicity in Astrological Signs and Ages* (Wheaton, IL: Quest Books, 1990), p. 125f. Jung started studying astrology in 1911, in the course of his study of mythology, and learned to cast horoscopes (Jung to Freud, May 8, 1911, *The Freud/Jung Letters*, p. 421). In terms of Jung's sources for the history of astrology, he cited Auguste Bouché-Leclercq's *L'Astrologie Grecque* on nine occasions in his later work (Paris: Ernest Leroux, 1899) – EDITORS.

12 This refers to the end of the Platonic month of Pisces and the beginning of the Platonic month of Aquarius. The precise dating of this is uncertain. In *Aion* (1951), Jung noted: "Astrologically the beginning of the next aeon, according to the starting point you select, falls between AD 2000 and 2200" (CW 9, 2. §149, note 88) – EDITORS.

13 In *Aion* (1951), Jung wrote: "If, as seems probable, the aeon of the fishes is ruled by the archetypal motif of the 'hostile brothers,' then the approach of the next Platonic month, namely Aquarius, will constellate the problem of the union of opposites. It will then no longer be possible to write off evil as a mere *privatio boni*; its real existence will have to be recognized" (CW 9, §142) – EDITORS.

14 "Flying Saucers: A Modern Myth," CW 10, par. 589.

15 The Arabic name for Alexander was Dhulqarnein, "two-horned." Cf. *Symbols of Transformation*, CW 5, par. 283, n. 32, also Pl. XXa.

16 Constellation of the "Southern Fish." Its mouth is formed by Fomalhaut (Arabic for "mouth of fish") below the constellation of the Water Bearer.

17 The constellation of Capricorn was originally called the "Goat-Fish."

8 The sign of the fishes

"The Sign of the Fishes" (1951) (*CW* 9ii), pars. 127–149

127 The figure of Christ is not as simple and unequivocal as one could wish. I am not referring here to the enormous difficulties arising out of a comparison of the Synoptic Christ with the Johannine Christ, but to the remarkable fact that in the hermeneutic writings of the Church Fathers, which go right back to the days of primitive Christianity, Christ has a number of symbols or "allegories" in common with the devil. Of these I would mention the lion, snake (*coluber*, "viper"), bird (devil = *nocturna avis*), raven (Christ = *nycticorax*, "night-heron"), eagle, and fish. It is also worth noting that Lucifer, the Morning Star, means Christ as well as the devil.[1] Apart from the snake, the fish is one of the oldest allegories. Nowadays we would prefer to call them symbols, because these synonyms always contain more than mere allegories, as is particularly obvious in the case of the fish symbol. It is unlikely that 'Ιχθῦς is simply an anagrammatic abbreviation of 'Ι[ησοῦς] Χ[ριστὸς] Θ[εοῦ] Υ[ἱὸς] Σ[ωτηρ],[2] but rather the symbolical designation for something far more complex. (As I have frequently pointed out in my other writings, I do not regard the symbol as an allegory or a sign, but take it in its proper sense as the best possible way of describing and formulating an object that is not completely knowable. It is in this sense that the creed is called a "symbolum.") The order of the words gives one more the impression that they were put together for the purpose of explaining an already extant and widely disseminated "Ichthys."[3] For the fish symbol, in the Near and Middle East especially, has a long and colourful prehistory, from the Babylonian fish-god Oannes and his priests who clothed themselves in fish-skins, to the sacred fish-meals in the cult of the Phoenician goddess Derceto-Atargatis and the obscurities of the Abercius inscription.[4] The symbol ranges from the redeemer fish of Manu in farthest India to the Eucharistic fish-feast celebrated by the "Thracian riders" in the Roman Empire.[5] For our purpose it is hardly necessary to go into this voluminous material more closely. As Doelger and others have shown, there are plenty of occasions for fish symbolism within the original, purely Christian world of ideas. I need only mention the regeneration in the font, in which the baptized swim like fishes.[6]

128 In view of this wide distribution of the fish symbol, its appearance at a particular place or at a particular moment in the history of the world is no cause for wonder. But the sudden activation of the symbol, and its identification with Christ even in the early days of the Church, lead one to conjecture a second source. This source is astrology, and it seems that Friedrich Muenter[7] was the first to draw attention to it. Jeremias[8] adopts the same view and mentions that a Jewish commentary on Daniel, written in the fourteenth century, expected the coming of the Messiah in the sign of the Fishes. This commentary is mentioned by Muenter in a later publication[9] as stemming from Don Isaac Abarbanel, who was born in Lisbon in 1437 and died in Venice in 1508.[10] It is explained here that the House of the Fishes (♓) is the house of justice and of brilliant splendour (♃ in ♓). Further, that in *anno mundi* 2365,[11] a great conjunction of Saturn (♄) and Jupiter (♃) took place in Pisces.[12] These two great planets, he says, are also the most important for the destiny of the world, and especially for the destiny of the Jews. The conjunction took place three years before the birth of Moses. (This is of course legendary.) Abarbanel expects the coming of the Messiah when there is a conjunction of Jupiter and Saturn in Pisces. He was not the first to express such expectations. Four hundred years earlier we find similar pronouncements; for instance, Rabbi Abraham ben Hiyya, who died about 1136, is said to have decreed that the Messiah was to be expected in 1464, at the time of the great conjunction in Pisces; and the same is reported of Solomon ben Gabirol (1020–70).[13] These astrological ideas are quite understandable when one considers that Saturn is the star of Israel, and that Jupiter means the "king" (of justice). Among the territories ruled by the Fishes, the house of Jupiter, are Mesopotamia, Bactria, the Red Sea, and Palestine.[14] Chiun (Saturn) is mentioned in Amos 5:26 as "the star of your god."[15] James of Sarug (d. 521) says the Israelites worshipped Saturn. The Sabaeans called him the "god of the Jews."[16] The Sabbath is Saturday, Saturn's Day. Albumasar[17] testifies that Saturn is the star of Israel.[18] In medieval astrology Saturn was believed to be the abode of the devil.[19] Both Saturn and Ialdabaoth, the demiurge and highest archon, have lion's faces. Origen elicits from the diagram of Celsus that Michael, the first angel of the Creator, has "the shape of a lion."[20] He obviously stands in the place of Ialdabaoth, who is identical with Saturn, as Origen points out.[21] The demiurge of the Naassenes is a "fiery god, the fourth by number."[22] According to the teachings of Apelles, who had connections with Marcion, there was a "third god who spoke to Moses, a fiery one, and there was also a fourth, the author of evil."[23] Between the god of the Naassenes and the god of Apelles there is evidently a close relationship, and also, it appears, with Yahweh, the demiurge of the Old Testament.

129 Saturn is a "black" star,[24] anciently reputed a "maleficus." "Dragons, serpents, scorpions, vipères, renards, chats et souris, oiseaux nocturnes et autres engeances sournoises sont le lot de Saturne," says Bouche-Leclercq.[25] Remarkably enough, Saturn's animals also include the ass,[26] which on that account was rated a theriomorphic form of the Jewish god. A pictorial representation of

it is the well-known mock crucifixion on the Palatine.[27] Similar traditions can be found in Plutarch,[28] Diodorus, Josephus,[29] and Tacitus.[30] Sabaoth, the seventh archon, has the form of an ass.[31] Tertullian is referring to these rumours when he says: "You are under the delusion that our God is an ass's head," and that "we do homage only to an ass."[32] As we have indicated, the ass is sacred to the Egyptian Set.[33] In the early texts, however, the ass is the attribute of the sun-god and only later became an emblem of the underworldly Apep and of evil (Set).[34]

130 According to medieval tradition, the religion the Jews originated in a conjunction of Jupiter with Saturn, Islam in ♃ ☌ ♀, Christianity ♃ ☌ ☿, and the Antichrist in ♃ ☌ ☽.[35]

Unlike Saturn, Jupiter is a beneficent star. In the Iranian view Jupiter signifies life, Saturn death.[36] The conjunction of the two therefore signifies the *union of extreme opposites*. In the year 7 B.C. this famed conjunction took place no less than three times in the sign of the Fishes. The greatest approximation occurred on May 29 of that year, the planets being only 0.21 degrees apart, less than half the width of the full moon.[37] The conjunction took place in the middle of the commissure, "near the bend in the line of the Fishes." From the astrological point of view this conjunction must appear especially significant, because the approximation of the two planets was exceptionally large and of an impressive brilliance. In addition, seen heliocentrically, it took place near the equinoctial point, which at that time was located between ♈ and ♓ that is, between fire and water.[38] The conjunction was characterized by the important fact that Mars was in opposition (♂ ☍ ♃ ♄), which means, astrologically, that the planet correlated with the instincts stood in a hostile relationship to it, which is peculiarly characteristic of Christianity. If we accept Gerhardt's calculation that the conjunction took place on May 29, in the year 7 B.C., then the position of the sun – especially important in a man's nativity – at Christ's birth would be in the double sign of the *Twins*.[39] One thinks involuntarily of the ancient Egyptian pair of hostile brothers, Horus and Set, the sacrificer and the sacrificed, who in a sense prefigure the drama of the Christian myth. In the Egyptian myth it is the evil one who is sacrificed on the "slave's post."[40] But the pair of brothers Heru-ur (the "older Horus") and Set are sometimes pictured as having one body with two heads. The planet Mercury is correlated with Set, and this is interesting in view of the tradition that Christianity originated in a conjunction of Jupiter with Mercury. In the New Kingdom (XIXth dynasty) Set appears as Sutech in the Nile delta. In the new capital built by Rameses II, one district was dedicated to Amon, the other to Sutech.[41] It was here that the Jews were supposed to have done slave-labour.

131 In considering the double aspect of Christ, mention might be made of the legend of Pistis Sophia (3rd cent.), which also originated in Egypt. Mary says to Jesus:

> When thou wert a child, before the spirit had descended upon thee, when thou wert in the vineyard with Joseph, the spirit came down from the height, and came unto me in the house, like unto thee, and I knew him not, but thought that he was thou. And he said unto me, "Where is Jesus,

> my brother, that I may go to meet him?" And when he had said this unto me, I was in doubt, and thought it was a phantom tempting me. I seized him and bound him to the foot of the bed which was in my house, until I had gone to find you in the field, thee and Joseph; and I found you in the vineyard, where Joseph was putting up the vine-poles. And it came to pass, when thou didst hear me saying this thing unto Joseph, that thou didst understand, and thou wert joyful, and didst say, "Where is he, that I may see him?" And it came to pass, when Joseph heard thee say these words, that he was disturbed. We went up together, entered into the house and found the spirit bound to the bed, and we gazed upon thee and him, and found that thou wert like unto him. And he that was bound to the bed was unloosed, he embraced thee and kissed thee, and thou also didst kiss him, and you became one.[42]

132 It appears from the context of this fragment that Jesus is the "truth sprouting from the earth," whereas the spirit that resembled him is "justice [*δικαιοσύνη*] looking down from heaven." The text says: "Truth is the power which issued from thee when thou wast in the lower regions of chaos. For this cause thy power hath said through David, 'Truth hath sprouted out of the earth,' because thou wert in the lower regions of chaos."[43] Jesus, accordingly, is conceived as a double personality, part of which rises up from the chaos or *hyle*, while the other part descends as pneuma from heaven.

133 One could hardly find the *φυλοκρίνησις*, or "discrimination of the natures" that characterizes the Gnostic Redeemer, exemplified more graphically than in the astrological determination of time. The astrological statements that were quite possible in antiquity all point to the prominent double aspect[44] of the birth that occurred at this particular moment of time, and one can understand how plausible was the astrological interpretation of the Christ-Antichrist myth when it entered into manifestation at the time of the Gnostics. A fairly old authority, earlier anyway than the sixth century, which bears striking witness to the antithetical nature of the Fishes is the Talmud. This says:

> Four thousand two hundred and ninety-one years after the Creation [A.D. 530], the world will be orphaned. There will follow the war of the *tanninim* [sea-monsters], the war of Gog and Magog,[45] and then the Messianic era: only after seven thousand years will the Holy One, blessed be He, set up his world anew. R. Abba, said, the son of Raba, said, It was taught: after five thousand years.[46]

The Talmud commentator Solomon ben Isaac, alias Rashi (1039–1105), remarks that the *tanninim* are fishes, presumably basing himself on an older source, since he does not give this as his own opinion, as he usually does. This remark is important, firstly because it takes the battle of the fishes as an eschatological event (like the fight between Behemoth and Leviathan), and secondly because it is probably the oldest testimony to the antithetical nature of the fishes. From about this period, too – the eleventh century – comes the apocryphal text of a Johannine Genesis in which the two fishes are mentioned, this time in unmistakably astrological form. Both documents fall within the critical epoch that opened with the second millennium of the Christian era, about which I shall have more to say in due course.

134 The year 531 is characterized astronomically by a conjunction of ♃ and ♄ in Gemini. This sign stands for a pair of brothers, and they too have a somewhat antithetical nature. The Greeks interpreted them as the Dioscuri ("boys of Zeus"), the sons of Leda who were begotten by the swan and hatched out of an egg. Pollux was immortal, but Castor shared the human lot. Another interpretation takes them as representing Apollo and Heracles or Apollo and Dionysus. Both interpretations suggest a certain polarity. Astronomically, at any rate, the air sign Gemini stands in a quartile and therefore unfavourable aspect to the conjunction that took place in the year 7 B.C. The inner polarity of ♊ may perhaps shed light on the prophecy about the war of the *tanninim*, which Rashi interprets as fishes. From the dating of Christ's birth it would appear, as said, that the sun was in Gemini. The motif of the brothers is found very early in connection with Christ, for instance among the Jewish Christians and Ebionites.[47]

135 From all this we may risk the conjecture that the Talmudic prophecy was based on astrological premises.

136 The precession of the equinoxes was a fact well known to the astrologers of antiquity. Origen, helped out by the observations and calculations of Hipparchus,[48] uses it as a cogent argument against an astrology based on the so-called "morphomata" (the actual constellations).[49] Naturally this does not apply to the distinction already drawn in ancient astrology between the morphomata and the *ζωδια νοητά* (the fictive signs of the zodiac).[50] If we take the 7,000 years mentioned in the prophecy as *anno mundi* 7000, the year denoted would be A.D. 3239. By then the spring-point will have moved from its present position 18 degrees into Aquarius, the next aeon, that of the Water Carrier. As an astrologer of the second or third century would be acquainted with the precession, we may surmise that these dates were based on astrological considerations. At all events the Middle Ages were much concerned with the calculation of *coniunctiones maximae* and *magnae*, as we know from Pierre d'Ailly and Cardan.[51] Pierre d'Ailly reckoned that the first *coniunctio maxima* (♃ ☌ ♄ in ♈) after the creation of the world took place in 5027 B.C., while Cardan relegated the tenth conjunction to A.D. 3613.[52] Both of them assumed the lapse of too large an interval between conjunctions in the same sign. The correct astronomical interval is about 795 years. Cardan's conjunction would accordingly take place in the year A.D. 3234. For astrological speculation this date is naturally of the greatest importance.

137 As to the 5,000 years, the date we get is A.D. 1239. This was an epoch noted for its spiritual instability, revolutionary heresies and chiliastic expectations, and at the same time it saw the founding of the mendicant orders, which injected new life into monasticism. One of the most powerful and influential voices to announce the coming of a "new age of the spirit" was Joachim

of Flora (d. 1202), whose teachings were condemned by the Fourth Lateran Council in 1215. He expected the opening of the seventh seal in the fairly near future, the advent of the "everlasting gospel" and the reign of the "intellectus spiritualis," the age of the Holy Ghost. This third aeon, he says, had already begun with St. Benedict, the founder of the Benedictine Order (the first monastery was supposed to have been built a few years after 529). One of Joachim's followers, the Franciscan friar Gerard of Borgo San Donnino, proclaimed in his *Introductorius in evangelium aeternum*, which appeared in 1254 in Paris, that Joachim's three main treatises were in fact the everlasting gospel, and that in the year 1260 this would replace the gospel of Jesus Christ.[53] As we know, Joachim saw monasticism as the true vehicle of the Holy Ghost and for this reason he dated the secret inception of the new era from the lifetime of St. Benedict, whose founding of the Benedictine Order revived monasticism in the West.

138 To Pierre d'Ailly the time of Pope Innocent III (1198–1216) had already seemed significant. About the year 1189, he says, the revolutions of Saturn were once again completed ("completae anno Christi 1189 vel circiter"). He complains that the Pope had condemned a treatise of Abbot Joachim,[54] and also the heretical doctrine of Almaricus.[55] This last is the theological philosopher Amalric of Bene (d. 1204), who took part in the widespread Holy Ghost movement of that age. It was then, too, he says, that the Dominican and Franciscan mendicant orders came into existence, "which was a great and wonderful thing for the Christian church." Pierre d'Ailly thus lays stress on the same phenomena that struck us as being characteristic of the time, and further regards this epoch as having been foretold in astrology.

139 The date for the founding of the monastery of Monte Cassino brings us very close to the year 530, which the Talmud prophesied would be a critical one. In Joachim's view not only does a new era begin then, but a new "status" of the world – the age of monasticism and the reign of the Holy Ghost. Its beginning still comes within the domain of the Son, but Joachim surmises in a psychologically correct manner that a new status – or, as we would say, a new attitude – would appear first as a more or less latent preliminary stage, which would then be followed by the *fructificatio*, the flower and the fruit. In Joachim's day the fruition was still in abeyance, but one could observe far and wide an uncommon agitation and commotion of men's spirits. Everyone felt the rushing wind of the pneuma; it was an age of new and unprecedented ideas which were blazoned abroad by the Cathari, Patarenes, Concorricci, Waldenses, Poor Men of Lyons, Beghards, Brethren of the Free Spirit, "Bread through God,"[56] and whatever else these movements were called. Their visible beginnings all lay in the early years of the eleventh century. The contemporary documents amassed by Hahn throw a revealing light on the ideas current in these circles:

> Item, they believe themselves to be God by nature without distinction . . . and that they are eternal. . . .

> Item, that they have no need of God or the Godhead.
>
> Item, that they constitute the kingdom of heaven.
>
> Item, that they are immutable in the new rock, that they rejoice in naught and are troubled by naught.
>
> Item, that a man is bound to follow his inner instinct rather than the truth of the Gospel which is preached every day. . . . They say that they believe the Gospel to contain poetical matters which are not true.[57]

140 These few examples may suffice to show what kind of spirit animated these movements. They were made up of people who identified themselves (or were identified) with God, who deemed themselves supermen, had a critical approach to the gospels, followed the promptings of the inner man, and understood the kingdom of heaven to be within. In a sense, therefore, they were modern in their outlook, but they had a religious inflation instead of the rationalistic and political psychosis that is the affliction of our day. We ought not to impute these extremist ideas to Joachim, even though he took part in that great movement of the spirit and was one of its outstanding figures. One must ask oneself what psychological impulse could have moved him and his adherents to cherish such bold expectations as the substitution of the "everlasting gospel" for the Christian message or the supersession of the second Person in the Godhead by the third, who would reign over the new era. This thought is so heretical and subversive that it could never have occurred to him had he not felt himself supported and swept along by the revolutionary currents of the age. He felt it as a revelation of the Holy Ghost, whose life and procreative power no church could bring to a stop. The numinosity of this feeling was heightened by the temporal coincidence – "synchronicity" – of the epoch he lived in with the beginning of the sphere of the "antichristian" fish in Pisces. In consequence, one might feel tempted to regard the Holy Ghost movement and Joachim's central ideas as a direct expression of the antichristian psychology that was then dawning. At any rate the Church's condemnation is thoroughly understandable, for in many ways his attitude to the Church of Jesus Christ comes very close to open insurrection, if not downright apostasy. But if we allow some credence to the conviction of these innovators that they were moved by the Holy Ghost, then another interpretation becomes not only possible but even probable.

141 That is to say, just as Joachim supposed that the status of the Holy Ghost had secretly begun with St. Benedict, so we might hazard the conjecture that a new status was secretly anticipated in Joachim himself. Consciously, of course, he thought he was bringing the status of the Holy Ghost into reality, just as it is certain that St. Benedict had nothing else in mind than to put the Church on a firm footing and deepen the meaning of the Christian life through monasticism. But, unconsciously – and this is psychologically what probably happened – Joachim could have been seized by the archetype of the spirit. There is no doubt that his activities were founded on a numinous experience, which is, indeed, characteristic of all those who are gripped by an archetype. He understood the

spirit in the dogmatic sense as the third Person of the Godhead, for no other way was possible, but not in the sense of the empirical archetype. This archetype is not of uniform meaning, but was originally an ambivalent dualistic figure[58] that broke through again in the alchemical concept of spirit after engendering the most contradictory manifestations within the Holy Ghost movement itself. The Gnostics in their day had already had clear intimations of this dualistic figure. It was therefore very natural, in an age which coincided with the beginning of the second Fish and which was, so to speak, forced into ambiguity, that an espousal of the Holy Ghost in its Christian form should at the same time help the archetype of the spirit to break through in all its characteristic ambivalence. It would be unjust to class so worthy a personage as Joachim with the bigoted advocates of that revolutionary and anarchic turbulence, which is what the Holy Ghost movement turned into in so many places. We must suppose, rather, that he himself unwittingly ushered in a new "status," a religious attitude that was destined to bridge and compensate the frightful gulf that had opened out between Christ and Antichrist in the eleventh century. The antichristian era is to blame that the spirit became non-spiritual and that the vitalizing archetype gradually degenerated into rationalism, intellectualism, and doctrinairism, all of which leads straight to the tragedy of modern times now hanging over our heads like a sword of Damocles. In the old formula for the Trinity, as Joachim knew it, the dogmatic figure of the devil is lacking, for then as now he led a questionable existence somewhere on the fringes of theological metaphysics, in the shape of the *mysterium iniquitatis*. Fortunately for us, the threat of his coming had already been foretold in the New Testament – for the less he is recognized the more dangerous he is. Who would suspect him under those high-sounding names of his, such as public welfare, lifelong security, peace among the nations, etc.? He hides under idealisms, under -isms in general, and of these the most pernicious is doctrinairism, that most unspiritual of all the spirit's manifestations. The present age must come to terms drastically with the facts as they are, with the absolute opposition that is not only tearing the world asunder politically but has planted a schism in the human heart. We need to find our way back to the original, living spirit which, because of its ambivalence, is also a mediator and uniter of opposites,[59] an idea that preoccupied the alchemists for many centuries.

142 If, as seems probable, the aeon of the fishes is ruled by the archetypal motif of the hostile brothers, then the approach of the next Platonic month, namely Aquarius, will constellate the problem of the union of opposites. It will then no longer be possible to write off evil as the mere privation of good; its real existence will have to be recognized. This problem can be solved neither by philosophy, nor by economics, nor by politics, but only by the individual human being, via his experience of the living spirit, whose fire descended upon Joachim, one of many, and, despite all contemporary misunderstandings, was handed onward into the future. The solemn proclamation of the *Assumptio Mariae* which we have experienced in our own day is an example of the way symbols develop through the ages. The impelling motive behind

it did not come from the ecclesiastical authorities, who had given clear proof of their hesitation by postponing the declaration for nearly a hundred years,[60] but from the Catholic masses, who have insisted more and more vehemently on this development. Their insistence is, at bottom, the urge of the archetype to realize itself.[61]

143 The repercussions of the Holy Ghost movement spread, in the years that followed, to four minds of immense significance for the future. These were Albertus Magnus (1193–1280); his pupil Thomas Aquinas, the philosopher of the Church and an adept in alchemy (as also was Albertus); Roger Bacon (*c.* 1214 – *c.* 1294), the English forerunner of inductive science; and finally Meister Eckhart (*c.* 1260–1327), the independent religious thinker, now enjoying a real revival after six hundred years of obscurity. Some people have rightly seen the Holy Ghost movement as the forerunner of the Reformation. At about the time of the twelfth and thirteenth centuries we find also the beginnings of Latin alchemy, whose philosophical and spiritual content I have tried to elucidate in my book *Psychology and Alchemy*. The image mentioned above (par. 139) of "immutability in the new rock" bears a striking resemblance to the central idea of philosophical alchemy, the *lapis philosophorum*, which is used as a parallel to Christ, the "rock," the "stone," the "corner-stone." Priscillian (4th cent.) says: "We have Christ for a rock, Jesus for a cornerstone."[62] An alchemical text speaks of the "rock which is smitten thrice with Moses' rod, so that the waters flow forth freely."[63] The lapis is called a "sacred rock" and is described as having four parts.[64] St. Ambrose says the water from the rock is a prefiguration of the blood that flowed from Christ's side.[65] Another alchemical text mentions the "water from the rock" as the equivalent of the universal solvent, the *aqua permanens*.[66] Khunrath, in his somewhat florid language, even speaks of the "Petroleum sapientum."[67] By the Naassenes, Adam was called the "rock" and the "cornerstone."[68] Both these allegories of Christ are mentioned by Epiphanius in his *Ancoratus*, and also by Firmicus Maternus.[69] This image, common to ecclesiastical and alchemical language alike, goes back to I Corinthians 10:4 and I Peter 2:4.

144 The new rock, then, takes the place of Christ, just as the everlasting gospel was meant to take the place of Christ's message. Through the descent and indwelling of the Holy Ghost the *υιοτης*, sonship, is infused into every individual, so that everybody who possesses the Holy Ghost will be a new rock, in accordance with I Peter 2:5: "Be you also as living stones built up."[70] This is a logical development of the teaching about the Paraclete and the filiation, as stated in Luke 6:35: "You shall be sons of the Highest," and John 10:34: "Is it not written in your law: I said, you are gods?" The Naassenes, as we know, had already made use of these allusions and thus anticipated a whole tract of historical development – a development that led via monasticism to the Holy Ghost movement, via the *Theologia Germanica* direct to Luther, and via alchemy to modern science.

145 Let us now turn back to the theme of Christ as the fish. According to Doelger, the Christian fish symbol first appeared in Alexandria around A.D. 200;[71]

similarly, the baptismal bath was described as a *piscina* (fish-pond) quite early. This presupposes that the believers were fishes, as is in fact suggested by the gospels (for instance Matt. 4:19). There Christ wants to make Peter and Andrew "fishers of men," and the miraculous draught of fishes (Luke 5:10) is used by Christ himself as a paradigm for Peter's missionary activity.

146 A direct astrological aspect of Christ's birth is given us in Matthew 2:1ff. The Magi from the East were star-gazers who, beholding an extraordinary constellation, inferred an equally extraordinary birth. This anecdote proves that Christ, possibly even at the time of the apostles, was viewed from the astrological standpoint or was at least brought into connection with astrological myths. The latter alternative is fully confirmed when we consider the apocalyptic utterances of St. John. Since this exceedingly complex question has been discussed by those who are more qualified than I, we can support our argument on the well-attested fact that glimpses of astrological mythology may be caught behind the stories of the worldly and otherworldly life of the Redeemer.[72]

147 Above all it is the connections with the age of the Fishes which are attested by the fish symbolism, either contemporaneously with the gospels themselves ("fishers of men," fishermen as the first disciples, miracle of loaves and fishes), or immediately afterwards in the post-apostolic era. The symbolism shows Christ and those who believe in him as fishes, fish as the food eaten at the Agape,[73] baptism as immersion in a fish-pond, etc. At first sight, all this points to no more than the fact that the fish symbols and mythologems which have always existed had assimilated the figure of the Redeemer; in other words, it was a symptom of Christ's assimilation into the world of ideas prevailing at that time. But, to the extent that Christ was regarded as the new aeon, it would be clear to anyone acquainted with astrology that he was born as the first fish of the Pisces era, and was doomed to die as the last ram[74] (*ἀρνίον*, lamb) of the declining Aries era.[75] Matthew 27:15ff. hands down this mythologem in the form of the old sacrifice of the seasonal god. Significantly enough, Jesus's partner in the ceremony is called Barabbas, "son of the father." There would be some justification for drawing a parallel between the tension of opposites in early Christian psychology and the fact the zodiacal sign for Pisces (♓) frequently shows two fishes moving in opposite directions, but only if it could be proved that their contrary movement dates from pre-Christian times or is at least contemporary with Christ. Unfortunately, I know of no pictorial representation from this period that would give us any information about the position of the fishes. In the fine bas-relief of the zodia from the Little Metropolis in Athens, Pisces and Aquarius are missing. There is one representation of the fishes, near the beginning of our era, that is certainly free from Christian influence. This is the globe of the heavens from the Farnese Atlas in Naples. The first fish, depicted north of the equator, is vertical, with its head pointing to the celestial Pole; the second fish, south of the equator, is horizontal, with its head pointing West. The picture follows the astronomical configuration and is therefore naturalistic.[76] The zodiac from the temple of Hathor at Denderah

(1st cent. B.C.) shows the fishes, but they both face the same way. The planisphere of Timochares,[77] mentioned by Hipparchus, has only *one* fish where Pisces should be. On coins and gems from the time of the emperors, and also on Mithraic monuments,[78] the fishes are shown either facing the same way or moving in opposite directions.[79] The polarity which the fishes later acquired may perhaps be due to the fact that the astronomical constellation shows the first (northerly) fish as vertical, and the second (southerly) fish as horizontal. They move almost at right angles to one another and hence form a cross. This countermovement, which was unknown to the majority of the oldest sources, was much emphasized in Christian times, and this leads one to suspect a certain tendentiousness.[80]

148 Although no connection of any kind can be proved between the figure of Christ and the inception of the astrological age of the fishes, the simultaneity of the fish symbolism of the Redeemer with the astrological symbol of the new aeon seems to me important enough to warrant the emphasis we place upon it. If we try to follow up the complicated mythological ramifications of this parallel, we do so with intent to throw light on the multifarious aspects of an archetype that manifests itself on the one hand in a *personality*, and on the other hand synchronistically, in a moment of time determined in advance, before Christ's birth. Indeed, long before that, the archetype had been written in the heavens by projection, so as then, "when the time was fulfilled," to coincide with the symbols produced by the new era. The fish, appropriately enough, belongs to the winter rainy season, like Aquarius and Capricorn (*αιγόκερως*, the goatfish).[81] As a zodiacal sign, therefore, it is not in the least remarkable. It becomes a matter for astonishment only when, through the precession of the equinoxes, the spring-point moves into this sign and thus inaugurates an age in which the "fish" was used as a name for the God who became a man, who was born as a fish and was sacrificed as a ram, who had fishermen for disciples and wanted to make them fishers of men, who fed the multitude with miraculously multiplying fishes, who was himself eaten as a fish, the "holier food," and whose followers are little fishes, the "pisciculi." Assume, if you like, that a fairly widespread knowledge of astrology would account for at least some of this symbolism in certain Gnostic-Christian circles.[82] But this assumption does not apply when it comes to eyewitness accounts in the synoptic gospels. There is no evidence of any such thing. We have no reason whatever to suppose that those stories are disguised astrological myths. On the contrary, one gets the impression that the fish episodes are entirely natural happenings and that there is nothing further to be looked for behind them. They are "Just So" stories, quite simple and natural, and one wonders whether the whole Christian fish symbolism may not have come about equally fortuitously and without premeditation. Hence one could speak just as well of the seemingly fortuitous coincidence of this symbolism with the name of the new aeon, the more so as the age of the fishes seems to have left no very clear traces in the cultures of the East. I could not maintain with any certainty that this is correct, because I know far too little about Indian and Chinese astrology. As against this, the fact

that the traditional fish symbolism makes possible a verifiable prediction that had already been made in the New Testament is a somewhat uncomfortable proposition to swallow.

149 The northerly, or easterly, fish, which the spring-point entered at about the beginning of our era,[83] is joined to the southerly, or westerly, fish by the so-called commissure. This consists of a band of faint stars forming the middle sector of the constellation, and the spring-point gradually moved along its southern edge. The point where the ecliptic intersects with the meridian at the tail of the second fish coincides roughly with the sixteenth century, the time of the Reformation, which as we know is so extraordinarily important for the history of Western symbols. Since then the spring-point has moved along the southern edge of the second fish, and will enter Aquarius in the course of the third millennium.[84] Astrologically interpreted, the designation of Christ as one of the fishes identifies him with the first fish, the vertical one. Christ is followed by the Antichrist, at the end of time. The beginning of the enantiodromia would fall, logically, midway between the two fishes. We have seen that this is so. The time of the Renaissance begins in the immediate vicinity of the second fish, and with it comes that spirit which culminates in the modern age.[85]

NOTES

1 Early collections of such allegories in the *Ancoratus* of Epiphanius, and in Augustine, *Contra Faustum*. For *nycticorax* and *aquila* see Eucherius, *Liber formularum spiritalis intelligentiae*, cap. 5 (Migne, *P.L.*, vol. 50, col. 740).

2 Augustine (*City of God*, trans, by J. Healey, II, p. 196) relates how the former proconsul Flaccianus, with whom he had a conversation about Jesus, produced a book containing the songs of the Erythraean Sibyl, and showed him the passage where the above words, forming the acrostic 'Ιχθῦς, are themselves the acrostic for a whole poem, an apocalyptic prophecy of the Sibyls:

> "Iudicii signum tellus sudore madescet,
> E coelo Rex adveniet per saecla futurus:
> Scilicet in came praesens ut iudicet orbem.
> Unde Deum cement incredulus atque fidelis
> Celsum cum Sanctis, aevi iam termino in ipso.
> Sic animae cum carne aderunt quas judicat ipse . . ."
> (In sign of doomsday the whole earth shall sweat.
> Ever to reign a king in heavenly seat
> Shall come to judge all flesh. The faithful and
> Unfaithful too before this God shall stand.
> Seeing him high with saints in time's last end.
> Corporeal shall he sit, and thence extend
> His doom on souls . . .)
>
> (Ibid., p, 437.)

The Greek original is in *Oracula Sibyllina*, ed. John Geffcken, p. 142. [For Augustine's explanation of the discrepancy in the acrostic, see Healey trans., II. p. 196. – EDITORS.]

3 Cf. Jeremias, *The Old Testament in the Light of the Ancient East*, I, p. 76, n. 2.

4 From this inscription I will cite only the middle portion, which says: "Everywhere I had a travelling companion, since I had Paul sitting in the chariot. But everywhere Faith

drew me onward, and everywhere he set before me for food a fish from the source, exceeding great and pure, which a holy virgin had caught. And he offered this fish to the friends to eat, having good wine, a mixed drink with bread." See Ramsay, "The Cities and Bishoprics of Phrygia," p. 424.

5 Cf. the material in Goodenough, *Jewish Symbols in the Greco-Roman Period*, V, pp. 13ff.

6 Doelger, 'ΙΧΘΤΣ: *Das Fischsymbol in frühchristlicher Zeit.*

7 *Sinnbilder und Kunstvorstellungen der alien Christen* (1825), p. 49. Muenter mentions Abrabanel (sic) here, "who in all probability drew on older sources."

8 Op. cit., p. 76.

9 *Der Stern der Weisen* (1827), pp. 54ff.

10 Isaac Abravanel (Abarbanel) ben Jehuda, *Ma'yene ha-Yeshu'ah* ("Sources of Salvation" – A Commentary on Daniel. Ferrara, 1551).

11 Corresponding to 1396 B.C.

12 Actually the conjunction took place in Sagittarius (♐). The *coniunctiones magnae* of the water trigon (♋, ♏, ♓) fall in the years 1800 to 1600 and 1000 to 800 B.C.

13 Anger, "Der Stern der Weisen und das Geburtsjahr Christi," p. 396, and Gerhardt, *Der Stern des Messias*, pp. 54f.

14 Gerhardt, p. 57. Ptolemy and, following him, the Middle Ages associate Palestine with Aries.

15 "Ye have borne Siccuth your king and Chiun your images, the star of your god, which ye made to yourselves" (RV). Stephen refers to this in his defence (Acts 7:43): "And you took unto you the tabernacle of Moloch and the star of your god Rempham." "Rempham" (*'Ρομφα*), is a corruption of Kewan (Chiun).

16 Dozy and de Goeje, "Nouveaux documents pour l'étude de la religion des Harraniens," p. 350.

17 Abu Ma'shar, d. 885.

18 Gerhardt, p. 57. Also Pierre d'Ailly, *Concordantia astronomiccum theologia*, etc., fol. g4 (Venice, 1490): "But Saturn, as Messahali says, has a meaning which concerns the Jewish people or their faith."

19 Reitzenstein, *Poimandres*, p. 76.

20 *Contra Celsum*, VI, 30 (trans. by H. Chadwick, p. 345).

21 Ibid., VI, 31: "But they say that this angel like unto a lion has a necessary connection with the star Saturn." Cf. *Pistis Sophia*, trans, by Mead, p. 47, and Bousset, *Hauptprobleme der Gnosis*, pp. 352ff.

22 Hippolytus, Elenchos, V, 7, 30 (Legge trans., I, p. 128).

23 Ibid., VII, 38, 1 (cf. Legge trans., II, p. 96).

24 Hence the image of Saturn worshipped by the Sabaeans was said to be made of lead or black stone. (Chwolsohn, *Die Ssabier und der Ssabismus*, II, p. 383.)

25 *L'Astrologie grecque*, p. 317.

26 Bouché-Leclercq (p. 318) conjectures one of the known classical "etymologies," namely an *onos* (ass) contained in *Kronos* (Saturn), based on a joke aimed at the Megarian philosopher Diodoros. But the reason for the Saturn-ass analogy probably lies deeper, that is, in the nature of the ass itself, which was regarded as a "cold, intractable, slow-witted, long-lived animal." (From the Greek bestiary cited by Bouché-Leclercq.) In Polemon's bestiary I find the following description of the wild ass: "Given to flight, timid, stupid, untamed, lustful, jealous, killing its females" (*Scriptores physiognomici graeci et latini*, I, p. 182).

27 A possible model might be the Egyptian tradition of the martyrdom of Set, depicted at Denderah. He is shown tied to the "slave's post," has an ass's head, and Horus stands before him with a knife in his hand. (Mariette, *Dendèrah*, plates vol. IV, pl. 56.)

28 *Quaestiones convivales*, IV, 5.

29 *Contra Apionem*, II, 7–8 (80ff.). (Cf. trans. by H. St. J. Thackeray and R. Marcus, I, pp. 325ff.)

30 *The Histories*, trans. by W. H. Fyfe, II, pp. 204ff.

31 Epiphanius, *Panarium* ed. Oehler, I, p. 184.

32 *Apologeticus adversus gentes*, XVI. (Migne, *PL.*, vol. 1, cols. 364–65; cf. trans. by S. Thelwall, I, pp. 84f.)

33 Plutarch, *De lside et Osiride*, in *Moralia*, pp. 77, 123. In ch. 31 Plutarch states that the legend of Set's flight on an ass and of the fathering of his two sons Hierosolymus and Judaeus is not Egyptian, but pertained to the *'Ιουδαϊκά.*

34 In the Papyrus of Ani (ed. E. A. W. Budge, p. 248) a hymn to Ra says: "May I advance upon the earth; may I smite the Ass; may I crush the evil one (Sebau); may I destroy Apep in his hour."

35 Albumasar, Lib. II, *De magnis coniunctionibus*, tract. I, diff. 4, p. a8r (1489): "If (Jupiter) is in conjunction with Saturn, it signifies that the faith of the citizens thereof is Judaism. . . . And if the moon is in conjunction with Saturn it signifies doubt and revolution and change, and this by reason of the speed of the corruption of the moon and the rapidity of its motion and the shortness of its delay in the sign." Cf. also Pierre d'Ailly, *Concordantia* etc., fol. d8r. J. H. Heidegger (*Quaestiones ad textum Lucae Vll*, 12–17, 1655) says in ch. IX that Abu Mansor (= Albumasar), in his sixth tractate, in the *Introductio maior*, connects the life of Christ, like that of Mahomet, with the stars. Cardan ascribes c1f to Christianity, c1 g to Judiasm, c1e to Islam, and according to him c1d signifies idolatry ("Commentarium in Ptolemaeum De astrorum Judiciis," p. 188).

36 Christensen, *Le Premier Homme et le premier roi dans l'histoire légendaire des Iraniens*, part 1, p. 24.

37 Gerhardt, *Stern des Messias*, p. 74.

38 Calculated on the basis of Peters and Knobel, *Ptolemy's Catalogue of Stars*.

39 Medieval astrologers cast a number of ideal horoscopes for Christ. Albumasar and Albertus Magnus took Virgo as the ascendent; Pierre d'Ailly (1356–1420), on the other hand, took Libra, and so did Cardan. Pierre d'Ailly says: "For Libra is the human sign, that is, of the Liberator of men, [the sign] of a prudent and just and spiritual man" (*Concordantia*, etc., cap. 2). Kepler, in his *Discurs von der grossen Conjunction* (1623; p. 701), says that God himself marked "such great conjunctions as these with extraordinary and marvellous stars visible in high heaven, also with notable works of his divine Providence." He continues: "Accordingly he appointed the birth of his Son Christ our Saviour exactly at time of the great conjunction in the signs of the Fishes and the Ram, near equinoctial point." Seen heliocentrically, the conjunction took place just in front of the equinoctial point, and this gives it a special significance astrologically. Pierre d'Ailly (*Concordantia*, etc., fol. br) says: "But a great conjunction is that of Saturn and Jupiter in the beginning of the Ram." These conjunctions occur every 20 years and take place every 200 years in the same trigon. But the same position can only recur every 800 years. The most significant positions are those between two trigons. Albumasar (*De magnis coniunc.*, tract. 3, diff. 1, fol. D 8r) says they manifest themselves "in changes of parties and offices and in changes of the laws and . . . in the coming of prophets and of prophesying and of miracles in parties and offices of state."

40 Crucifixion was a well-known punishment for slaves. The Cross with a snake on it, instead of the Crucified, is often found in medieval times [*Psychology and Alchemy*, fig. 217], and also in the dreams and fantasy-images of modern people who know nothing of this tradition. A characteristic dream of this sort is the following: *The dreamer was watching a Passion play in the theatre. On the way to Golgotha, the actor taking the part of the Saviour suddenly changed into a snake or crocodile.*

41 Erman, *Die Religion der Ägypter*, p. 137.

42 *Pistis Sophia*, Mead trans., pp. 118f., slightly modified.

43 Cf. the fish that Augustine says was "drawn from the deep."

44 In this connection mention should be made of the "Saviour of the twins" (σωτῆρες) in *Pistis Sophia* (Mead trans., pp. 2, 17, and elsewhere).

45 Also mentioned in the *Chronique* of Tabari (I, ch. 23, p. 67). There Antichrist is the king of the Jews, who appears with Gog and Magog. This may be an allusion to Rev. 20:7f.: "And when the thousand years are expired, Satan shall be loosed out of his prison, and shall go out to deceive the nations which are in the four comers of the earth, Gog and Magog, to gather them together to battle" (AV).

Graf von Wackerbarth (*Merkwürdige Geschichte der weltberühmten Gog und Magog*, p. 19) relates from an English "History of the World," which came out in German in 1760, that the Arab writers say the "Yajui" were "of more than ordinary size," whereas the "Majui" were "not more than three spans high." This story, despite the obscurity of its origins, points to the antithetical nature of Gog and Magog, who thus form a parallel to the Fishes. Augustine interprets "the nations which are in the four corners of the earth, Gog and Magog" as, respectively (Gog), *tectum*, "roof" or "house," and (Magog) *de tecto*, "he that comes out of the house": "Ut illae sint tectum, ipse de tecto." That is to say the nations are the house, but the devil dwells in the house and comes out of it. (*City of God*, Healey trans., II, p. 286.) On Augustine is based the *Compendium theologicae veritatis* (Venice, 1492), which was attributed in turn to Albertus Magnus, Hugh of Strasbourg, and John of Paris. It is our main source for the Antichrist legend. With reference to Augustine it says (Libell. 7, cap. 11) that Gog means "occultatio" (concealment), Magog "detectio" (revelation). This corroborates the antithetical nature of Gog and Magog at least for the Middle Ages. It is another instance of the motif of the hostile brothers, or of duplication. Albumasar (tract. 4, diff. 12, f. 8r) calls the sixth "clima" (inclination towards the Pole) that of Gog and Magog, and correlates it with Gemini and Virgo.

46 *Nezikin* VI, Sanhedrin II (*BT*, p. 658). R. Hanan ben Tahlifa, into whose mouth this prophecy is put, is mentioned in the list of Amoraim (teachers of the Talmud) and lived in the 2nd cent. A.D.

47 Epiphanius, *Panarium*, XXX (Oehler edn., I, pp. 240ff.).

48 Hipparchus is supposed to have discovered the precession. Cf. Boll, *Sphaera*, p. 199, n. 1.

49 Origen, *Commentaria in Genesim*, tom. Ill, i, 14, 11 (Migne, *P.G.*, vol. 12, col. 79): "There is indeed a theory that the zodiacal circle, just like the planets, is carried back from setting to rising [or: from west to east], within a century by one degree; . . . since the twelfth part [1 zodion] is one thing when conceived in the mind, another when perceived by the senses; yet from that which is conceived only in the mind, and can scarcely, or not even scarcely, be held for certain, the truth of the matter appears." The Platonic year was then reckoned as 36,000 years. Tycho Brahe reckoned it at 24,120 years. The constant for the precession is 50.3708 seconds and the total cycle (360°) takes 25,725.6 years.

50 Bouché-Leclercq, p. 591, n. 2; Knapp, *Antiskia*; Boll, *Sphaera*.

51 The theory of the conjunctions was set down in writing by the Arabs about the middle of the 9th cent., more particularly by Messahala. Cf. Strauss, *Die Astrologie des Johannes Kepler*.

52 With his estimate of 960 years between two *coniunctiones maximae*, Pierre d'Ailly would also arrive at A.D. 3613.

53 This period around the year 1240 would, from the astrological standpoint, be characterized by the great conjunction of Jupiter and Saturn in Libra, in 1246. Libra is another double sign with a pneumatic nature (air trigon), like Gemini, and for this reason it was taken by Pierre d'Ailly as Christ's ascendent.

54 At the Lateran Council, 1215. Cf. Denzinger and Bannwart, *Enchiridion symbolorum*, pp. 190ff.

55 "His teaching is to be held not so much heretical as insane," says the decree.

56 Hahn, *Geschichte der Ketzer im Mittelalter*, II, p. 779: ". . . some who under the name of a false and pretended religious order, whom the common folk call Beghards and Schwestrones or 'Brod durch Gott'; but they call themselves Little Brethren and Sisters of the fellowship of the Free Spirit and of Voluntary Poverty."

57 "Item credunt se esse Deum per naturam sine esse aeternos . . .
"Item quod nullo indigent nec Deo nec Deitate.
"Item quod sunt ipsum regnum coelorum.
"Item quod sunt etiam immutabiles in nova rupe, quod de nullo gaudent, et de nullo turbantur.
"Item quod homo magis tenetur sequi instinctum interiorem quam veritatem Evangelii quod cottidie praedicatur . . . dicunt, se credere ibi (in Evangelio) esse poëtica quae non sunt vera."

(Hahn, II, pp. 779f.)

58 Cf. "The Phenomenology of the Spirit in Fairytales," pars. 396ff.
59 "The Spirit Mercurius," pars. 284ff., and "A Psychological Approach to the Dogma of the Trinity," pars. 257ff.
60 [Although Mary's Immaculate Conception was declared *de fide* by Pope Pius IX in 1854, by the bull *Ineffabilis Deus*, her Assumption was not defined as part of divine revelation until 1950. – EDITORS.]
61 [Cf. "Psychology and Religion," par. 122, and "Answer to Job," pars. 748ff.]
62 *Opera*, ed. G. Schepps, p. 24.
63 Cf. *Aurora Consurgens* (ed. von Franz), p. 127: "this great and wide sea smote the rock and the metallic waters flowed forth."
64 *Musaeum hermeticum* (1678), p. 212: "Our stone is called the sacred rock, and is understood or signified in four ways." Cf. Ephesians 3 : 18. The Pyramid Text of Pepi I mentions a god of resurrection with four faces: "Homage to thee, O thou who hast four faces. . . . Thou art endowed with a soul, and thou dost rise (like the sun) in thy boat . . . carry thou this Pepi with thee in the cabin of thy boat, for this Pepi is the son of the Scarab." (Budge, *Gods of the Egyptians*, I, p. 85.)
65 *Explanationes in Psalmos*, XXXVIII: "In the shadow there was water from the rock, as it were the blood of Christ."
66 Mylius, *Philosophia reformata* (1622), p. 112: "Whence the philosopher brought forth water from the rock and oil out of the flinty stone."
67 *Von hylealischen Chaos* (1597), p. 272.
68 Hippolytus, *Elenchos*, V, 7, 34f. (Legge trans., I, p. 129). Reference is also made here to the "stone cut from the mountain without hands" (Daniel 2 : 45), a metaphor used by the alchemists.
69 *De errore profanarum religionum*, 20, 1.
70 Cf. the building of the seamless tower (church) with "living stones" in the "Shepherd" of Hermas.
71 Doelger, ΙΧΘΥΣ: *Das Fischsymbol*, I, p. 18. Though the Abercius inscription, which dates from the beginning of the 3rd cent, (after A.D. 216), is of importance in this connection, it is of doubtful Christian origin. Dieterich (*Die Grabschrift des Aberkios*), in the course of a brilliant argument, demonstrates that the "holy shepherd" mentioned in the inscription is Attis, the Lord of the sacred Ram and the thousand-eyed shepherd of glittering stars. One of his special forms was Elogabal of Emera, the god of the emperor Heliogabalus, who caused the *hieros gamos* of his god to be celebrated with Urania of Carthage, also called *Virgo coelestis*. Heliogabalus was a *gallus* (priest) of the Great Mother, whose fish only the priests might eat. The fish had to be caught by a virgin. It is conjectured that Abercius had this inscription written in commemoration of his journey to Rome to the great *hieros gamos*, sometime after A.D. 216. For the same reasons there are doubts about the Christianity of the Pectorios inscription at Autun, in which the fish figures too: "*Εσθιε πν* . . . , *ιχθυν εχων παλάμαις 'Ιχθυϊ χορταξ αρα λιλαιω σεσποτα σωτερ*: Eat . . . (reading uncertain), holding the fish in the hands. Nourish now with the fish, I yearn, Lord Saviour." Probable reading: *πιάων* instead of *πεινάων*. Cf. Cabrol and Leclercq, *Dictionnaire d'archéologie chrétienne*, XIII, cols. 2884ff., "Pectorios." The first three distichs of the inscription make the acrostic Ichthys. Dating is uncertain (3rd–5th cent.). Cf. Doelger, I, pp. 12ff.

72 I refer particularly to Boll, *Aus der Offenbarung Johannis*. The writings of Arthur Drews have treated the astrological parallels with – one can well say – monomaniacal thoroughness, not altogether to the advantage of this idea. See *Der Sternenhimmel in der Dichtung und Religion der alten Völker und des Christentums*.

73 Religious meal. According to Tertullian (*Adversus Marcionem*, I, cap. XIV; Migne, *P.L.*, vol. 2, col. 262) the fish signifies "the holier food." Cf. also Goodenough, *Jewish Symbols*, V, pp. 41ff.

74 Origen, In *Genesim hom*. VIII, g (Migne, *P.G.*, vol. 12, col. 208): "We said . . . that Isaac bore the form of Christ, but that the ram also seems no less to bear the form of Christ." Augustine (*City of God*, XVI, 32, 1) asks: "Who was that ram by the offering whereof was made a complete sacrifice in typical blood . . . who was prefigured thereby but Jesus . . . ?" For the Lamb as Aries in the Apocalypse see Boll, *Aus der Offenbarung Johannis*.

75 Eisler, *Orpheus – The Fisher*, pp. 51ff. There is also a wealth of material in Eisler's paper "Der Fisch als Sexualsymbol," though it contains little that would help to interpret the fish-symbol, since the question puts the cart before the horse. It has long been known that *all the instinctual forces of the psyche* are involved in the formation of symbolic images, hence sexuality as well. Sex is not "symbolized" in these images, but leaps to the eye, as Eisler's material clearly shows. In whatsoever a man is involved, there his sexuality will appear too. The indubitably correct statement that St. Peter's is made of stone, wood, and metal hardly helps us to interpret its meaning, and the same is true of the fish symbol if one continues to be astonished that this image, like all others, has its manifest sexual components. With regard to the terminology, it should be noted that something known is never "symbolized," but can only be expressed *allegorically* or *semiotically*.

76 Thiele, *Antike Himmelsbilder*, p. 29.

77 Boll, *Sphaera*, Pl. I, and Eisler, *The Royal Art of Astrology*, Pl. 5, following p. 164.

78 Gaedechens, *Der Marmorne Himmelsglobus*.

79 Cumont, *Textes et monuments*, II.

80 See the two fishes in Lambspringk's symbols (*Mus. herm*., p. 343), representing at the same time the opposites to be united. Aratus (*Phaenomena*, Mair trans., p. 401) mentions only the higher position of the northern fish as compared with the southern one, without emphasizing their duality or opposition. Their double character is, however, stressed in modern astrological speculation. (E. M. Smith, *The Zodia*, p. 279.) Senard (*Le Zodiaque*, p. 446) says: "The fish . . . swimming from above downwards symbolizes the movement of involution of Spirit in Matter; that . . . which swims from below upwards, the movement of evolution of the Spirit-Matter composite returning to its Unique Principle."

81 Capricorn ♑

82 A clear reference to astrology can be found in *Pistis Sophia*, where Jesus converses with the "ordainers of the nativity": "But Jesus answered and said to Mary: If the ordainers of the nativity find Heimarmene and the Sphere turned to the left in accordance with their first circulation, then their words will be true, and they will say what must come to pass. But if they find Heimarmene or the Sphere turned to the right, then they will not say anything true, because I have changed their influences and their squares and their triangles and their octants." (Cf. Mead trans., p. 29.)

83 The meridian of the star "O" in the commissure passed through the spring-point in A.D. 11, and that of the star "a 113" in 146 B.C. calculated on the basis of Peters and Knobel, *Ptolemy's Catalogue of Stars*.

84 Since the delimitation of the constellations is known to be somewhat arbitrary, this date is very indefinite. It refers to the actual constellation of fixed stars, not to the *zodion noeton*, i.e., the zodiac divided into sectors of 30° each. Astrologically the beginning of the next aeon, according to the starting-point you select, falls between A. D. 2000 and 2200. Starting from star "O" and assuming a Platonic month of 2,143 years, one would

arrive at A.D. 2154 for the beginning of the Aquarian Age, and at A.D. 1997 if you start from star "a 113." The latter date agrees with the longitude of the stars in Ptolemy's Almagest.

85 Modern astrological speculation likewise associates the Fishes with Christ: "The fishes . . . the inhabitants of the waters, are fitly an emblem of those whose life being hid with Christ in God, come out of the waters of judgment without being destroyed [an allusion to the fishes which were not drowned in the Deluge! – C.G.J.] and shall find their true sphere where life abounds and death is not: where, for ever surrounded with the living water and drinking from its fountain, they 'shall not perish, but have everlasting life.' . . . Those who shall dwell for ever in the living water are one with Jesus Christ the Son of God, the Living One." (Smith, *The Zodia*, pp. 280f.)

9 The prophecies of Nostradamus

"The Prophecies of Nostradamus" (1951) (*CW* 9ii), pars. 150–161

150 The course of our religious history as well as an essential part of our psychic development could have been predicted more or less accurately, both as regards time and content, from the precession of the equinoxes through the constellation of Pisces. The prediction, as we saw, was actually made and coincides with the fact that the Church suffered a schism in the sixteenth century. After that an enantiodromian process set in which, in contrast to the "Gothic" striving *upwards* to the heights, could be described as a horizontal movement *outwards*, namely the voyages of discovery and the conquest of Nature. The vertical was cut across by the horizontal, and man's spiritual and moral development moved in a direction that grew more and more obviously antichristian, so that today we are confronted with a crisis of Western civilization whose outcome appears to be exceedingly dubious.

151 With this background in mind, I would like to mention the astrological prophecies of Nostradamus, written in a letter[1] to Henry II of France, on June 27, 1558. After detailing a year characterized, among other things, by ♃ ☌ ☿ with ♂ □ ☿,[2] he says:

> Then the beginning of that year shall see a greater persecution against the Christian Church than ever was in Africa,[3] and it shall be in the year 1792, at which time everyone will think it a renovation of the age. . . . And at that time and in those countries the infernal power shall rise against the Church of Jesus Christ. This shall be the second Antichrist, which shall persecute the said Church and its true vicar by means of the power of temporal kings, who through their ignorance shall be seduced by tongues more sharp than any sword in the hands of a madman. . . . The persecution of the clergy shall have its beginning in the power of the Northern Kings joined by the Eastern ones. And that persecution shall last eleven years, or a little less, at which time the chief Northern king shall fail.[4]

152 However, Nostradamus thinks that "a united Southern king" will outlast the Northern one by three years. He sees a return of paganism ("the sanctuary

destroyed by paganism"), the Bible will be burned, and an immense bloodbath will take place: "So great tribulations as ever did happen since the first foundation of the Christian Church." All Latin countries will be affected by it.

153 There are historical determinants that may have moved Nostradamus to give the year 1792 as the beginning of the new aeon. For instance, Cardinal Pierre d'Ailly, basing himself on Albumasar, writes in his *Concordantia*[5] on the eighth *coniunctio maxima* (f1gin A), which had been calculated for 1693:

> And after that shall be the fulfilment of ten revolutions of Saturn in the year 1789, and this will happen after the said conjunction, in the course of ninety-seven years or thereabouts. . . . This being so, we say that if the world shall endure until then, which God alone knows, then there will be many and great and marvellous changes and transformations of the world, especially as concerns law-giving and religious sects, for the said conjunction and the revolutions of Saturn will coincide with the revolution or reversal of the upper orb, i.e., the eighth sphere, and from these and other premises the change of sects will be known. . . . Whence it may be concluded with some probability that this is the time when the Antichrist shall come with his law and his damnable sects, which are utterly contrary and inimical to the law of Christ; for, being human, we can have no certainty with regard to the time and the moment of his coming. . . . Yet, despite the indeterminate statement that he will come at approximately that time, it is possible to have a probable conjecture and a credible hypothesis in accordance with the astronomical indications. If, therefore, the astronomers say that a change of sects will occur about that time, then, according to them, a Mighty One will come after Mahomet, who will set up an evil and magical law. Thus we may surmise with credible probability that after the sect of Mahomet none other will come save the law of the Antichrist.[6]

154 In connection with the calculation of the year 1693, Pierre d'Ailly quotes Albumasar as saying that the first *coniunctio maxima* of Saturn and Jupiter took place *anno mundi* 3200. To this Albumasar added 960 years, which brings us to A.D. 1693 as the year of the eighth *coniunctio maxima.*[7] In Part III of his book, chapter 17, Pierre d'Ailly criticizes this view and calls it a "false deduction." In his treatise against "superstitiosos astronomos," 1410, he maintains that the Christian religion should not be brought under astrological laws. He was alluding in particular to Roger Bacon, who had revived the theory that Christianity was under the influence of the planet Mercury. Pierre d'Ailly held that only superstitions and heretical opinions were astrologically influenced, and especially the coming of the Antichrist.[8]

155 We are probably right in assuming that these calculations were known to Nostradamus, who proposed 1792 as an improvement on 1789. Both dates are suggestive, and a knowledge of subsequent events confirms that the things that happened around that time were significant forerunners of developments

in our own day. The enthronement of the "Déesse Raison" was, in fact, an anticipation of the antichristian trend that was pursued from then onwards.

156 The "renovation of the age" might mean a new aeon, and it coincides in a remarkable way with the new system of dating, the revolutionary calendar, which began with September 22, 1792, and had a distinctly antichristian character.[9] What had been brewing up long beforehand then became a manifest event; in the French Revolution men witnessed the enantiodromia that had set in with the Renaissance and ran parallel with the astrological fish symbol. The time seemed a significant one astrologically, for a variety of reasons. In the first place this was the moment when the precession of the equinoxes reached the tail of the second fish.[10] Then, in the year 1791, Saturn was in ♈, a fiery sign. Besides that, tradition made use of the theory of maximal conjunctions[11] and regarded the year of the eighth *coniunctio maxima* – 1693 – as a starting-point for future calculations.[12] This critical year was combined with another tradition basing itself on periods of ten revolutions of Saturn, each period taking three hundred years. Pierre d'Ailly cites Albumasar, who says in his *Magnae coniunctiones*: "They said that the change shall come when ten revolutions of Saturn have been completed, and that the permutation of Saturn is particularly appropriate to the movable signs" (♈, ♋, ♎, ♑).[13] According to Pierre d'Ailly, a Saturn period came to an end in 11 B.C., and he connects this with the appearance of Christ. Another period ended in A.D. 289: this he connects with Manichaeism. The year 589 foretells Islam, and 1189 the significant reign of Pope Innocent III; 1489 announces a schism of the Church, and 1789 signalizes – by inference – the coming of the Antichrist. Fantasy could do the rest, for the archetype had long been ready and was only waiting for the time to be fulfilled. That a usurper from the North would seize power[14] is easily understood when we consider that the Antichrist is something infernal, the devil or the devil's son, and is therefore Typhon or Set, who has his fiery abode in the North. Typhon's power is triadic, possessing two confederates, one in the East and one in the South. This power corresponds to the "lower triad."[15]

157 Nostradamus, the learned physician and astrologer, would certainly have been familiar with the idea of the North as the region of the devil, unbelievers, and all things evil. The idea, as St. Eucherius of Lyons (d. 450) remarks,[16] goes back to Jeremiah 1:14: "From the north shall an evil wind break forth upon all the inhabitants of the land,"[17] and other passages such as Isaiah 14:12f.:

> How art thou fallen from heaven, O Lucifer, son of the morning! how art thou cut down to the ground, which didst weaken the nations! For thou hast said in thine heart, I will ascend into heaven, I will exalt my throne above the stars of God, I will sit on the mount of assembly in the far north.[18]

The Benedictine monk Rhabanus Maurus (d. 856) says that "the north wind is the harshness of persecution" and "a figure of the old enemy."[19] The north wind, he adds, signifies the devil, as is evident from Job 26:7: "He stretcheth out the north over the empty space, and hangeth the earth upon nothing."[20]

Rhabanus interprets this as meaning that "God allows the devil to rule the minds of those who are empty of his grace."[21] St. Augustine says: "Who is that north wind, save him who said: I will set up my seat in the north, I will be like the most High? The devil held rule over the wicked, and possessed the nations," etc.[22]

158 The Victorine monk Garnerius says that the "malign spirit" was called Aquilo, the north wind. Its coldness meant the "frigidity of sinners."[23] Adam Scotus imagined there was a frightful dragon's head in the north from which all evil comes. From its mouth and snout it emitted smoke of a triple nature,[24] the "threefold ignorance, namely of good and evil, of true and false, of fitting and unfitting."[25] "That is the smoke," says Adam Scotus, "which the prophet Ezekiel, in his vision of God, saw coming from the north,"[26] the "smoke" of which Isaiah speaks.[27] The pious author never stops to think how remarkable it is that the prophet's vision of God should be blown along on the wings of the north wind, wrapped in this devilish smoke of threefold ignorance. Where there is smoke, there is fire. Hence the "great cloud" had "brightness round about it, and fire flashing forth continually, and in the midst of the fire, as it were gleaming bronze."[28] The north wind comes from the region of fire and, despite its coldness, is a "ventus urens" (burning wind), as Gregory the Great calls it, referring to Job 27 : 21.[29] This wind is the malign spirit, "who rouses up the flames of lust in the heart" and kindles every living thing to sin. "Through the breath of evil incitement to earthly pleasures he makes the hearts of the wicked to burn." As Jeremiah 1:13 says, "I see a boiling pot, facing away from the north." In these quotations from Gregory we hear a faint echo of the ancient idea of the fire in the north, which is still very much alive in Ezekiel, whose cloud of fire appears from the north, whence "an evil shall break forth upon all the inhabitants of the land."[30]

159 In these circumstances it is hardly surprising that Nostradamus warns against the usurper from the north when foretelling the coming of the Antichrist. Even before the Reformation the Antichrist was a popular figure in folklore, as the numerous editions of the "Entkrist"[31] in the second half of the fifteenth century show.[32] This is quite understandable in view of the spiritual events then impending: the Reformation was about to begin. Luther was promptly greeted as the Antichrist, and it is possible that Nostradamus calls the Antichrist who was to appear after 1792 the "second Antichrist" because the first had already appeared in the guise of the German reformer, or much earlier with Nero or Mohammed.[33] We should not omit to mention in this connection how much capital the Nazis made out of the idea that Hitler was continuing and completing the work of reformation which Luther had left only half finished.

160 From the existing astrological data, therefore, and from the possibilities of interpreting them it was not difficult for Nostradamus to predict the imminent enantiodromia of the Christian aeon; indeed, by making this prediction, he placed himself firmly in the antichristian phase and served as its mouthpiece.

161 After this excursion, let us turn back to our fish symbolism.

NOTES

1 Printed in the Amsterdam edition of the *Vrayes Centuries et Prophéties de Maistre Michel Nostredame* (1667), pp. 96ff.

2 According to the old tradition the conjunction of Jupiter and Mercury, as mentioned above, is characteristic of Christianity. The quartile aspect between Mercury and Mars "injures" Mercury by "martial" violence. According to Cardan, ☿ ☌ ♂ signifies "the law of Mahomet" (*Comment. in Ptol.*, p. 188). This aspect could therefore indicate an attack by Islam. Albumasar regards ♃ ☌ ♂ in the same way: "And if Mars shall be in conjunction with him (Jupiter), it signifies the fiery civilization and the pagan faith" (*De magn. coniunct.*, tract. I, diff. 4, p. a8r). On the analogy of history the evil events to come are ascribed to the crescent moon, but one never reflects that the opponent of Christianity dwells in the European unconscious. History repeats itself.

3 Where Roman Christendom succumbed to Islam.

4 *The Complete Prophecies of Nostradamus*, trans, and ed. by H. C. Roberts, pp. 231ff.

5 D 7v to 8r, div. 2, cap. 60 and 61. Cf. also Thorndike, *A History of Magic and Experimental Science*, IV, p. 102.

6 "Et post illam erit complementum 10 revolutionum saturnalium anno Christi 1789 et hoc erit post dictam coninnctionem per annos 97 vel prope. . . . His itaque praesuppositis dicimus quod si mundus usque ad ilia tempora duraverit, quod solus deus novit, multae tunc et magnae et mirabiles alterationes mundi et mutationes futurae sunt, et *maxime circa leges et sectas*, nam cum praedicta coniunctione et illis Tevolutionibus Saturni ad hoc concurret revolutio seu reversio superioris orbis, id est, octavae sphaerae per quam et per alia praemissa cognoscitur sectarum mutatio . . . Unde ex his probabiliter conduditur quod forte circa ilia tempora veniet *Antichristus* cum lege sua vel secta damnabili, quae maxime adversa erit et contraria Iegi Christi; nam licet de adventu sui determinato tempore vel momento haberi non possit humanitus certitudo. . . . Tamen indeterminate loquendo quod circa ilia tempora venturus sit potest haberi probabilis coniectura et verisimilis suspicio per astronomica iudicia. Cum enim dictum sit secundum astronomos circa ilia tempora fieri mutationem sectarum et secundum eos post *machometum* erit aliquis potens, qui legem foedam et magicam constituet. Ideo verisimili probabilitate credi potest, quod post sectam machometi nulla secta veniet, nisi lex antichristi."

7 *Concordantia*, etc., fol. b 5.

8 Cf. Thorndike, IV, p. 103.

9 In classical usage *renovatio* can have the meaning of the modern word "revolution." whereas even in late Latin *revolutio* still retains its original meaning of "revolving." As the text shows, Nostradamus thought of this moment (1791) as the climax of a long-standing persecution of the Church. One is reminded of Voltaire's "écrasez l'inflâme!"

10 There is nothing to suggest that a conscious attempt was made to prophesy on the basis of the precession.

11 Conjunctions in Aries were regarded as such, at least as a rule. 0° Aries is the spring-point.

12 I cannot claim to have understood Pierre d'Ailly's argument. Here is the text (Second treatise, ch. 60, "De octava coniunctione maxima"): "Et post illam erit complementum 10 revolutionum saturnalium anno Christi 1789 et hoc erit post dictam coniunctionem per annos 97 vel prope et inter dictam coniunctionem et illud complementum dictarum 10 revolutionum erit status octavae sphaerae circiter per annos 25 quod sic patet: quia status octavae sphaerae erit anno 444 post situm augmentationum [reading uncertain], quae secundum tabulas astronomicas sunt adaequatae ad annum Christi 1330 perfectum, et ideo anno Christi 1764, quibus annis si addas 25, sunt anni 1789 quos praediximus. Unde iterum patet quod ab hoc anno Christi 1414 usque ad statum octavae sphaerae erunt anni 253 perfecti." (And after that shall be the fulfilment of 10 revolutions of Saturn to the year 1789, and this shall be after the said conjunction for 97 years or thereabouts, and between the said conjunction and that fulfilment of the

10 revolutions there shall be a standstill of the eighth sphere for about 25 years, which is evident from this: that the standstill of the eighth sphere shall be in the 444th year after the position of the augmentations, which according to the astronomical tables are assigned to the end of the year of Christ 1320, that is the year of Christ 1764, and if you add 85 years to this, you arrive at the year 1789 aforesaid. Hence it is again evident that from this year of Christ 1414 to the standstill of the eighth sphere there will be 253 complete years.)

13 Fol. d 6.

14 It is not clear from the text whether the same "persecution" is meant, or a new one. The latter would be possible.

15 Cf. "The Phenomenology of the Spirit in Fairytales," pars. 425f., 436ff.

16 Migne, *P.L.*, vol. 50, col. 740.

17 "Ab Aquilone pendetur malum super omnes habitatores terrae" (DV).

18 "Quomodo cecidisti de coelo, Lucifer, qui mane oriebaris? corruisti in terram qui vulnerabas gentes? Qui dicebas in corde tuo: in caelum conscendam, super astra Dei exaltabo solium meum, sedebo in monte testamenti, in lateribus Aquilonis" (trans. is AV; last line RSV).

19 Migne, *P.L.*, vol. 112, col. 860.

20 This is an obvious analogy of the pneuma brooding on the face of the deep.

21 ". . . quod illorum mentibus, qui gratia sua vacui, diabolum Deus dominari permittit."

22 *Enar. in Ps.* XLVII, 3; Migne, *P.L.*, vol. 36, col. 534.

23 *Sancti Victoris Parisiensis Gregorianum*; Migne, *P.L.*, vol. 193, cols. 59f.

24 Allusion to the lower triad.

25 *De tripartito tabernaculo*, III, c. 9; Migne, *P.L.*, vol. 198, col 761. Adam Scotus speaks of the "darkness of the smoke from the north." Pseudo-Clement (Homilies, XIX, 22) stresses "the sins of unconsciousness" (*agnoia*). Honorius of Autun (*Speculum de mysteriis ecclesiae*; Migne, *P.L.*, vol. 172, col. 833) says: "By the north, where the sun lies hidden under the earth, Matthew is meant, who describes the divinity of Christ hidden under the flesh." This confirms the chthonic nature of the triad.

26 Ezek. 1:4: "And I saw, and behold a whirlwind came out of the north, and a great cloud . . ."

27 Isaiah 14:31: "Howl, O gate, cry, O city, all Philistia is thrown down, for a smoke shall come from the north, and there is none that shall escape his troop."

28 Ezek. 1:4.

29 "A burning wind shall take him up and carry him away: and as a whirlwind shall snatch him from his place" (*In Expositicmem beati Job Moralia*; Migne, *P.L.*, vol. 76, cols. 54, 55).

30 Jer. 1:13f.

31 Cf. *Symbols of Transformation*, par. 565.

32 The text of the various mss. is supposed to go back to the *Compendium theologicae veritatis* of Hugh of Strasbourg (13th cent.). Cf. Kelchner, *Der Enndkrist*, p. 7.

33 So in Giovanni Nanni (1432–1502). See Thorndike, IV, pp. 263ff.

10 The historical significance of the fish

"The Historical Significance of the Fish" (1951) (*CW* 9ii), pars. 172–180

172 . . . Through the fish symbolism, Christ was assimilated into a world of ideas that seems far removed from the gospels – a world of pagan origin, saturated with astrological beliefs to an extent that we can scarcely imagine today. Christ was born at the beginning of the aeon of the Fishes. It is by no means ruled out that there were educated Christians who knew of the *coniunctio maxima* of Jupiter and Saturn in Pisces in the year 7 B.C., just as, according to the gospel reports, there were Chaldaeans who actually found Christ's birthplace. The Fishes, however, are a double sign.

173 At midnight on Christmas Eve, when (according to the old time-reckoning) the sun enters Capricorn, Virgo is standing on the eastern horizon, and is soon followed by the Serpent held by Ophiuchus, the "Serpent-bearer." This astrological coincidence seems to me worth mentioning, as also the view that the two fishes are mother and son. The latter idea has a quite special significance because this relationship suggests that the two fishes were originally one. In fact, Babylonian and Indian astrology know of only one fish.[1] Later, this mother evidently gave birth to a son, who was a fish like her. The same thing happened to the Phoenician Derceto-Atargatis, who, half fish herself, had a son called Ichthys. It is just possible that "the sign of the prophet Jonah"[2] goes back to an older tradition about an heroic night sea journey and conquest of death, where the hero is swallowed by a fish ("whale-dragon") and is then reborn.[3] The redemptory name Joshua[4] (Yehoshua, Yeshua, Gr. *Iesous*) is connected with the fish: Joshua is the son of Nun, and Nun means "fish." The Joshua ben Nun of the Khidr legend had dealings with a fish that was meant to be eaten but was revived by a drop of water from the fountain of life.[5]

174 The mythological Great Mothers are usually a danger to their sons. Jeremias mentions a fish representation on an early Christian lamp, showing one fish devouring the other.[6] The name of the largest star in the constellation known as the Southern Fish – Fomalhaut, "the fish's mouth" – might be interpreted in this sense, just as in fish symbolism every conceivable form of devouring *concupiscentia* is attributed to fishes, which are said to be "ambitious,

libidinous, voracious, avaricious, lascivious" – in short, an emblem of the vanity of the world and of earthly pleasures ("voluptas terrena").[7] They owe these bad qualities most of all to their relationship with the mother- and love-goddess Ishtar, Astarte, Atargatis, or Aphrodite. As the planet Venus, she has her "exaltatio" in the zodiacal sign of the fishes. Thus, in astrological tradition as well as in the history of symbols, the fishes have always had these opprobrious qualities attached to them,[8] while on the other hand laying claim to a special and higher significance. This claim is based – at least in astrology – on the fact that anyone born under Pisces may expect to become a fisherman or a sailor, and in that capacity to catch fishes or hold dominion over the sea – an echo of the primitive totemistic identity between the hunter and his prey. The Babylonian culture-hero Oannes was himself a fish, and the Christian Ichthys is a fisher of men par excellence. Symbologically, he is actually the hook or bait on God's fishing-rod with which the Leviathan – death or the devil – is caught.[9] In Jewish tradition the Leviathan is a sort of eucharistic food stored up for the faithful in Paradise. After death, they clothe themselves in fishrobes.[10] Christ is not only a fisher but the fish that is "eucharistically" eaten.[11] Augustine says in his *Confessions*: "But [the earth] eats the fish that was drawn from the deep, at the table which you have prepared for them that believe; for the fish was drawn from the deep in order to nourish the needy ones of the earth."[12] St. Augustine is referring to the meal of fishes eaten by the disciples at Emmaus (Luke 24:43). We come across the "healing fish" in the story of Tobit: the angel Raphael helps Tobit to catch the fish that is about to eat him, and shows him how to make a magic "smoke" against evil spirits from the heart and liver of the fish, and how he can heal his father's blindness with its gall (Tobit 6:1ff.).

175 St. Peter Damian (d. 1072) describes monks as fishes, because all pious men are little fishes leaping in the net of the Great Fisher.[13] In the Pectorios inscription (beginning of the fourth century), believers are called the "divine descendants of the heavenly fish."[14]

176 The fish of Manu is a saviour,[15] identified in legend with Vishnu, who had assumed the form of a small goldfish. He begs Manu to take him home, because he was afraid of being devoured by the water monsters.[16] He then grows mightily, fairytale fashion, and in the end rescues Manu from the great flood.[17] On the twelfth day of the first month of the Indian year a golden fish is placed in a bowl of water and invoked as follows: "As thou, O God, in the form of a fish, hast saved the Vedas that were in the underworld, so save me also, O Keshava!"[18] De Gubernatis and other investigators after him tried to derive the Christian fish from India.[19] Indian influence is not impossible, since relations with India existed even before Christ and various spiritual currents from the East made themselves felt in early Christianity, as we know from the reports of Hippolytus and Epiphanius. Nevertheless, there is no serious reason to derive the fish from India, for Western fish symbolism is so rich and at the same time so archaic that we may safely regard it as autochthonous.

177 Since the Fishes stand for mother and son, the mythological tragedy of the son's early death and resurrection is already implicit in them. Being the twelfth sign of the Zodiac, Pisces denotes the end of the astrological year and also a new beginning. This characteristic coincides with the claim of Christianity to be the beginning and end of all things, and with its eschatological expectation of the end of the world and the coming of God's kingdom.[20] *Thus the astrological characteristics of the fish contain essential components of the Christian myth; first, the cross; second, the moral conflict and its splitting into the figures of Christ and Antichrist; third, the motif of the son of a virgin; fourth, the classical mother-son tragedy; fifth, the danger at birth; and sixth, the saviour and bringer of healing*. It is therefore not beside the point to relate the designation of Christ as a fish to the new aeon then dawning. If this relationship existed even in antiquity, it must obviously have been a tacit assumption or one that was purposely kept secret; for, to my knowledge, there is no evidence in the old literature that the Christian fish symbolism was derived from the zodiac. Moreover, the astrological evidence up to the second century A.D. is by no means of such a kind that the Christ/Antichrist antithesis could be derived *causally* from the polarity of the Fishes, since this, as the material we have cited shows, was not stressed as in any way significant. Finally, as Doelger rightly emphasizes, the Ichthys was always thought of as only *one* fish, though here we must point out that in the astrological interpretation Christ is in fact only one of the fishes, the role of the other fish being allotted to the Antichrist. There are, in short, no grounds whatever for supposing that the zodion of the Fishes could have served as the Ichthys prototype.

178 Pagan fish symbolism plays in comparison a far greater role.[21] The most important is the Jewish material collected by Scheftelowitz. The Jewish "chalice of benediction"[22] was sometimes decorated with pictures of fishes, for fishes were the food of the blessed in Paradise. The chalice was placed in the dead man's grave as a funerary gift.[23] Fishes have a wide distribution as sepulchral symbols. The Christian fish occurs mainly in this connection. Devout Israelites who live "in the water of the doctrine" are likened to fishes. This analogy was self-evident around A.D. 100.[24] The fish also has a Messianic significance.[25] According to the Syrian Apocalypse of Baruch, Leviathan shall rise from the sea with the advent of the Messiah.[26] This is probably the "very great fish" of the Abercius inscription, corresponding to the "fish from the fountain" mentioned in a religious debate at the court of the Sassanids (5th century). The fountain refers to the Babylonian Hera, but in Christian language it means Mary, who in orthodox as well as in Gnostic circles (Acts of Thomas) was invoked as *πηγή*, "fountain." Thus we read in a hymn of Synesius (*c.* 350): *Παγά παγϖν, άρχϖν άρχα,ριζϖν ριζα, μονας ει μοναϑων, κτλ*. (Fountain of fountains, source of sources, root of roots, monad of monads art thou.)[27] The fountain of Hera was also said to contain the one fish (*μόνον ίχθυν*) that is caught by the "hook of divinity" and "feeds the whole world with its flesh."[28] In a Boeotian vase-painting the "lady of the beasts"[29] is shown with a fish between her legs, or in her body,[30] presumably indicating that the

fish is her son. Although, in the Sassanid debate, the legend of Mary was transferred to Hera, the "one fish" that is hooked does not correspond to the Christian symbol, for in Christian symbology the crucifix is the hook or bait with which God catches Leviathan,[31] who is either death or the devil ("that ancient serpent") but not the Messiah. In Jewish tradition, on the other hand, the *pharmakon athanasias* is the flesh of Leviathan, the "Messianic fish," as Scheftelowitz says. The Talmud Sanhedrin says that the Messiah "will not come until a fish is sought for an invalid and cannot be procured."[32] According to the Apocalypse of Baruch, Behemoth as well as Leviathan[33] is a eucharistic food. This is assiduously overlooked. As I have explained elsewhere,[34] Yahweh's two prehistoric monsters seem to represent a pair of opposites, the one being unquestionably a land animal, and the other aquatic.

179 Since olden times, not only among the Jews but all over the Near East, the birth of an outstanding human being has been identified with the rising of a star. Thus Balaam prophesies (Num. 24:17):

> I shall see him, but not now,
> I shall behold him, but not nigh;
> a star shall come forth out of Jacob. . . .

180 Always the hope of a Messiah is connected with the appearance of a star. According to the Zohar, the fish that swallowed Jonah died, but revived after three days and then spewed him out again. "Through the fish we shall find a medicament for the whole world."[35] This text is medieval but comes from a trustworthy source. The "very great[36] and pure fish from the fountain" mentioned in the Abercius inscription is, in the opinion of Scheftelowitz,[37] none other than Leviathan, which is not only the biggest fish but is held to be pure, as Scheftelowitz shows by citing the relevant passages from Talmudic literature. In this connection we might also mention the "one and only fish" (*εἶς μονος ιχθυς*) recorded in the "Happenings in Persia."[38]

NOTES

1 Namely *Piscis Austrinus*, the "Southern Fish," which merges with Pisces and whose principal star is Fomalhaut.
2 Matt. 12:39, 16:4; Luke 11:29f.
3 Cf. Frobenius, *Das Zeitalter des Sonnengottes*, and my *Symbols of Transformation*, pars. 308ff.
4 "Yahweh is salvation."
5 Koran, Sura 18. Cf. "Concerning Rebirth," pars. 244f., and Vollers, "Chidher," p. 241.
6 Jeremias, *The Old Testament in the Light of the Ancient East*, p. 76. This lamp has never been traced.
7 Picinellus, *Mundus symboticus* (1680–81), Lib. VI, cap. I.
8 Bouché-Leclercq, p. 147.
9 How closely the negative and the positive meanings are related can be seen from the fish-hook motif, attributed to St. Cyprian: "Like a fish which darts at a baited hook, and not only does not lay hold of the bait along with the hook, but is itself hauled up out of the sea; so he who had the power of death did indeed snatch away the body of Jesus

unto death, but did not observe that the hook of the Godhead was concealed therein, until he had devoured it: and thereupon remained fixed thereto."

Stephen of Canterbury (*Liber allegoricus in Habacuc*, unavailable to me) says: "It is the bait of longed-for enjoyment that is displayed in the hook, but the tenacious hidden hook is consumed along with the bait. So in fleshly concupiscence the devil displays the bait of pleasure, but the sting of sin lies hid therein." In this regard see Picinellus, Lib. VI, cap. 1.

10 Scheftelowitz, "Das Fisch-Symbol im Judentum und Christentum," p. 365.

11 Cf. Goodenough, *Jewish Symbols*, V, pp. 41ff.

12 Lib. XIII, cap. XXI. (Cf. trans, by F. J. Sheed, p. 275, modified.)

13 "The cloister of a monastery is indeed a fishpond of souls, and fish live therein" (Picinellus, *Mundus*).

An Alexandrian hymn from the 2nd cent, runs:

> "Fisher of men, whom Thou to life dost bring!
> From the evil sea of sin
> And from the billowy strife
> Gathering pure fishes in,
> Caught with sweet bait of life."

(Writings of Clement of Alexandria, trans, by W. Wilson, I, p. 344.) Cf. Doelger, 'ΙΧΘΤΣ, I, p. 4. Tertullian (*De baptismo*, cap. I) says: "But we little fishes, after the example of our 'ΙΧΘΤΣ Jesus Christ, are born in water, nor have we safety in any other way than by permanently abiding in (that) water." (Trans, by S. Thelwall, I, pp. 231–32.) The disciples of Gamaliel the Elder (beginning of 1st cent.) were named after various kinds of fishes. (*Abot de Rabbi Nathan*, cap. 40 [cf. trans, by J. Goldin, p. 166], cited in Scheftelowitz, p. 5.)

14 Pohl, *Das Ichthysmonument von Autun*, and Doelger, I, pp. 12ff.

15 "I will save thee." Shatapatha Brahmana (trans. by J. Eggeling, I [i.e., XII], p. 216).

16 De Gubematis, *Zoological Mythology*, II, pp. 334f.

17 Shatapatha Brahmana (Eggeling trans., pp. 216ff.).

18 Doelger, I, p. 23. Keshava means "having much or fine hair," a cognomen of Vishnu.

19 Ibid., pp. 21ff.

20 Origen (*De oratione*, cap. 27): ". . . as the last month is the end of the year, after which the beginning of another month ensues, so it may be that, since several ages complete as it were a year of ages, the present age is 'the end," after which certain 'ages to come' will ensue, of which the age to come is the beginning, and in those coming ages God will 'shew the riches of his grace in kindness' [Eph. 2:7]" (Oulton/Chadwick trans., p. 304).

21 Especially noteworthy is the cult of the dove and the fish in the Syrian area. There too the fish was eaten as "Eucharistic" food. (Cumont, *Les Religions orientales dans le paganisme romain*, pp. 108–9, 255–57) The chief deity of the Philistines was called Dagon, derived from *dag*, "fish.'

22 *τὸ ποτήριον της ευλοΥιας*: *calix benedictionis* (I Cor. 10:16, DV).

23 Scheftelowitz, p. 375.

24 Ibid., p. 3.

25 Cf. Goodenough, V, pp. 35ff.

26 At the same time "Behemoth shall be revealed from his place . . . and then they shall be food for all that are left." (Charles, *Apocrypha and Pseudepigrapha*, II, p. 497.) The idea of Leviathan rising from the sea also links up with the vision in II Esdras 13 : 25, of the "man coming up from the midst of the sea". Cf. Charles, II, p. 579, and Wischnitzer-Bernstein, *Symbole und Gestalten der jüdischen Kunst*, pp. 122f. and 134f.

27 Wirth, *Aus orientalischen Chroniken*, p. 199.

28 Ibid., pp. 161, 19f.

29 [Cf. Neumann, *The Great Mother*, ch. 14 and pl. 134. – EDITORS.]
30 Eisler, *Orpheus – The Fisher*, Pl. LXIV.
31 See *Psychology and Alchemy*, fig. 28.
32 Scheftelowitz, p. 9; from the Talmud *Nezikin* VI, Sanhedrin II (*BT*, p. 662). Cf. the εσθιε πιναων in the Pectorios inscription, supra, p. 89n.
33 A passage in Moses Maimonides (*Guide for the Perplexed*, trans, by M. Friedlander, p. 303) has bearing on the interpretation of Leviathan. Kirclimaier (*Disputationes Zoologicae*, 1736, p. 73) cites it as follows: "Speaking of these same things Rabbi Moses Maimon says that Leviathan possesses a [universal] combination (*complexum generalem*) of bodily peculiarities found separate in different animals." Although this rationalistic author dismisses the idea as "nugatory," it nevertheless seems to me to hint at an archetype ("complexum generalem") of the "spirit of gravity."
34 *Psychological Types*, pars. 456ff.
35 Scheftelowitz, p. 10. Cf. Matt. 12 : 39 and 16 : 4, where Christ takes the sign of the prophet Jonah as a sign of the Messianic age and a prefiguration of his own fate. Cf. also Goodenough, *Jewish Symbols*, V, pp. 47ff.
36 *Παμμεγεθης*.
37 Ibid., pp. 7f.
38 *Τα εν Περσιδι πραχθεντα* (Wirth, p. 151).

Part IV

Explanations of astrology

INTRODUCTION

Jung entertained multiple explanations of astrology. In the selections in Part IV, we witness the shifts in his position as they unfold in response to material he read and to his own reflections and research. To aid comprehension, his various hypotheses regarding astrology are placed into separate chapters (11 to 17). The commentary that follows offers some analysis of each hypothesis, drawing out the essential line of argument of the more complex theories. Jung pursues up to seven possible explanations, some overlapping and some contradictory.

1. Astrology can be understood in terms of the classical and medieval principles of the "sympathy of all things" and a microcosm-macrocosm correspondence. These ideas, considered in Chapter 11, are extracted primarily from "Synchronicity: An Acausal Connecting Principle," which surveys a range of related ideas that support an astrological conception of the world, including ancient Greek philosophical speculation (Hippocrates, Philo, Theophrastus), Neoplatonism (Plotinus), Renaissance philosophy (Pico della Mirandola), alchemy and medieval natural philosophy (Zosimos, Paracelsus, Agrippa, Aegidius de Vadis), and Kepler's view of "astrological character."

It is an axiom of esoteric thought that the human being is a miniature version or reflection of the entire cosmos. The celestial heavens are deemed to exist within us all ("heaven . . . is infused into man the microcosm").[1] Similarly, classical and medieval thought posits bonds of sympathy linking disparate parts of the universe in a grand system of *correspondentia* connecting the human, worldly, and celestial – an idea captured by the statement "as above, so below." This correspondence ultimately rests in the unity of God or the *anima mundi* or *spiritus mundi* (the world soul and world spirit, respectively).

Jung presents these perspectives as essential background to his theory of synchronicity and to his research into astrology. "Synchronicity," he notes, "is a modern differentiation of the obsolete concept of correspondence, sympathy, and harmony."[2] Especially significant for Jung was the classical and medieval belief, also present in Chinese thought, that there are connections between discrete events and experiences that are not causal, in that there is no apparent causal chain linking them. Rather, such connections or correspondences are deemed by Jung to be acausal, existing in parallel with each other and connected solely by meaning. Regarding astrology, for example, if one were to express anger and assertive force at a time when the planet Mars (associated with the Greco-Roman god of war) is aligned with the sun in one's astrological chart, it would, on this view, not be due to any causal influence of the planet Mars, but on the "meaningful coincidence" of that planetary alignment with a psychological state or a constellation of archetypes in one's psyche.

2. Astrology is a projection of the collective unconscious into the heavens. The practice of astrology might be understood as a symbolic system or perspective in which the planets represent the "gods," that is, the archetypes of the collective unconscious. This second hypothesis, covered in Chapter 12, is perhaps Jung's most consistent and oft-repeated position. Astrology, Jung claims, is a "complete projected theory of human character."[3] To a large extent, as we have already seen in Part III, Jung is led to the conclusion that astrology is projected psychology by the consideration of the phenomenon of the precession of the equinoxes. Because the signs of the zodiac are no longer aligned with the constellations after which they were originally named, he reasons, there is no physical basis to the alleged influence of the signs on human life. The same line of argument does not necessarily apply to the planets, of course, for these obviously possess substantive physical existence, even though they exert no demonstrable causal influence on human life. Jung's concern here is primarily understanding the alleged influence of zodiacal signs and constellations (which he often refers to as the "stars"), but it is conceivable that the zodiacal signs might be explicable as a form of projected psychology while the astrology of the planets might be explicable in other terms.

Generalizing from his reflection on the signs, Jung concludes that the source of astrological meanings is not from the cosmos but from archetypes in the unconscious psyche, from the microcosm of the individual human being. That is, although astrologers might believe that the planets and signs are the determining factors shaping the human personality, what are taken to be celestial causes are really psychological ones. Just as alchemy is understood by Jung as a projection into the *prima materia* in the alchemical vessel of the psychological transformation process (individuation) occurring within the alchemist's psyche, so astrology is seen as a projection of the qualities and traits of the human personality into the heavens. In both cases, the implication is that the alchemist and astrologer were working under something of a delusion.

Over the centuries, in Jung's view, the increasing differentiation of the ego, the subject of experience, from the world, as object, made it possible to become more conscious of our psychological projections as we progressively left behind the primal condition of *participation mystique*, in which there is no clear distinction between the inner world of thoughts and emotions and external happenings in the environment. To the epistemologically naïve mind, Jung believes, inner and outer blur, or are not adequately distinguished, and psychological reality is mistakenly construed as cosmology or metaphysical reality – a critique Jung levels at theosophy, for instance. Modern science and psychology, Jung maintains, now enable us to recognize these projections for what they are and to withdraw them.

Jung does not address how his view of astrology as projection meshes with his explanations in terms of synchronicity and acausal correspondences. Nor does he attempt to reconcile projection with his numerous assertions that appear to contradict the Cartesian separation of the inner world of the human subject from the outer world – a premise on which the theory of astrology as projection depends. For example, Jung describes the unconscious as a "field of experience of unlimited extent"[4] and likens it to the "atmosphere in which we live."[5] As we see in Chapter 17, he goes so far as to posit the existence of a *psyche tou kosmou*, a cosmic psyche, and to connect the collective unconscious to the Platonic idea of an *anima mundi*, a world soul.[6] If such speculations are accurate, it might be that the unconscious actually pervades the environment all around us and is not an encapsulated realm located exclusively within the individual, as we tend to assume. This implies, in turn, that archetypal meaning might be inherent to the universe itself, and not restricted to a separate, isolated psyche, projecting its meanings into the external world and into the heavens. Jung's reflections on the psychoid nature of the archetypes, discussed under points 6 and 7, also support this supposition.

3. Astrology is a mantic method, a means of divination, in which astrological interpretations and predictions are forms of synchronicity manifesting as meaningful "lucky hits."[7] In considering Jung's view of astrology as divination, Chapter 13 sets forth the rationale behind his "astrological experiment" and presents the conclusions he drew from it, despite the experiment's fatal errors in calculation – indeed, because of these errors.

Jung's experiment proposed to investigate whether there are statistically significant correlations between marriage and certain planetary configurations formed between the astrological birth charts of husband and wife in married pairs, compared to unmarried pairs. As noted in the editorial comments within the chapter, although the results of Jung's astrology experiment ultimately concluded that correlations between the astrological factors and marriages were *not* statistically significant, initial errors were made in calculation such that the data appeared at first to lend support to astrology. Jung took this susceptibility to error, distorting the results in favor of corroborating astrology, as itself significant, viewing it as a synchronistic occurrence through which the unconscious conspired to influence the outcome in line with the researcher's "lively interest" and personal investment in astrology.[8] In Jung's view, synchronistic factors had produced something like an experimenter bias.

Addressing this matter in *Jung and Astrology*, Maggie Hyde makes a helpful distinction between two different kinds of synchronicity discussed in Jung's writing, which she terms "Synchronicity I" and "Synchronicity II." She describes the former as "the (meaningful) interdependence of events among themselves,"[9] emphasizing something like an "objective pattern" in the nature of things, with synchronistic acausal correlations between the objective fact of the planetary positions and meanings or events observed in human experience.[10] The latter, Synchronicity II, emphasizes the "subjective participation of the observing psyche," with synchronicity recognized as a significant factor in the subjective act of interpreting astrological meanings, much in the manner that Jung attributed the mathematical errors in calculation in his astrology experiment to synchronicity, with the expectations and emotional state of the researcher unconsciously entangled with the calculation of the results.[11] Hyde emphasizes that the astrologer cannot escape his or her subjectivity when reading the chart and seeking to uncover meaning in the astrological configurations. What emerges as significant during any particular reading is guided by a synchronistic collusion between astrologer, client, and the astrological symbols.

Impressed by what had happened during his experiment, Jung was led to conclude that in the practice of the astrology "a secret, mutual connivance existed between the material and the psychic state of the astrologer."[12] Astrology works, in this view, because of the astrologer's and the client's psychological investment and participation in the horoscope reading, with the emotionally charged context of the reading providing the necessary conditions for synchronicity to occur. Thus, even if the astrologer uses the wrong birth data, and therefore an incorrect astrological chart, the horoscope reading can still be valid since astrology, the reasoning goes, depends not on accessing an objective order in the universe, but on the astrologer using chart symbols, unconsciously guided by synchronicity, as a way to divine the meaning of the moment. Synchronicity II therefore goes hand in hand with the view of astrology as divination. In this respect, casting a horoscope is similar to doing a reading with Tarot cards in which the unconscious seemingly directs the selection of cards in answer to a question posed by the querent. Astrology, in the divinatory view, accesses the inner world of psychological meanings, functioning as a kind of symbolic mirror of the psyche, irrespective of whether there is an objective order to which astrological factors refer.[13] Because all things can be read symbolically, it does not necessarily matter which particular astrological variables are used, for, as Cornelius, Hyde, and Webster note, "every factor conceivable by an astrologer is capable of generating valid symbolism"[14]

Jung later refers to this (Synchronicity II) as "our narrower conception of synchronicity" that "needs expanding" since it is restricted to specific exceptional incidents of the revelation of subjective meaning during astrology readings rather than constituting a general principle of consistent correspondence between human experience and an objective order in the nature of things.[15] He comes to the conclusion that "synchronicity in the narrow sense is only a particular instance of general acausal orderedness" – a topic addressed in Chapter 17 and summarized under point 7.[16]

4. There is a physical mechanism to explain astrology in the form of photon radiation emitted by the sun impacting the Earth's magnetic field. Astrology, therefore, works via efficient and material causation: there is a physical cause producing an effect in human beings. To date, there is no satisfactory causal explanation in terms of the four known forces – the strong and weak nuclear forces, electromagnetism, and gravity – to account for how planets and signs could physically influence human beings.[17] Perhaps for this reason, a survey of literature in the field suggests most astrologers today eschew explanations of astrology in causal terms, with many preferring to construe astrology as symbolic or synchronistic.[18] As we read in the selections included in Chapter 2, Jung himself rejected explanations of astrology based on the idea of physical "vibration," a view he attributed to theosophy.

However, even late into his life Jung was reluctant to abandon causal explanations entirely, pivoting back to this line of inquiry as he worked on the astrology chapter in the synchronicity monograph in the 1950s. Having argued in other places that astrology should be viewed as synchronistic, the selections in Chapter 14 show Jung – influenced by the reading of German physicist Max Knoll's theory connecting solar proton radiation and planetary constellations – giving serious consideration to the possibility of there being a physical, causal explanation of astrology. Indeed, he goes as far as to explicitly reject the idea that astrology is a mantic method and also argues that both synchronistic and causal explanations might be simultaneously valid. The causal influence, he conjectures, might be based on the influence of the seasons, manifest through the date of one's birth – an influence transmitted via photon radiation from the sun impacting the Earth's magnetic field. With this kind of explanation, he fancies that there is "some prospect today of a causal explanation in conformity with natural law,"[19] and he is therefore "inclined to rank astrology alongside the natural sciences."[20]

5. Astrology depends upon the qualitative significance of time. Time is not an empty frame of reference, as we commonly assume, for each unique moment possesses a certain quality, which astrological horoscopes symbolize. "Whatever is born or done at this particular moment of time," Jung declared, "has the quality of this moment of time."[21] He devotes considerable energy to articulating this view, especially in his seminars and writing from the late 1920s and 1930s, which comprise many of the extracts included in Chapter 15. Jung argues that the astrological study of the movements of the planets in the heavens is a method of understanding the changing qualities of moments in time. He employs something like the following line of argument:

- a Time is derived from the observation of the flux of things, of change in the universe.
- b Change is generated by the movement of energy, or the transformation of energy from one form to another.
- c Therefore, time is an aspect of energy.
- d Astrology is an indication of the condition of universal energy at particular moments in time, functioning like a cosmic clock or watch, with the positions of the planets like the hands of a clock indicating the state of things at a particular moment.
- e Fate is identical with time. To observe the movements of the planets as an indication of passing time is thus to observe fate as it fulfills itself.

By the 1950s, however, Jung felt impelled to qualify his position, noting in a letter to André Barbault that he chose to replace the notion of the qualitative significance of time with the concept of synchronicity, which he develops more fully in the material presented in Chapter 17.[22]

6. Astrology rests upon transcendental numerical archetypes, as in the Pythagorean and Platonic understanding of number as an a priori ordering principle. Astrology has its foundation in the qualitative significance of number, "in conjunction," Jung notes, "with the numinous assemblage of gods which the horoscope represents."[23] For Jung, as in astrology, numbers are held not only to be instruments for counting and calculation (the quantitative aspect of number), but they are also thought to possess universal symbolic meaning. The number one, for example, implies unity and beginning; two is associated with duality and the tension of opposites; and three suggests harmony arising from the reconciliation of opposites. This kind of numerical symbolic logic runs throughout astrology. The twelve signs of the zodiac are derived from the qualities of number, generated by the subdivision of the 360 degrees of the zodiac. Similarly, the meanings of specific aspects (the geometric relationships between the planets) are also based on the meanings of the small whole numbers from which they are derived – the conjunction pertains to the number one, the opposition to two, the trine to three, the square to four, and so forth.

Although he was initially concerned with the role of number as a psychological ordering factor in the unconscious (he called number the "archetype of order"[24]), his later reflections on the psychoid dimension of the archetype led him, as we read in his letters, towards a Pythagorean view of number as an ordering principle intrinsic to all of reality, both the inner world of the psyche and the external world, although he did not make this position explicit in his formal writing. Jung introduced the term *psychoid* in the 1950s to designate the tendency of the archetype, at its deepest level, to pass over from instinct into an "organic substrate"[25] and to "fall in with fundamental forms of the physical process in general."[26] "Archetypes," he proposes, "are not found exclusively in the psychic sphere, but can occur just as much in circumstances that are not psychic."[27]

In the selections in Chapter 16, then, Jung poses the question as to the relationship between number and "something as archetypal as astrology."[28] The answer, in terms of Jung's own statements, might be formulated as something like the following argument:

a Number is an archetypal ordering principle in the unconscious psyche ("the unconscious uses number as an ordering factor"); numbers "have an archetypal foundation."[29]
b At its deeper levels, archetypes in the unconscious have a psychoid dimension, such that they also pertain to physical processes in the material world. Presumably, then, this implies that numbers, as archetypes, also have a psychoid dimension.
c This supposition accords with Jung's assertion that "number, like Meaning, inheres in the nature of all things,"[30] which draws Jung close to a Pythagorean position, as he himself recognizes: "The fact is that the numbers pre-existing

in nature are presumably the most fundamental archetypes, being the very matrix of all others. Here Pythagoras was certainly on the right track . . ."[31]

d It is possible, therefore (and this seems to be the implication of Jung's speculations on number), that astrology is based on a transcendental numerical order, manifest both in the psyche and in the universe at large.

As we will consider here, Jung's reflections on number should be viewed alongside his theory of synchronicity.

7. Astrology is a form of synchronicity, reflecting an acausal parallelism or correspondence between planetary positions and experiences in human life, partly explicable in terms of the psychoid nature of archetypes. Focusing on synchronicity in general rather than astrology specifically, the hypothesis presented in Chapter 17 is not explicitly applied by Jung to understand astrology, yet it constitutes what is, arguably, his most developed and sophisticated explanation of it. Arising out of and subsuming Jung's view of astrology as archetypal, synchronistic, and rooted in numerical forms is the idea that astrology might be explained in terms of a "general acausal orderedness."[32] Jung understands this as an "underlying principle"[33] of arrangement, an a priori archetypal order in the nature of things, which stands behind specific instances of synchronicity (this is Synchronicity I, in Hyde's scheme).

As an example of "synchronicity on a grand scale,"[34] astrology might conceivably be understood as the expression of this acausal orderedness, which Jung considers to be an "all-pervading factor or principle in the universe."[35] This position emerges from Jung's speculations on the intersection of depth psychology and physics and from his reflections on the mind-matter relationship. Contemplating these questions also led him to posit the existence of a "transcendental psychophysical background"[36] to the empirical world and drew him close to the medieval notion of the *unus mundus*, "where there is no incommensurability between so-called matter and so-called psyche."[37] The psyche and the cosmos are considered to be two related aspects of the unitary reality that is neither psychological nor material.[38] Thus Jung: "The common background of microphysics and depth psychology is as much physical as psychic and therefore neither, but rather a third thing, a neutral nature which can a most be grasped in hints since its essence is transcendental."[39]

Proceeding further, Jung ventures to suggest that the archetypal background can be viewed as a "potential world"[40] and as a "universal factor existing from all eternity," which manifests itself in acts of "continuous creation" in time.[41] It stretches the limits of our comprehension to fully grasp Jung's intended meaning here, but he seems to be proposing that what is eternally present, in the transcendental background of reality, appears to us as a succession – as an ordered unfolding of the ground in a series of temporal moments, supporting specific synchronistic and acausal correlations between the psyche and cosmos, of which astrology is one form. Recalling here Jung's explanation of astrology in terms of the quality of time, we could say that astrology, as an indication of the changing qualities of moments in time, might be used to map the unfolding of eternal archetypal reality of the "potential world" into a temporal sequence.

To summarize briefly, then, this explanation of astrology depends upon the idea that there is a psychoid archetypal order, at a deeper dimension of reality, functioning as a kind of organizing principle of both the psyche and the cosmos – hence Jung's enthusiasm, in a letter of 1957, for the idea of a "transcendental 'arranger'" behind acausal synchronistic correlations.[42] If there is indeed such an organizing principle underlying the psyche and the cosmos, it is conceivable that the physical configurations formed by the planets in the solar system might be organized according to the same transcendent numerical archetypes that also order and inform the collective unconscious – thereby helping to account for the relationship posited in some forms of astrology between planetary configurations and archetypes. Such a view contradicts the idea that astrology might be wholly explained as an unconscious projection of the psyche into the heavens, for the observed correspondences between planetary configurations and activated archetypal themes in human experience could conceivably be better explained as a special kind of constant synchronicity based on the underlying order described earlier.[43]

Although speculative, this hypothesis perhaps constitutes the most coherent and comprehensive position emerging from Jung's engagement with synchronicity and astrology, one that is broadly in accord with certain perspectives in the new-paradigm sciences.[44] This hypothesis also has much in common with the classical and medieval explanations of astrology (point 1), covered in Chapter 11.

Jung does not further develop these reflections in relation to astrology. The material in Chapter 17 and in Chapter 16, on numerical archetypes, represents the terminus of his exploratory thinking on synchronicity and, by inference, astrology. Thus, he concedes, in the same letter of 1957:

> It seems to me that for the time being I have exhausted my psychological ammunition. I have got stuck, one the one hand, in the acausality (or "synchronicity") of certain phenomena of unconscious provenance and, on the other hand, in the qualitative statements of numbers, for here I set foot on territories where I cannot advance without the help and understanding of other disciplines.[45]

In concluding this overview of Part IV, it should be stressed that in most cases the various explanations summarized here are not mutually exclusive. As the basis of astrology, there could, for example, be an objective order of archetypal meaning inherent in the underlying structure of reality and, at the same time, projections of the unconscious into observed patterns in the heavens. Indeed, given the plethora of astrological techniques and variables employed today, with astrologers finding significance in their own preferred approaches, it is almost certain that projection shapes the interpretation of the celestial patterns symbolized in astrology. Equally, there are surely synchronistic elements at play in the subjective act of the interpretation of astrological charts, evident in those instances in which valid meaning is conveyed even when an astrologer inadvertently works with the wrong chart data.

Whatever explanation of astrology one finds most compelling, what is most striking is just how many elements of Jung's theories and understanding of the psyche are pertinent to an astrological view of the world. Taking seriously the claims of astrology, alongside the evidence of synchronicity, led Jung to contemplate the deepest mysteries and fundamental questions of existence, such as the nature of space and time, the relationship between mind and matter, and the possibility of meaning existing outside of human consciousness. That he was not able to provide conclusive explanations of astrology is, in the face of these great mysteries, entirely to be expected, although his speculations present rich possibilities for further theoretical elaboration.

Keiron Le Grice

NOTES

1 Jung, "Synchronicity: An Acausal Connecting Principle," in *Structure and Dynamics of the Psyche* (*CW* 8), p. 490, par. 926.
2 Jung, "On Synchronicity," in *Structure and Dynamics of the Psyche* (*CW* 8), p. 531, par. 995.
3 Jung, "Religious Ideas in Alchemy" (1937), in *Psychology and Alchemy* (*CW* 12), p. 245, par. 346.
4 Jung, "Relations between the Ego and the Unconscious" (1928), in *Two Essays on Analytical Psychology* (*CW* 7), p. 184, par. 292.
5 Jung to Fritz Künkel, 10 July 1946, in *Letters I*, p. 433.
6 Jung to Stephen Abrams, 21 October 1957, in *Letters II*, p. 399.
7 Jung to Hans Bender, 10 April 1958, in *Letters II*, p. 428.
8 Jung, "Synchronicity: An Acausal Connecting Principle" (1952), in *Structure and Dynamics of the Psyche* (*CW* 8), p. 478, par. 905.
9 Hyde, *Jung and Astrology*, p. 128.
10 Ibid., p. 134.
11 Ibid., pp. 128 and 131. The divinatory approach to astrology is also advanced in Geoffrey Cornelius, *The Moment of Astrology*.
12 Jung, "Synchronicity: An Acausal Connecting Principle" (1952), in *Structure and Dynamics of the Psyche* (*CW* 8), 478, par. 905.
13 As Cornelius, Hyde, and Webster put it: "Astrology-as-divination is a metaphoric mirror. Horoscope factors are treated 'as if' they are metaphors revealing salient features of the subject of the horoscope" (*Astrology for Beginners*, p. 165).
14 Cornelius, Hyde, and Webster, *Astrology for Beginners*, p. 172.
15 Jung, "Synchronicity: An Acausal Connecting Principle" (1952), in *Structure and Dynamics of the Psyche* (*CW* 8), p. 516, par. 965.
16 Jung, "Synchronicity: An Acausal Connecting Principle" (1952), in *Structure and Dynamics of the Psyche* (*CW* 8), p. 516, par. 965.
17 The term *causal*, as used by Jung, implies physical and efficient causation, which are two of the four types of causation identified by Aristotle. Efficient causation is what we today think of as cause and effect, the billiard-ball model in which A causes B causing C, and so on. Physical causation is the matter of which something is comprised. Although he flirts with explanations in terms of cause and effect, Jung far more often describes astrology as synchronistic and acausal, a form of connection between discrete phenomena in which there is no direct influence or causal chain between them. The Aristotelian categories of formal and final causation, pertaining, respectively, to the organizing pattern and the end or goal of a process or organism, have clearer associations with synchronicity and the functioning of archetypes in human experience. See, for example, Jung's reflections on teleology and finality in Jung, "Synchronicity: An Acausal Connecting Principle" (1952), in *Structure and Dynamics of the Psyche* (*CW* 8), p. 493, par. 931, and his view of the archetype as an organizing form.

18 For one notable advocate of causal explanations of astrology, see Seymour, *Astrology: The Evidence of Science*.
19 Jung, "Synchronicity: An Acausal Connecting Principle" (1952), in *Structure and Dynamics of the Psyche* (*CW* 8), p. 528, par. 988.
20 Jung to Hans Bender, 10 April 1958, in *Letters II*, p. 429.
21 Jung, "Richard Wilhelm: In Memoriam" (1930), in *Spirit in Man, Art, and Literature* (*CW* 15), pp. 56–57, par. 82.
22 See Jung to André Barbault, 26 May 1954, in *Letters II*, pp. 175–177.
23 Jung, "An Astrological Experiment" (1958), in *Symbolic Life* (*CW* 18), pp. 497–498, par. 1183.
24 Jung, "Synchronicity: An Acausal Connecting Principle" (1952), in *Structure and Dynamics of the Psyche* (*CW* 8), p. 456, par. 870.
25 Jung, "On the Nature of the Psyche," in *Structure and Dynamics of the Psyche* (*CW* 8), p. 177, par. 368.
26 Jung to H. Rossteutscher, 3 May 1958, in *Letters II*, p. 437.
27 Jung, "Synchronicity: An Acausal Connecting Principle" (1952), in *Structure and Dynamics of the Psyche* (*CW* 8), p. 515, par. 964.
28 Jung, "An Astrological Experiment" (1958), in *Symbolic Life* (*CW* 18), pp. 497–498, par. 1183.
29 Jung, "Synchronicity: An Acausal Connecting Principle" (1952), in *Structure and Dynamics of the Psyche* (*CW* 8), pp. 456–457, par. 870.
30 Jung to Robert Dietrich, 27 May 1956, in *Letters II*, p. 302.
31 Jung to Patrick Evans, 1 September 1956, in *Letters II*, p. 327.
32 Jung, "Synchronicity: An Acausal Connecting Principle" (1952), in *Structure and Dynamics of the Psyche* (*CW* 8), p. 516, par. 965.
33 Jung, "Synchronicity: An Acausal Connecting Principle" (1952), in *Structure and Dynamics of the Psyche* (*CW* 8), pp. 500–501, par. 938.
34 Jung, "Richard Wilhelm: In Memoriam" (1930), in *Spirit in Man, Art, and Literature* (*CW* 15), p. 56, par. 81.
35 Jung to Stephen Abrams, 21 October 1957, in *Letters II*, p. 400.
36 Jung, *Mysterium Coniunctionis* (*CW* 14), p. 538, par. 769.
37 Jung to Stephen Abrams, 21 October 1957, in *Letters II*, p. 400.
38 Jung here advocates a form of neutral or dual-aspect monism with regards to the mind-matter relationship. For a discussion on neutral monism, see Leopold Stubenberg, "Neutral Monism," *The Stanford Encyclopedia of Philosophy* (Winter 2016 Edition). For a discussion on dual-aspect monism, see Harald Atmanspacher, "Quantum Approaches to Consciousness," *The Stanford Encyclopedia of Philosophy* (Summer 2015 Edition).
39 Jung, *Mysterium Coniunctionis* (*CW* 14), p. 538, par. 768.
40 Ibid., par. 769.
41 Jung, "Synchronicity: An Acausal Connecting Principle" (1952), in *Structure and Dynamics of the Psyche* (*CW* 8), p. 519, par. 968.
42 Jung to Werner Nowacki, 22 March 1957, in *Letters II*, p. 352.
43 A number of the ideas discussed in this chapter are taken up by Jung's foremost collaborator, Marie-Louise von Franz, in *Psyche and Matter*. See especially, "The Synchronicity Principle of C. G. Jung," pp. 203–228.
44 For a synthesis of Jungian psychology and the new-paradigm sciences, in support of an astrological worldview, see Le Grice, *Archetypal Cosmos*.
45 Jung to Werner Nowacki, 22 March 1957, in *Letters II*, p. 352.

BIBLIOGRAPHY

Atmanspacher, Harald, "Quantum Approaches to Consciousness." In *The Stanford Encyclopedia of Philosophy*. Summer 2015 Edition. Edited by Edward N. Zalta. URL = <http://plato.stanford.edu/archives/sum2015/entries/qt-consciousness/> (accessed November 25, 2016).

Cornelius, Geoffrey. *The Moment of Astrology: Origins in Divination*. London: Arkana, 1994.

Cornelius, Geoffrey, Maggie Hyde, and Chris Webster. *Astrology for Beginners*. London: Icon Books, 1995.

Hyde, Maggie. *Jung and Astrology*. London: The Aquarian Press, 1992.

Jung, Carl Gustav. "An Astrological Experiment." 1958. In *The Symbolic Life*, 494–501. Vol. 18 of *The Collected Works of C. G. Jung*. Translated by R.F.C. Hull. London: Routledge & Kegan Paul, 1977.

———. *C. G. Jung Letters I: 1906–1950*. Edited by Gerald Adler and Aniela Jaffé. Translated by R.F.C. Hull. London: Routledge & Kegan Paul, 1973.

———. *C. G. Jung Letters II: 1951–1961*. Edited by Gerald Adler and Aniela Jaffé. Translated by R.F.C. Hull. London: Routledge & Kegan Paul, 1973.

———. *Dream Analysis: Notes on the Seminar Given in 1928–1930*. Bollingen Series XCIX. Edited by William McGuire. Princeton, NJ: Princeton University Press, 1984.

———. *Mysterium Coniunctionis*. 2nd Edition. 1955–1956. Vol. 14 of *The Collected Works of C. G. Jung*. Translated by R.F.C. Hull. Princeton, NJ: Princeton University Press, 1989.

———. "On the Nature of the Psyche." 1947/1954. In *The Structure and Dynamics of the Psyche*, 159–234. Vol. 8 of *The Collected Works of C. G. Jung*. Translated by R.F.C. Hull. London: Routledge & Kegan Paul, 1960.

———. "The Relations between the Ego and the Unconscious." 1928. In *Two Essays on Analytical Psychology*, 121–241. Second Edition. Vol. 7 of *The Collected Works of C. G. Jung*. Translated by R.F.C. Hull. London: Routledge & Kegan Paul, 1966.

———. "Religious Ideas in Alchemy." 1937. In *Psychology and Alchemy*, 225–472. 2nd Edition. Vol. 12 of *The Collected Works of C. G. Jung*. Translated by R.F.C. Hull. Princeton, NJ: Princeton University Press, 1968.

———. "Richard Wilhelm: In Memoriam." 1930. In *The Spirit in Man, Art, and Literature*, 53–62. Vol. 15 of *The Collected Works of C. G. Jung*. Translated by R.F.C. Hull. Reprint, Princeton, NJ: Princeton University Press, 1966/1971.

———. "On Synchronicity." 1951. In *The Structure and Dynamics of the Psyche*, 520–531. Vol. 8 of *The Collected Works of C. G. Jung*. Translated by R.F.C. Hull. London: Routledge & Kegan Paul, 1960.

———. "Synchronicity: An Acausal Connecting Principle." 1952. In *The Structure and Dynamics of the Psyche*, 417–552. Vol. 8 of *The Collected Works of C. G. Jung*. Translated by R.F.C. Hull. London: Routledge & Kegan Paul, 1960.

Le Grice, Keiron. *The Archetypal Cosmos: Rediscovering the Gods in Myth, Science and Astrology*. Edinburgh, UK: Floris Books, 2010.

Seymour, Percy. *Astrology: The Evidence of Science*. Revised Edition. London: Arkana, 1990.

Stubenberg, Leopold. "Neutral Monism." In *The Stanford Encyclopedia of Philosophy*. Winter 2016 Edition. Edited by Edward N. Zalta. Forthcoming URL = http://plato.stanford.edu/archives/win2016/entries/neutral-monism/ (accessed 25 November, 2016).

von Franz, Marie-Louise. *Psyche and Matter*. 1988. Reprint, Boston, MA: Shambhala Publications, 1992.

11 As above, so below

The microcosm-macrocosm correspondence

From: "Synchronicity: An Acausal Connecting Principle" (1952) (*CW* 8), pars. 924–936

924 With us details are important for their own sakes; for the Oriental mind they always complete a total picture. In this totality, as in primitive or in our own medieval, pre-scientific psychology (still very much alive!), are included things which seem to be connected with one another only "by chance," by a coincidence whose meaningfulness appears altogether arbitrary. This is where the theory of *correspondentia*[1] comes in, which was propounded by the natural philosophers of the Middle Ages, and particularly the classical idea of the *sympathy of all things*.[2] Hippocrates says:

> There is one common flow, one common breathing, all things are in sympathy. The whole organism and each one of its parts are working in conjunction for the same purpose . . . the great principle extends to the extremest part, and from the extremest part it returns to the great principle, to the one nature, being and not-being.[3]

The universal principle is found even in the smallest particle, which therefore corresponds to the whole.

925 In this connection there is an interesting idea in Philo (25 B.C.–A.D. 42):

> God, being minded to unite in intimate and loving fellowship the beginning and end of created things, made heaven the beginning and man the end, the one the most perfect of imperishable objects of sense, the other the noblest of things earthborn and perishable, being, in very truth, a miniature heaven. He bears about within himself, like holy images, endowments of nature that correspond to the constellations. . . . For since the corruptible and the incorruptible are by nature contrary the one to the other, God assigned the fairest of each sort to the beginning and the end, heaven (as I have said) to the beginning, and man to the end.[4]

926 Here the great principle[5] or beginning, heaven, is infused into man the microcosm, who reflects the star-like natures and thus, as the smallest part and end of the work of Creation, contains the whole.

927 According to Theophrastus (371–288 B.C.) the suprasensuous and the sensuous are joined by a bond of community. This bond cannot be mathematics, so must presumably be God.[6] Similarly in Plotinus the individual souls born of the one World Soul are related to one another by sympathy or antipathy, regardless of distance.[7] Similar views are to be found in Pico della Mirandola:

> Firstly there is the unity in things whereby each thing is at one with itself, consists of itself, and coheres with itself. Secondly there is the unity whereby one creature is united with the others and all parts of the world constitute one world. The third and most important (unity) is that whereby the whole universe is one with its Creator, as an army with its commander.[8]

By this threefold unity Pico means a simple unity which, like the Trinity, has three aspects: "a unity distinguished by a threefold character, yet in such a way as not to depart from the simplicity of unity."[9] For him the world is *one* being, a visible God, in which everything is naturally arranged from the very beginning like the parts of a living organism. The world appears as the *corpus mysticum* of God, just as the Church is the *corpus mysticum* of Christ, or as a well-disciplined army can be called a sword in the hand of the commander. The view that all things are arranged according to God's will is one that leaves little room for causality. Just as in a living body the different parts work in harmony and are meaningfully adjusted to one another, so events in the world stand in a meaningful relationship which cannot be derived from any immanent causality. The reason for this is that in either case the behaviour of the parts depends on a central control which is supraordinate to them.

928 In his treatise *De hominis dignitate* Pico says: "The Father implanted in man at birth seeds of all kinds and the germs of original life."[10] Just as God is the "copula" of the world, so, within the created world, is man. "Let us make man in our image, who is not a fourth world or anything like a new nature, but is rather the fusion and synthesis of three worlds (the supracelestial, the celestial, and the sublunary)."[11] In body and spirit man is "the little God of the world," the microcosm.[12] Like God, therefore, man is a centre of events, and all things revolve about him.[13] This thought, so utterly strange to the modern mind, dominated man's picture of the world until a few generations ago, when natural science proved man's subordination to nature and his extreme dependence on causes. The idea of a correlation between events and meaning (now assigned exclusively to man) was banished to such a remote and benighted region that the intellect lost track of it altogether. Schopenhauer remembered it somewhat belatedly after it had formed one of the chief items in Leibniz's scientific explanations.

929 By virtue of his microcosmic nature man is a son of the firmament or macrocosm. "I am a star travelling together with you," the initiate confesses in the Mithraic liturgy.[14] In alchemy the microcosmos has the same significance as the *rotundum*, a favourite symbol since the time of Zosimos of Panopolis, which was also known as the Monad.

930 The idea that the inner and outer man together form the whole, the *οὐλομελίη* of Hippocrates, a microcosm or smallest part wherein the "great principle" is undividedly present, also characterizes the thought of Agrippa von Nettesheim. He says:

> It is the unanimous consent of all Platonists, that as in the archetypal World, all things are in all; so also in this corporeal world, all things are in all, albeit in different ways, according to the receptive nature of each. Thus the Elements are not only in these inferiour bodies, but also in the Heavens, in Stars, in Divels, in Angels, and lastly in God, the maker, and archetype of all things.[15]

The ancients had said: "All things are full of gods."[16] These gods were "divine powers which are diffused in things."[17] Zoroaster had called them "divine allurements,"[18] and Synesius "symbolic incitements."[19] This latter interpretation comes very close indeed to the idea of archetypal projections in modern psychology, although from the time of Synesius until quite recently there was no epistemological criticism, let alone the newest form of it, namely psychological criticism. Agrippa shares with the Platonists the view that "there is in the lower beings a certain virtue through which they agree in large measure with the higher," and that as a result the animals are connected with the "divine bodies" (i.e., the stars) and exert an influence on them.[20] Here he quotes Virgil: "I for my part do not believe that they [the rooks] are endowed with divine spirit or with a foreknowledge of things greater than the oracle."[21]

931 Agrippa is thus suggesting that there is an inborn "knowledge" or "perception" in living organisms, an idea which recurs in our own day in Hans Driesch.[22] Whether we like it or not, we find ourselves in this embarrassing position as soon as we begin seriously to reflect on the teleological processes in biology or to investigate the compensatory function of the unconscious, not to speak of trying to explain the phenomenon of synchronicity. Final causes, twist them how we will, postulate a *foreknowledge of some kind*. It is certainly not a knowledge that could be connected with the ego, and hence not a conscious knowledge as we know it, but rather a self-subsistent "unconscious" knowledge which I would prefer to call "absolute knowledge." It is not cognition but, as Leibniz so excellently calls it, a "perceiving" which consists – or to be more cautious, seems to consist – of images, of subjectless "simulacra." These postulated images are presumably the same as my archetypes, which can be shown to be formal factors in spontaneous fantasy products. Expressed in modern language, the microcosm which contains "the images of all creation" would be the collective unconscious.[23] By the *spiritus mundi*, the *ligamentum animae et corporis*, the *quinta essentia*,[24] which he shares with the alchemists, Agrippa probably means what we would call the unconscious. The spirit that "penetrates all things," or shapes all things, is the World Soul: "The soul of the world therefore is a certain only thing, filling all things, bestowing all things, binding, and knitting together all things, that it might make one frame

of the world . . ."[25] Those things in which this spirit is particularly powerful therefore have tendency to "beget their like,"[26] in other words to produce correspondences or meaningful coincidences.[27] Agrippa gives long list of these correspondences, based on the numbers 1 to 12.[28] A similar but more alchemical table of correspondences can be found in a treatise of Aegidius de Vadis.[29] Of these I would only mention the *scala unitatis*, because it is especially interesting from the point of view of the history of symbols: "Yod [the first letter of the tetragrammaton, the divine name] – anima mundi – sol – lapis philosophorum – cor – Lucifer."[30] I must content myself with saying that this is an attempt to set up a hierarchy of archetypes, and that tendencies in this direction can be shown to exist in the unconscious.[31]

932 Agrippa was an older contemporary of Theophrastus Paracelsus and is known to have had a considerable influence on him.[32] So it is not surprising if the thinking of Paracelsus proves to be steeped in the idea of correspondence. He says:

> If a man will be a philosopher without going astray, he must lay the foundations of his philosophy by making heaven and earth a microcosm, and not be wrong by a hair's breadth. Therefore he who will lay the foundations of medicine must also guard against the slightest error, and must make from the microcosm the revolution of heaven and earth, so that the philosopher does not find anything in heaven and earth which he does not also find in man, and the physician does not find anything in man which heaven and earth do not have. And these two differ only in outward form, and yet the form on both sides is understood as pertaining to one thing.[33]

The *Paragranum*[34] has some pointed psychological remarks to make about physicians:

> For this reason, [we assume] not four, but one arcanum, which is, however, four-square, like a tower facing the four winds. And as little as a tower may lack a corner, so little may the physician lack one of the parts. . . . At the same [time he] knows how the world is symbolized [by] an egg in its shell, and how a chick with all its substance lies hidden within it. Thus everything in the world and in man must lie hidden in the physician. And just as the hens, by their brooding, transform the world prefigured in the shell into a chick, so Alchemy brings to maturity the philosophical arcana lying in the physician. . . . Herein lies the error of those who do not understand the physician aright.[35]

What this means for alchemy I have shown in some detail in my *Psychology and Alchemy*.

933 Johannes Kepler thought in much the same way. He says in his *Tertius interveniens* (1610):[36]

> This [viz., a geometrical principle underlying the physical world] is also, according to the doctrine of Aristotle, the strongest tie that links the lower world to the heavens and unifies it therewith so that all its forms are governed

from on high; for in this lower world, that is to say the globe of the earth, there is inherent a spiritual nature, capable of *Geometria*, which *ex instinctu creatoris, sine ratiocinatione* comes to life and stimulates itself into a use of its forces through the geometrical and harmonious combination of the heavenly rays of light. Whether all plants and animals as well as the globe of the earth have this faculty in themselves I cannot say. But it is not an unbelievable thing. . . . For, in all these things [e.g., in the fact that flowers have a definite colour, form, and number of petals] there is at work the *instinctus divinus, rationis particeps*, and not at all man's own intelligence. That man, too, through his soul and its lower faculties, has a like affinity to the heavens as has the soil of the earth can be tested and proven in many ways.[37]

934 Concerning the astrological "Character," i.e., astrological synchronicity, Kepler says:

This *Character* is received, not into the body, which is much too inappropriate for this, but into the soul's own nature, which behaves like a point (for which reason it can also be transformed into the point of the *confluxus radiorum*). This [nature of the soul] not only partakes of their reason (on account of which we human beings are called reasonable above other living creatures) but also has another, innate reason [enabling it] to apprehend instantaneously, without long learning, the *Geometriam* in the *radiis* as well as in the *vocibus*, that is to say, in *Musica*.[38]

Thirdly, another marvellous thing is that the nature which receives this *Characterem* also induces a certain correspondence *in constellationibus coelestibus* in its relatives. When a mother is great with child and the natural time of delivery is near, nature selects for the birth a day and hour which correspond, on account of the heavens [scil., from an astrological point of view], to the nativity of the mother's brother or father, and this *non qualitative, sed astronomice et quantitative*.[39]

Fourthly, so well does each nature know not only its *characterem coelestem* but also the celestial *configurationes* and courses of every day that, whenever a planet moves *de praesenti* into its *characteris ascendentem* or *loca praecipua*, especially into the *Natalitia*,[40] it responds to this and is affected and stimulated thereby in various ways.[41]

935 Kepler supposes that the secret of the marvellous correspondence is to be found in the *earth*, because the earth is animated by an *anima telluris*, for whose existence he adduces a number of proofs. Among these are: the constant temperature below the surface of the earth; the peculiar power of the earth-soul to produce metals, minerals, and fossils, namely the *facultas formatrix*, which is similar to that of the womb and can bring forth in the bowels of the earth shapes that are otherwise found only outside – ships, fishes, kings, popes, monks, soldiers, etc.;[42] further the practice of geometry, for it produces the five geometrical bodies and the six-cornered figures in crystals. The *anima telluris* has all this from an original impulse, independent of the reflection and ratiocination of man.[43]

936 The seat of astrological synchronicity is not in the planets but in the earth;[44] not in matter, but in the *anima telluris*. Therefore every kind of natural or living power in bodies has a certain "divine similitude."[45]

From: *Symbols of Transformation* (1911–1912/1952) (*CW* 5), par. 198

198 Numerous mythological and philosophical attempts have been made to formulate and visualize the creative force which man knows only by subjective experience. To give but a few examples, I would remind the reader of the cosmogonic significance of Eros in Hesiod,[46] and also of the Orphic figure of Phanes,[47] The Shining One, the First-Created, the "Father of Eros." Orphically, too, he has the significance of Priapus; he is bisexual and equated with the Theban Dionysus Lysius.[48] The Orphic significance of Phanes is akin to that of the Indian Kama, the god of love, who is likewise a cosmogonic principle. To the Neoplatonist Plotinus, the world-soul is the energy of the intellect.[49] He compares the One, the primordial creative principle, with light, the intellect with the sun (♂), and the world-soul with the moon (♀).[50] Or again, he compares the One with the Father and the intellect with the Son.[51] The One, designated as Uranos, is transcendent; the Son (Kronos) has dominion over the visible world; and the world-soul (Zeus) is subordinate to him. The One, or the *ousia* of existence in totality, is described by Plotinus as hypostatic, and so are the three forms of emanation; thus we have *μία οὐσία ἐν τρισὶν ὑποστάσεσιν* (one being in three hypostases). As Drews has observed, this is also the formula for the Christian Trinity as laid down at the councils of Nicaea and of Constantinople.[52] We might add that certain early Christian sects gave a maternal significance to the Holy Ghost (world-soul or moon). According to Plotinus, the world-soul has a tendency towards separation and divisibility, the *sine qua non* of all change, creation, and reproduction. It is an "unending All of life" and wholly energy; a living organism of ideas which only become effective and real in it.[53] The intellect is its progenitor and father, and what the intellect conceives the world-soul brings to birth in reality.[54] "What lies enclosed in the intellect comes to birth in the world-soul as Logos, fills it with meaning and makes it drunken as if with nectar."[55] Nectar, like soma, is the drink of fertility and immortality. The soul is fructified by the intellect; as the "oversoul" it is called the heavenly Aphrodite, as the "undersoul" the earthly Aphrodite. It knows "the pangs of birth."[56] It is not without reason that the dove of Aphrodite is the symbol of the Holy Ghost.

NOTES

1 Professor W. Pauli kindly calls my attention to the fact that Niels Bohr used "correspondence" as a mediating term between the representation of the discontinuum (particle) and the continuum (wave). Originally (1913–18) he called it the "principle of correspondence," but later (1927) it was formulated as the "argument of correspondence."

2 "*συμπάθεια τῶν ὅλων*."

3 *De alimento*, a tract ascribed to Hippocrates. (Trans. by John Precope in *Hippocrates on Diet and Hygiene*, p. 174, modified.) "*Σύρροια μία, συμπνοία μία, πάντα συμπαθέα*

κατὰ μὲν οὐλομελίην πάντα κατὰ μέρς δὲ τὰ ἐν ἑκάστῳ μέρει μέρεα πρὸς τό ἔργον. . .άρχή μεγάλη ἐς ἔσχατον μέρος ἀφικνέεται, ἐξ ἐσχάτου μέρος είς άρχήν μεγάλην άφικνέεται, μία φῦσις είναι καί είναι."

4 *De opificio mundi*, 82 (trans. by F. H. Colson and G. H. Whitaker, I, p. 67).
5 "*ἀρχή μεγάλη*"
6 Eduard Zeller, *Die Philosophie der Griechen*, II, part ii, p. 654.
7 *Enneads*, IV, 3, 8 and 4, 32 (in A. C. H. Drews, *Plotin und der Untergang der antiken Weltanschauung*, p. 179).
8 *Heptaplus*, VI, prooem., in *Opera omnia*, pp. 40f. ("Est enim primum ea in rebus unitas, qua unumquodque sibi est unum sibique constat atque cohaeret. Est ea secundo, per quam altera alteri creatura unitur, et per quam demum omnes mundi partes unus sunt mundus. Tertia atque omnium principalissima est, qua totum universum cum suo opifice quasi exercitus cum suo duce est unum.")
9 "unitas ita ternario distincta, ut ab unitatis simplicitate non discedat."
10 *Opera omnia*, p. 315. ("Nascenti homini omnifaria semina et origenae vitae germina indidit pater.")
11 *Heptaplus*, V, vi, in ibid., p. 38. ("Faciamus hominem ad imaginem nostram, qui non tam quartus est mundus, quasi nova aliqua natura, quam trium (mundus supercoelestis, coelestis, sublunaris) complexus et colligatio.")
12 "God . . . placed man in the centre [of the world] after his image and the similitude of forms" ("Deus . . . hominem in medio [mundi] statuit ad imaginem suam et similitudinem formarum").
13 Pico's doctrine is a typical example of the medieval correspondence theory. A good account of cosmological and astrological correspondence is to be found in Alfons Rosenberg, *Zeichen am Himmel: Das Weltbild der Astrologie*.
14 Dieterich, *Eine Mithrasliturgie*, p. 9.
15 Henricus Cornelius Agrippa von Nettesheim, *De occulta philosophia Libri tres*, I, viii, p. 12. Trans, by "J. F," as *Three Books of Occult Philosophy* (1651 edn.), p. 20; republished under the editorship of W. F. Whitehead, p. 55. [Quotations from the J. F. translation have been slightly modified. – TRANS.] ("Est Platonicorum omnium unanimis sententia quemadmodum i ı archetypo mundo omnia sunt in omnibus, ita etiam in hoc corporeo mundo, omnia in omnibus esse, modis tamen diversis, pro natura videlicet suscipientium: sic et elementa non solum sunt in istis inferioribus, sed in coelis, in stellis, in daemonibus, in angelis, in ipso denique omnium opifice et archetypo.")
16 "Omna plena diis esse."
17 "virtutes divinae in rebus diffusae."
18 "divinae illices."
19 "symbolicae illecebrae." [In J. F. original edn., p. 32; Whitehead edn., p. 69. – TRANS.] Agrippa is basing himself here on the Marsilio Ficino translation (*Auctores Platonici*, II, vo). In Synesius (*Opuscula*, ed. by Nicolaus Terzaghi, p. 148), the text of *Περί ἐνυπνίων* III B has *τὸ θελγόμενον*, from *θελγειν*, "to excite, charm, enchant."
20 *De occulta philosophia*, I, iv, p. 69. (J. F. edn., p. 117; Whitehead edn., p. 169.) Similarly in Paracelsus.
21 "Haud equidem credo, quia sit divinius illis
Ingenium aut rerum fato prudentia maior."
– *Georgics*, I, 415f.

22 *Die "Seele" als elementarer Naturfaktor*, pp. 80, 82.
23 Cf. supra, "On the Nature of the Psyche," pars. 392f.
24 Agrippa says of this (op. cit., I, xiv, p. 29; J. F. edn., p. 33; Whitehead edn., p. 70): "That which we call the quintessence: because it is not from the four Elements, but a certain fifth thing, having its being above, and besides them." ("Quoddam quintum super ilia [elementa] aut praeter illa subsistens.")

25 II, lvii, p. 203 (J. F. edn., p. 331): "Est itaque anima mundi, vita quaedam unica omnia replens, omnia perfundens, omnia colligens et connectens, ut unam reddat totius mundi machinam. . . ."
26 Ibid.: ". . . potentius perfectiusque agunt, turn etiam promptius generant sibi simile."
27 The zoologist A. C. Hardy reaches similar conclusions: "Perhaps our ideas on evolution may be altered if something akin to telepathy – unconscious no doubt – were found to be a factor in moulding the patterns of behaviour among members of a species. If there was such a non-conscious group-behaviour plan, distributed between, and linking, the individuals of the race, we might find ourselves coming back to something like those ideas of subconscious racial memory of Samuel Butler, but on a group rather than an individual basis." "The Scientific Evidence for Extra-Sensory Perception," in *Discovery*, X, 328, quoted by Soal, q.v.
28 Op. cit., II, iv–xiv.
29 "Dialogus inter naturam et filium philosophiae." *Theatrum chemicum*, II (1602), p. 123.
30 Cited in Agrippa, op. cit., II, iv, p. 104 (J. F. edn., p. 176).
31 Cf. Aniela Jaffé, "Bilder und Symbole aus E. T. A. Hoffmann's Märchen 'Der goldene Topf,'" and Marie-Louise von Franz, "Die Passio Perpetuae."
32 Cf. *Alchemical Studies*, index, *s.v.* "Agrippa."
33 *Das Buch Paragranum*, ed. by Franz Strunz, pp. 35f. Much the same in *Labyrinthus medicorum*, in the *Sämtliche Werke*, ed. Sudhoff, XI, pp. 204ff.
34 Strunz edn., p. 34.
35 Similar ideas in Jakob Böhme, *The Signature of All Things*, trans. by John Ellistone, p. 10: "Man has indeed the forms of all the three worlds in him, for he is a complete image of God, or of the Being of all beings. . . ." (*Signatura rerum*, I, 7.)
36 *Opera omnia*, ed. by C. Frisch, I, pp. 605ff.
37 Ibid., No. 64.
38 Ibid., No. 65.
39 Ibid., No. 67.
40 ["in die Natalitia" = "into those [positions presiding] at birth," if "in die" is construed as German. The *Gesammelte Werke*, ed. by M. Caspar and F. Hammer, IV, p. 211, has "in die Natalitio" = "in the day of birth," the words "in die" being construed as Latin. – TRANS.]
41 Ibid., No. 68.
42 See the dreams mentioned below [KLG: In "Synchronicity: An Acausal Connecting Principle," par. 945].
43 Kepler, *Opera*, ed. by Frisch, V, p. 254; cf. also II, pp. 270f and VI, pp. 178f. ". . . formatrix facultas est in visceribus terrae, quae feminae praegnantis more occursantes foris res humanas veluti eas videret, in fissibilibus lapidibus exprimit, ut militum, monachorum, pontificum, regum et quidquid in ore hominum est. . . ."
44 ". . . quod scl. principatus causae in terra sedeat, non in planetis ipsis." Ibid., II, p. 642.
45 ". . . ut omne genus naturalium vel animalium facultatum in corporibus Dei quandam gerat similitudinem," Ibid. I am indebted to Dr. Liliane Frey-Rohn and Dr. Marie-Louise von Franz for this reference to Kepler.
46 *Theogony*, 120.
47 [KLG: See Jung, *Symbols of Transformation,* pl. XII.]
48 Cf. Roscher, *Lexikon*, III, II, 2248ff.
49 Drews, *Plotin*, p. 127.
50 [KLG: Jung, apparently in error, uses the glyphs for Mars and Venus rather than the glyphs for the Sun and the Moon.]
51 Ibid., p. 132.
52 Ibid., p. 135.
53 Plotinus, *Enneads*, II, 5, 3.
54 Ibid., IV, 8, 3.
55 Ibid., Ill, 5, 9.
56 Drews, p. 141.

12 Astrology as a projection of the unconscious

From: "19 November 1930," *Visions I*

Astrology is the projected psychology of the unconscious . . .

From: "The Theory of Psychoanalysis" (1913/1955) (*CW* 4), par. 477

477 . . . The whole of astro-mythology is at bottom nothing but psychology – unconscious psychology – projected into the heavens; for myths never were and never are made consciously, they arise from man's unconscious.

From: "On the Nature of the Psyche" (1947/1954) (*CW* 8), par. 392

392 It strikes me as significant, particularly in regard to our hypothesis of a multiple consciousness and its phenomena, that the characteristic alchemical vision of sparks scintillating in the blackness of the arcane substance should, for Paracelsus, change into the spectacle of the "interior firmament" and its stars. He beholds the darksome psyche as a star-strewn night sky, whose planets and fixed constellations represent the archetypes in all their luminosity and numinosity.[1] The starry vault of heaven is in truth the open book of cosmic projection, in which are reflected the mythologems, i.e., the archetypes. In this vision astrology and alchemy, the two classical functionaries of the psychology of the collective unconscious, join hands.

From: "Religious Ideas in Alchemy" (1937) (*CW* 12), par. 346

346 As we all know, science began with the stars, and mankind discovered in them the dominants of the unconscious, the "gods," as well as the curious psychological qualities of the zodiac: a complete projected theory of human character. Astrology is a primordial experience similar to alchemy. Such projections repeat themselves whenever man tries to explore an empty darkness and involuntarily fills it with living form.

From: "The Spirit Mercurius" (1943/1948) (*CW* 13), par. 285

285 So long as one knows nothing of psychic actuality, it will be projected, if it appears at all. Thus the first knowledge of psychic law and order was found in the stars, and was later extended by projections into unknown matter. These two realms of experience branched off into sciences: astrology became astronomy, and alchemy chemistry. On the other hand, the peculiar connection between character and the astronomical determination of time has only very recently begun to turn into something approaching an empirical science. The really important psychic facts can neither be measured, weighed, nor seen in a test tube or under a microscope. They are therefore supposedly indeterminable, in other words they must be left to people who have an inner sense for them, just as colours must be shown to the seeing and not to the blind.

From: "Archetypes of the Collective Unconscious" (1934/1954) (*CW* 9i), par. 7

7 What the word "archetype" means in the nominal sense is clear enough, then, from its relations with myth, esoteric teaching, and fairytale. But if we try to establish what an archetype is *psychologically*, the matter becomes more complicated. So far mythologists have always helped themselves out with solar, lunar, meteorological, vegetal, and other ideas of the kind. The fact that myths are first and foremost psychic phenomena that reveal the nature of the soul is something they have absolutely refused to see until now. Primitive man is not much interested in objective explanations of the obvious, but he has an imperative need – or rather, his unconscious psyche has an irresistible urge – to assimilate all outer sense experiences to inner, psychic events. It is not enough for the primitive to see the sun rise and set; this external observation must at the same time be a psychic happening: the sun in its course must represent the fate of a god or hero who, in the last analysis, dwells nowhere except in the soul of man. All the mythologized processes of nature, such as summer and winter, the phases of the moon, the rainy seasons, and so forth, are in no sense allegories[2] of these objective occurrences; rather they are symbolic expressions of the inner, unconscious drama of the psyche which becomes accessible to man's consciousness by way of projection – that is, mirrored in the events of nature. The projection is so fundamental that it has taken several thousand years of civilization to detach it in some measure from its outer object. In the case of astrology, for instance, this age-old "scientia intuitiva" came to be branded as rank heresy because man had not yet succeeded in making the psychological description of character independent of the stars. Even today, people who still believe in astrology fall almost without exception for the old superstitious assumption of the influence of the stars. And yet anyone who can calculate a horoscope should know that, since the days of Hipparchus of Alexandria, the spring-point has been fixed at 0° Aries, and that the zodiac on

which every horoscope is based is therefore quite arbitrary, the spring-point having gradually advanced, since then, into the first degrees of Pisces, owing to the precession of the equinoxes.

From: "6 November 1935," *Nietzsche's Zarathustra I*

Jung is discussing Nietzsche's concept of the individual, from the 1880s, and contrasting the modern idea of the individual in relationship to the cosmos with the medieval conception of the individual self as a microcosm reflecting the whole of existence.

Our more modern idea of the individual is entirely different from that statistical way of envisaging problems. We look at the individual from the inside, and then the individual means the man, the subjective man, the single man being a sort of microcosm and not an atom in a continuum. So our psychological concept of the individual, in comparison with that of the eighties, seems like a most extraordinary exaggeration. When that era was in full bloom, the individual was of course nothing but a sort of contrivance of nature and the main goal of the whole life-process was the life of the species; the individual meant no more than a cell means in a body. Moreover, the individual contained nothing. There was nothing inside but his conscious psyche; everything else was just the body. So that time was utterly unable to see the individual as a microcosm, in contradistinction to a previous time, the early Middle Ages. Then the individual *was* seen as a microcosm, but then they saw the macrocosm – the sky with the stars and the planets and God as the ruling spirit of the universe – and every individual was the mirror reflex of that wholeness; it was as if the whole cosmos had descended into the individual entity *man* and made him a microcosm.

Now we have again a similar idea, yet it is very different: namely, we discover the microcosm in the individual as the origin of the macrocosm. Our idea is that as you find certain archetypal ideas in man, you also discover them in the universe, but man put them there: they were not there before. For instance, the eternal constellations in the heavens to the medieval man had had a meaningful existence for an eternity. God himself expressed his power and his might in those constellations, and he caused them to be in man too; he created man as the microcosm. We would turn the thing round and say the individual man was the origin of such a universe; we see the universe largely depending upon man. He fills this universe with meaning, but in itself it is without meaning; it is even quite futile to ask whether it is eternal. Moreover, we are convinced that it is not eternal in its present form. There are no eternal constellations, because they all change their position in the course of untold centuries. So what was an eternal and unshakeable truth to the primitive man – namely, the unchangeable nature of the zodiac signs – is relative to us; we know that in the course of many thousands of years all those stars will change their positions and the universe will have an entirely different shape; and to call them "eternal" or to name them "The Fishes," "Capricorn," and so on, is merely a projection. You see, we also find the archetypal images in man, but instead of making them derive from the great cosmos, we make them derive from the constellations in man. Now, I don't want to discuss the ulterior philosophical question, "Which is older, the ape or then hen?" – but I say that for our time we have a tendency to think in this way. Of course this may be a continuation of materialism, an *enantiodromia*, an overestimate of the individual over against the time when he was utterly depreciated. That is quite possible, but even if we know that, we cannot get away from such a point of view, because this is a necessary concept at present. We have to live it, have to accept it; for the time being, such a standpoint would be the natural thing.

From: "1 February 1939," *Nietzsche's Zarathustra II*

You see, our whole mental life, our consciousness, began with projections. Our mind under primitive conditions was entirely projected, and it is interesting that those internal contents, which made the foundation of real consciousness, were projected the farthest into space – into the stars. So the first science was astrology. That was an attempt of man to establish a line of communication between the remotest objects and himself. Then he slowly fetched back all those projections out of space into himself. Primitive man – well, even up to modern times – lives in a world of animated objects. Therefore that term of Tylor's, *animism*, which is simply the state of projection where man experiences his psychical contents as parts of the objects of the world. Stones, trees, human beings, families are all alive along with my own psyche and therefore I have a *participation mystique* with them. I influence them and I am influenced by them in a magical way, which is only possible because there is a bond of sameness. What appears in the animal say, is identical with myself because it is myself – it is a projection. So our psychology has really been a sort of coming together, a confluence of projections. The old gods, for instance, were very clearly psychical functions, or events, or certain emotions; some are thoughts and some are definite emotions. A wrathful god is your own wrathfulness. A goddess like Venus or Aphrodite is very much your own sexuality, but projected. Now, inasmuch as these figures have been deflated, inasmuch as they do not exist any longer, you gradually become conscious of having those qualities or concepts; you speak of *your* sexuality. That was no concept in the early centuries, but was the god, Aphrodite or Cupid or Kama or whatever name it was called by. Then slowly we sucked in those projections and that accumulation made up psychological consciousness.

From: "Commentary on the Secret of the Golden Flower" (1929) (*CW* 13), par. 49

49 Activated unconscious contents always appear at first as projections upon the outside world, but in the course of mental development they are gradually assimilated by consciousness and reshaped into conscious ideas that then forfeit their originally autonomous and personal character. As we know, some of the old gods have become, via astrology, nothing more than descriptive attributes (martial, jovial, saturnine, erotic, logical, lunatic, and so on).

From*: "9 March 1932," *Visions I

Discussion of a vision that includes a patient who sees stars falling into a fire: "I entered a room. In the center of the room there shot up a great fire which reached high into the sky and melted many stars which fell into the fire."

DR. JUNG: . . . *(continuing to read the vision text)*: "I passed through the fire and emerged into a garden. I walked along the path until I came to a pool." What is this?

MR. ALLEMANN: A mandala.

DR. JUNG: Yes, and it has a rim of fire apparently, through which she passes and enters the garden. It is like the Eastern mandala. In the center is a pool, which would be the disk of gold, or the great void, or the germinal vescicle, or the place of rebirth, or the fountain. So this fire that melts the stars and makes them fall is really the fire round the mandala, round the Self. . . .

I once saw such a mandala. The figure of the patient was in the center, and stars were falling into the center too, meaning that even the stars form constituents of that body which is called the Self. This idea is very difficult because it has something to do with man's cosmic correspondences, an entirely unscientific idea out of the unconscious which is a very hot and angry thing to hold; the whole thing is very fantastic, yet it is a strange psychological fact. The idea of souls becoming stars, or descending from the stars, is very old. The star of Bethlehem was the soul of Christ that descended upon the earth. And there was that well-known idea, to us almost childish, that after death souls traveled up to the stars and were then like stars. As the old Romans thought that their emperors after death transformed into stars. Or the Manichaeans thought that the souls of dying people who had light enough in their essence, were sucked up by the waxing moon; then when it was quite full of souls, the moon approached the sun and there gradually discharged its contents; so all the souls that contained enough light went over to the sun, thus forming the so-called Pillar of Light in which they were taken up to the highest heaven. I have not yet investigated this idea sufficiently – the story is in only one Persian manuscript – but the point is that the soul of man has something to do with the stars, and of course that has to do with astrology.

It is as if the human soul consisted of qualities coming from the stars; apparently the stars have qualities that fit in with our psychology. This is because of the original fact that astrology is a projection of man's unconscious psychology into the stars. There is an amazing knowledge of unconscious functioning there, which we consciously do not possess, and it appeared first in the remotest stars, the stars of the zodiacal constellations. What we possess, as the most intimate and secret knowledge of ourselves, is apparently written in the heavens. In order to know my individual and true character, I have to search the heavens, I cannot see it directly in myself. When I discover that my sun is in Leo and my moon in Taurus, for instance, something has been explained to me; and when I find that I have a particular touch with modern times, and the rising sign in my horizon is Aquarius, it is as if I had learned something more than

I already knew of myself. The projection still holds good. This has nothing to do with the stars, yet my most unconscious laws are written there.

There must, therefore, be some connection in the unconscious of man with – well, one might say – with the universe. Something in man must be universal, otherwise he would not make such a projection, he could not read himself in the most remote constellations. One cannot project something which one does not possess; whatever one projects into someone else is within oneself even if it is the devil himself. So the fact that we project something into the stars means that we must possess something of the stars. You see, we really are part of the universe. We must never forget that we are living on a planet, and a planet is a satellite of the sun, it is just a body moving about in space, and we are a kind of living slime on the surface of that body flying through the eternal heavens. So we are cosmic and every particle of our bodies, we are the dust of eternity and of limitless space. All that is within us, and that is why we can project it, why we can perceive space at all, and why we have such ideas as infinite space or infinite time. It is because we have it in ourselves, we are parts of the cosmos.

And so the symbol of stars falling down has the eternal meaning of the soul of man descending. The star that appeared at the birth of Christ announced a cosmic phenomenon, a cosmic soul had descended. In other words, a man who was conscious of his cosmic fate, of the absolute regularity of his fate; that is, one could say, a man with the understanding that his life was law abiding, that it was an expression of the ordinances of heaven. The Chinese would call it a complete expression of Tao, for Tao is the condition which is in tune with the ordinances of heaven, a complete expression of the order that rules heaven and earth. So when one creates something which is right, one should be conscious of the fact that it is imbued with the stars. That explains the idea of the choice of days, why people study the stars to find out whether a certain time is favorable to their psychological condition, in tune with them or not. It is because they instinctively realize that whatever one does should be the expression of the universe; since one is part of the cosmos everything one does should be in accordance with the laws of the cosmos. That is the idea here, the coming down of the stars means the coming into consciousness of the cosmic laws, that one's life evolves like the revolution of planets, or like the rising and setting of the sun. You see, that brings in what is called the eternal aspect, the envisaging of things *sub specie eternitatis*; one then sees human life not in the ordinary personal perspective but in the impersonal objective perspective of a cosmic procedure. I hope I have made myself clear. I admit it is almost impossible to see all that from this little hint, but this hint is worth more than all the rest.

NOTES

1 In the *Hieroglyphica* of Horapollo the starry sky signifies God as ultimate Fate, symbolized by a "5," presumably a quincunx. [Trans by George Boas, p. 66. – EDITORS.]

2 An allegory is a paraphrase of a conscious content, whereas a symbol is the best possible expression for an unconscious content whose nature can only be guessed, because it is still unknown.

13 Astrology as a mantic method

From: "To Robert L. Kroon, 15 November 1958," *Letters II*

Astrology is one of the intuitive methods like the *I Ching*, geomantics, and other divinatory procedures. It is based upon the synchronicity principle, i.e., meaningful coincidence. I have explored experimentally three intuitive methods: the method of the *I Ching*, geomantics, and astrology.

From "Synchronicity: An Acausal Connecting Principle" (1952) (*CW* 8), par. 987

987 We are in a somewhat more favourable situation [compared to the *I Ching*] when we turn to the astrological method, as it presupposes a meaningful coincidence of planetary aspects and positions with the character or the existing psychic state of the questioner.

From: "On the Nature of the Psyche" (1947/1954) (*CW* 8), note 118 to par. 405

Occasionally it [the archetype] is associated with synchronistic or parapsychic effects. I mean by synchronicity, as I have explained elsewhere, the not uncommonly observed "coincidence" of subjective and objective happenings, which just cannot be explained causally, at least in the present state of our knowledge. On this premise astrology is based and the methods of the *I Ching*. These observations, like the astrological findings, are not generally accepted, though as we know this has never hurt the facts. I mention these special effects solely for the sake of completeness and solely for the benefit of those readers who have had occasion to convince themselves of the reality of parapsychic phenomena.

From: "Synchronicity: An Acausal Connecting Principle" (1952) (*CW* 8), pars. 867–869, 875, 901

867 Though the results of both procedures [geomancy and the *I Ching*] point in the desired direction, they do not provide any basis for a statistical evaluation.

I have, therefore, looked round for another intuitive technique and have hit on astrology, which, at least in its modern form, claims to give a more or less total picture of the individual's character. There is no lack of commentaries here; indeed, we find a bewildering profusion of them – a sure sign that interpretation is neither simple nor certain. The meaningful coincidence we are looking for is immediately apparent in astrology, since the astronomical data are said by astrologers to correspond to individual traits of character; from the remotest times the various planets, houses, zodiacal signs, and aspects have all had meanings that serve as a basis for a character study or for an interpretation of a given situation. It is always possible to object that the result does not agree with our psychological knowledge of the situation or character in question, and it is difficult to refute the assertion that knowledge of character is a highly subjective affair, because in characterology there are no infallible or even reliable signs that can be in any way measured or calculated – an objection that also applies to graphology, although in practice it enjoys widespread recognition.

868 This criticism, together with the absence of reliable criteria for determining traits of character, makes the meaningful coincidence of horoscope structure and individual character postulated by astrology seem inapplicable for the purpose here under discussion. If, therefore, we want astrology to tell us anything about the acausal connection of events, we must discard this uncertain diagnosis of character and put in its place an absolutely certain and indubitable fact. One such fact is the marriage connection between two persons.[1]

869 Since antiquity, the main traditional astrological and alchemical correspondence to marriage has been the *coniunctio Solis* (☉) et *Lunae* (☽), the *coniunctio Lunae et Lunae*, and the conjunction of the moon with the ascendent.[2] There are others, but these do not come within the main traditional stream. The ascendent-descendent axis was introduced into the tradition because it has long been regarded as having a particularly important influence on the personality.[3] As I shall refer later to the conjunction and opposition of Mars (♂) and Venus (♀), I may say here that these are related to marriage only because the conjunction or opposition of these two planets points to a love relationship, and this may or may not produce a marriage. So far as my experiment is concerned, we have to investigate the coincident aspects ☉ ☽ , ☽ ☽ , and ☽ *Asc.* in the horoscopes of married pairs in relation to those of unmarried pairs. It will, further, be of interest to compare the relation of the above aspects to those of the aspects which belong only in a minor degree to the main traditional stream. No belief in astrology is needed to carry out such an investigation, only the birth-dates, an astronomical almanac, and a table of logarithms for working out the horoscope.

875 Marriage is a well-characterized fact, though its psychological aspect shows every conceivable sort of variation. According to the astrological view, it is precisely this aspect of marriage that expresses itself most markedly in the horoscopes. The possibility that the individuals characterized by the horoscopes married one another, so to say, by accident will necessarily recede

into the background; all external factors seem capable of astrological evaluation, but only inasmuch as they are represented psychologically. Owing to the very large number of characterological variations, we would hardly expect marriage to be characterized by only *one* astrological configuration; rather, if astrological assumptions are at all correct, there will be several configurations that point to a predisposition in the choice of a marriage partner.

901 From the scientific point of view the result of our investigation is in some respects not encouraging for astrology, as everything seems to indicate that in the case of large numbers the differences between the frequency values for the marriage aspects of married and unmarried pairs disappear altogether. Thus, from the scientific point of view, there is little hope of proving that astrological correspondence is something that conforms to law. At the same time, it is not so easy to counter the astrologer's objection that my statistical method is too arbitrary and too clumsy to evaluate correctly the numerous psychological and astrological aspects of marriage.

From: "Synchronicity: An Acausal Connecting Principle" (1952) (*CW* 8), pars. 905–907, 911–912

Although the results of Jung's astrology experiment ultimately yielded statistically insignificant correlations between the astrological factors and marriages, initial errors were made in calculations that appeared to lend support to astrology. Jung took this susceptibility to error as itself significant.

905 . . . We can regard what happened in our case as a synchronistic phenomenon. The statistical material shows that a practically as well as theoretically improbable chance combination occurred which coincides in the most remarkable way with traditional astrological expectations. That such a coincidence should occur at all is so improbable and so incredible that nobody could have dared to predict anything like it. It really does look as if the statistical material had been manipulated and arranged so as to give the appearance of a positive result. The necessary emotional and archetypal conditions for a synchronistic phenomenon were already given, since it is obvious that both my co-worker and myself had a lively interest in the outcome of the experiment, and apart from that the question of synchronicity had been engaging my attention for many years. What seems in fact to have happened – and seems often to have happened, bearing in mind the long astrological tradition – is that we got a result which has presumably turned up many times before in history. Had the astrologers (with but few exceptions) concerned themselves more with statistics and questioned the justice of their interpretations in a scientific spirit, they would have discovered long ago that their statements rested on a precarious foundation. But I imagine that in their case too, as with me, a secret, mutual connivance existed between the material and the psychic state of the astrologer. This correspondence is simply *there* like any other agreeable or annoying accident, and it seems doubtful to me whether it can be proved scientifically

to be anything more than that.[4] One may be fooled by coincidence, but one has to have a very thick skin not to be impressed by the fact that, out of fifty possibilities, three times precisely those turned up as maxima which are regarded by tradition as typical.

906 As though to make this startling result even more impressive, we found that use had been made of unconscious deception. On first working out the statistics I was put off the trail by a number of errors which I fortunately discovered in time. . . . *The errors all tend to exaggerate the results in a way favourable to astrology*, and add most suspiciously to the impression of an artificial or fraudulent arrangement of the facts, which was so mortifying to those concerned that they would probably have preferred to keep silent about it.

907 I know, however, from long experience of these things that spontaneous synchronistic phenomena draw the observer, by hook or by crook, into what is happening and occasionally make him an accessory to the deed. That is the danger inherent in all parapsychological experiments. The dependence of ESP on an emotional factor in the experimenter and subject is a case in point. I therefore consider it a scientific duty to give as complete an account as possible of the result and to show how not only the statistical material, but the psychic processes of the interested parties, were affected by the synchronistic arrangement. Although, warned by previous experience, I was cautious enough to submit my original account (in the Swiss edition) to four competent persons, among them two mathematicians, I allowed myself to be lulled into a sense of security too soon.

911 The result of our experiment tallies with our experience of mantic procedures. One has the impression that these methods, and others like them, create favourable conditions for the occurrence of meaningful coincidences.

912 In view of the levelling influence which the statistical method has on the quantitative determination of synchronicity, we must ask how it was that Rhine succeeded in obtaining positive results. I maintain that he would never have got the results he did if he had carried out his experiments with a single subject,[5] or only a few. He needed a constant renewal of interest, an emotion with its characteristic *abaissement mental*, which tips the scales in favour of the unconscious. Only in this way can space and time be relativized to a certain extent, thereby reducing the chances of a causal process. What then happens is a kind of *creatio ex nihilo*, an act of creation that is not causally explicable. The mantic procedures owe their effectiveness to this same connection with emotionality: by touching an unconscious aptitude they stimulate interest, curiosity, expectation, hope, and fear, and consequently evoke a corresponding preponderance of the unconscious. The effective (numinous) agents in the unconscious are the archetypes. By far the greatest number of spontaneous synchronistic phenomena that I have had occasion to observe and analyse can easily be shown to have a direct connection with an archetype. This, in itself, is an irrepresentable, psychoid factor[6] of the collective unconscious. The latter cannot be localized, since either it is complete in principle in every individual or is found to be the same everywhere. You can never say with certainty

whether what appears to be going on in the collective unconscious of a single individual is not also happening in other individuals or organisms or things or situations.

From: "Synchronicity: An Acausal Connecting Principle" (1952) (*CW* 8), par. 994

994 Although I was obliged to express doubt, earlier, about the mantic character of astrology, I am now forced as a result of my astrological experiment to recognize it again.[7]

NOTES

1 Other obvious facts would be murder and suicide. Statistics are to be found in Herbert von Kloeckler (*Astrologie als Erfahrungswissenschaft*, pp. 232ff. and 260ff.), but unfortunately they fail to give comparisons with normal average values and cannot be used for our purpose. On the other hand, Paul Flambart (*Preuves et bases de l'astrologie scientifique*, pp. 79ff.) shows a graph of statistics on the ascendents of 123 outstandingly intelligent people. Definite accumulations occur at the corners of the airy trigon (♊, ♎, ♒). This result was confirmed by a further 300 cases.

2 This view dates back to Ptolemy: "Apponit [Ptolemaeus] autem tres gradus concordiae: Primus cum Sol in viro, et Sol vel Luna in femina. aut Luna in utrisque, fuerint in locis se respicientibus trigono, vel hexagono aspectu. Secundus cum in viro Luna, in uxore Sol eodem modo disponuntur. Tertius si cum hoc alter alterum recipiat." (Ptolemy postulates three degrees of harmony. The first is when the sun in the man's [horoscope], and the sun or moon in the woman's, or the moon in both, are in their respective places in a trine or sextile aspect. The second degree is when the moon in a man's [horoscope] and the sun in a woman's are constellated in the same way. The third degree is when the one is receptive to the other.) On the same page, Cardan quotes Ptolemy (*De iudiciis astrorum*): "Omnino vero constantes et diurni convictus permanent quando in utriusque conjugis genitura luminaria contigerit configurata esse concorditer" (Generally speaking, their life together will be long and constant when in the horoscopes of both partners the luminaries [sun and moon] are harmoniously constellated). Ptolemy regards the conjunction of a masculine moon with a feminine sun as particularly favourable for marriage. – Jerome Cardan, *Commentaria in Ptolemaeum de astrorum iudiciis*, Book IV (in his *Opera omnia*, V, p. 332).

3 The practising astrologer can hardly suppress a smile here, because for him these correspondences are absolutely self-evident, a classic example being Goethe's connection with Christiane Vulpius: ☉ 5° ♍ ☌ ☽ 7° ♍.

I should perhaps add a few explanatory words for those readers who do not feel at home with the ancient art and technique of astrology. Its basis is the horoscope, a circular arrangement of sun, moon, and planets according to their relative positions in the signs of the zodiac at the moment of an individual's birth. There are three main positions, viz., those of sun (☉), moon (☽), and the so-called ascendent (*Asc.*); the last has the greatest importance for the interpretation of a nativity: the *Asc.* represents the degree of the zodiacal sign rising over the eastern horizon at the moment of birth. The horoscope consists of 12 so-called "houses," sectors of 30° each. Astrological tradition ascribes different qualities to them as it does to the various "aspects," i.e., angular relations of the planets and the *luminaria* (sun and moon), and to the zodiacal signs.

4 As my statistics show, the result becomes blurred with larger figures. So it is very probable that if more material were collected it would no longer produce a similar result.

We have therefore to be content with this apparently unique *lusus naturae*, though its uniqueness in no way prejudices the facts.

5 By which I mean a subject chosen at random, and not one with specific gifts.

6 Cf. "On the Nature of the Psyche," pars. 417f.

7 [KLG: Compare to Jung's previous rejection of the mantic nature of astrology occurring three pages earlier in the same essay, which is included in this volume in Chapter 14, "Astrology as Causal Influence," p. 175.]

14 Astrology as causal influence

From: "To Hans Bender, 6 March 1958," *Letters II*

With regard to the horoscope I have serious doubts whether it can be understood as a purely synchronistic phenomenon, for there are unquestionable causal connections between the planetary aspects and the powerful effects of proton radiation,[1] though we are still very much in the dark as to what its physiological effects might be.

From: "To Aniela Jaffé, 8 September 1951," *Letters II*

I must rework the chapter on astrology [in Jung's monograph on synchronicity]. An important change has to be made – Knoll[2] put me on to it. Astrology is not a mantic method but appears to be based on proton radiation[3] (from the sun). I must do a statistical experiment in order to be on sure ground.

From: "To Hans Bender, 10 April 1958," *Letters II*

It is indeed very difficult to explain the astrological phenomenon. I am not in the least disposed to an either-or explanation. I always say that with a psychological explanation there is only the alternative: either *and* or! This seems to me to be the case with astrology too. The readiest explanation, as you quite rightly point out, would seem to be the parallelistic view. It is in line with the Geulincx-Leibniz theory of collateral correspondences which you will find formulated most clearly in Schopenhauer.[4]

My objection to this theory is that it presupposes a strict causality, or rather, is founded on an axiomatic causality. Accordingly, the correspondence would have to conform to law. This is to some extent so with very large numbers, as Rhine has shown; but nevertheless so seldom that the limits of mathematical probability are exceeded only by a little. From this we could conclude that in the realm of smaller numbers the correspondence lies within the limits of probability and so cannot be rated a phenomenon that conforms to law, as your clock and watch simile demonstrates.[5] You set your watch by the clock, and this amounts to a causal dependence, just as in Leibniz's mondaology all the monadic watches were originally wound up by the same creator.

The synchronicity concept discards this *harmonia praestabilita*, or parallelism, because if this principle operated there would necessarily be a far greater and more regular number of correspondences than is the case in reality. Making due allowance for errors, one gets the impression that these "lucky hits" occur relatively seldom. Although we cannot conceive of a causal law and hence necessary connection between an event and its determination in time (horoscope), it nevertheless looks as though such a connection did exist; for on it is based the traditional interpretation of the horoscope, which presupposes and establishes a certain regularity of events. So even if we ascribe only a limited meaning to the horoscope, we are already assuming a necessary connection between the event and the heavenly constellation.

The fact, however, is that our whole astrological determination of time does not correspond to any actual constellation in the heavens because the vernal equinox has long since moved out of Aries into Pisces and from the time of Hipparchus has been artificially set at 0° Aries. Consequently the correlations with planetary houses[6] are purely fictitious, and this rules out the possibility of a causal connection with the actual positions of the stars, so that the astrological determination of time is purely symbolic. Even so, the rough correlation with the actual seasons remains unimpaired, and this is of great significance so far as the horoscope is concerned. There are, for instance, spring births and autumn births, which play an especially important role in the animal world. Then, beside the seasonal influences there are also fluctuations of proton radiation, which have been proved to exert a considerable influence on human life. These are all causally explicable influences and argue in favour of astrological correlations that conform to law. To that extent, therefore, I would be inclined to rank astrology among the natural sciences.

On the other hand, astrological observation yields cases where one hesitates to maintain the validity of a purely causalistic explanation. Cases of astonishing predictions, for instance, give me at any rate the feeling of a meaningful "lucky hit," a meaningful coincidence, since they seem to me to make excessive demands on a causal explanation by their extreme improbability, and to that extent I would rather adduce synchronicity as an explanatory principle. An historical example of this kind is the reputed coincidence of Christ's birth with the triple royal conjunction in Pisces in the year 7 B.C.[7]

As I have said, astrology seems to require differing hypotheses, and I am unable to opt for an either-or. We shall probably have to resort to a mixed explanation, for nature does not give a fig for the sanitary neatness of the intellectual categories of thought.

From: "Synchronicity: An Acausal Connecting Principle" (1952) (*CW* 8), pars. 875–876

875 . . . I must call the reader's attention to the well-known correspondence between the sun-spot periods and the mortality curve. The connecting link appears to be the disturbances of the earth's magnetic field, which in their turn are due to fluctuations in the proton radiation from the sun. These fluctuations also have an influence on "radio weather" by disturbing the ionosphere that

reflects the radio waves.[8] Investigation of these disturbances seems to indicate that the conjunctions, oppositions, and quartile aspects of the planets play a considerable part in increasing the proton radiation and thus causing electromagnetic storms. On the other hand, the astrologically favourable trine and sextile aspects have been reported to produce uniform radio weather.

876 These observations give us an unexpected glimpse into a possible causal basis for astrology. At all events, this is certainly true of Kepler's weather astrology. But it is also possible that, over and above the already established physiological effects of proton radiation, psychic effects can occur which would rob astrological statements of their chance nature and bring them within range of a causal explanation. Although nobody knows what the validity of a nativity horoscope rests on, it is just conceivable that there is a causal connection between the planetary aspects and the psycho-physiological disposition. One would therefore do well not to regard the results of astrological observation as synchronistic phenomena, but to take them as possibly causal in origin. For, wherever a cause is even remotely thinkable, synchronicity becomes an exceedingly doubtful proposition.

From: "Synchronicity: An Acausal Connecting Principle" (1952) (*CW* 8), pars. 987–988

987 In the light of the most recent astrophysical research, astrological correspondence is probably not a matter of synchronicity but, very largely, of a causal relationship. As Professor Max Knoll has demonstrated,[9] the solar proton radiation is influenced to such a degree by planetary conjunctions, oppositions, and quartile aspects that the appearance of magnetic storms can be predicted with a fair amount of probability. Relationships can be established between the curve of the earth's magnetic disturbances and the mortality rate that confirm the unfavourable influence of conjunctions, oppositions, and quartile aspects and the favourable influence of trine and sextile aspects. So it is probably a question here of a causal relationship, i.e., of a natural law that excludes synchronicity or restricts it. . . . Astrology presupposes that . . . time has a determining quality. It is possible that this quality, like the disturbances in the earth's magnetic field, is connected with the seasonal fluctuations to which solar proton radiation is subject. It is therefore not beyond the realm of possibility that the zodiacal positions may also represent a causal factor.

988 Although the psychological interpretation of horoscopes is still a very uncertain matter, there is nevertheless some prospect today of a causal explanation in conformity with natural law. Consequently, we are no longer justified in describing astrology as a mantic method. Astrology is in the process of becoming a science.[10]

NOTES

1 Cf. Jaffé, 8 Sept. 51, n. 2.

2 Max Knoll (1897–1970), German physicist, 1948–55 professor of electrical engineering at Princeton U.; after 1956 director of the Institute for Technical Electronics, Munich.

3 According to Knoll, solar proton radiation is strongly influenced by planetary constellations. Cf. Knoll, "Transformation of Science in Our Age," *Man and Time*, Papers from the Eranos Yearbooks, 3 (1957); Jung "On Synchronicity," CW 8, Appendix, par. 987, and "Synchronicity," par. 875.

4 Schopenhauer, in his "Transcendent Speculations on the Apparent Design in the Fate of the Individual," *Parerga und Paralipomena*, I (1891), employs a geographical analogy to illustrate the simultaneity of causally unconnected events, where the parallels of latitude intersect the meridians of longitude, which are thought of as causal chains; by virtue of this cross-connection even simultaneous events are linked to causality. Cf. "Synchronicity," par. 828.

5 B. spoke of "a structure of order which would probably have to be understood in a parallelistic sense, as in the oft-quoted relationship between clock and watch, where the directing *tertium* [third] remains open."

6 [KLG: Presumably Jung means the zodiacal signs rather than the planetary houses.]

7 The conjunction of Jupiter and Saturn, the astrological signs of life and death, signifies the union of extreme opposites. This conjunction occurred three times in the year 7 B.C. (*Aion*, CW 9, ii, par. 130). [KLG: Many modern astrologers would not equate Jupiter with "life" but rather with growth, excess, optimism, expansion, abundance, and similar characteristics. Jupiter and Saturn are not "astrological signs," of course, but planets and the names of associated "planetary archetypes."]

8 For a comprehensive account of this, see Max Knoll, "Transformations of Science in Our Age," in *Man and Time*.

9 ["Transformations of Science in Our Age," ibid.] [KLG: This was a part of a 1952 lecture by Dr. Hellmut Wilhelm at Eranos.]

10 [KLG: Compare Jung's comment on the mantic nature of astrology three pages later in the same essay – see Chapter 13, "Astrology as a Mantic Method," p. 171.]

15 Synchronicity and the qualities of time

From: "Richard Wilhelm: In Memoriam" (1930) (*CW* 15), pars. 81–82

81 The science of the *I Ching* is based not on the causality principle but on one which – hitherto unnamed because not familiar to us – I have tentatively called the *synchronistic* principle. My researches into the psychology of unconscious processes long ago compelled me to look around for another principle of explanation, since the causality principle seemed to me insufficient to explain certain remarkable manifestations of the unconscious. I found that there are psychic parallelisms which simply cannot be related to each other causally, but must be connected by another kind of principle altogether. This connection seemed to lie essentially in the relative simultaneity of the events, hence the term "synchronistic." It seems as though time, far from being an abstraction, is a concrete continuum which possesses qualities or basic conditions capable of manifesting themselves simultaneously in different places by means of an acausal parallelism, such as we find, for instance, in the simultaneous occurrence of identical thoughts, symbols, or psychic states. Another example, pointed out by Wilhelm, would be the coincidence of Chinese and European periods of style, which cannot have been causally related to one another. Astrology would be an example of synchronicity on a grand scale if only there were enough thoroughly tested findings to support it. But at least we have at our disposal a number of well-tested and statistically verifiable facts which make the problem of astrology seem worthy of scientific investigation . . .

82 The fact that it is possible to reconstruct a person's character fairly accurately from his birth data shows the relative validity of astrology. It must be remembered, however, that the birth data are in no way dependent on the actual astronomical constellations, but are based on an arbitrary, purely conceptual time system. Owing to the precession of the equinoxes, the spring-point has long since moved out of the constellation of Aries into Pisces, so that the astrological zodiac on which horoscopes are calculated no longer corresponds to the heavenly one. If there are any astrological diagnoses of character that are in fact correct, this is due not to the influence of the stars but to our own

hypothetical time qualities. In other words, whatever is born or done at this particular moment of time has the quality of this moment of time.

From: "To H. J. Barrett, 26 March 1957," *Letters II*

Jung is responding to Barrett's discussion of synchronicities between his own experience and that of a Mr. Percy, who shared his birthday. One coincidence was that the two men both swallowed a stone.

If anybody is born on the same day and possibly in the same hour, he is like a grape of the same vineyard ripening at the same time. All the grapes of the same site produce the same wine. This is the truth stated by astrology and experience since time immemorial. Thus it is very probable that you have quite a lot of things in common with Mr. Percy who was born on the same day as you. If you go critically through your list you will find a number of points in common not only with Mr. Percy but with any amount of other individuals . . .

I regard such a case not at all as a *Doppelgänger*, which would be to me an unaccountable phenomenon, but rather as a peculiar synchronistic fact, if anything at all. I am not dense enough to overlook the curious fact of the considerable number of coincidences and particularly not the remarkable fact of swallowing a stone,[1] but I hold that there are quite a number of individuals born at the same time with an equally remarkable biographical likeness to you. I remember having read a case of a man born in the vicinity of Buckingham Palace on the same day and at the same hour as Edward VII. His life was the most ridiculous and close-fitting caricature of the King's life.

I don't want to offend you but I should like to call your attention to astrology, which has dealt with such phenomena for about 5000 years.

From: "Foreword to the 'I Ching'" (1950) (*CW* 11), par. 970

Jung is discussing the meaning of the divinatory practice of the I Ching *for the "Chinese mind."*

970 With us [Westerners] it would be a banal and almost meaningless statement (at least on the face of it) to say that whatever happens in a given moment has inevitably the quality peculiar to that moment. This is not an abstract argument but a very practical one. There are certain connoisseurs who can tell you merely from the appearance, taste, and behaviour of a wine the site of its vineyard and the year of its origin. There are antiquarians who with almost uncanny accuracy will name the time and place of origin and the maker of an *objet d'art* or piece of furniture on merely looking at it. And there are even astrologers who can tell you, without any previous knowledge of your nativity, what the position of your sun and moon was and what zodiacal sign rose above the horizon at the moment of your birth. In the face of such facts, it must be admitted that moments can leave long-lasting traces.

From: "To B. Baur, 20 January 1934," *Letters I*

So far as the argument of the precession[2] is concerned, this is no objection to the validity of astrology but rather to the primitive theory that the stars themselves radiate certain effects. The precession argument says that a person born today in Aries 1, when ostensibly Aries has risen one degree over the Eastern horizon, is not born at this point of time at all but in Pisces 1. The secret powers of the sun are in Aries 1. Moon for instance in Cancer 7, Venus, Jupiter in similar positions, are therefore not right astronomically and so cannot be derived from these merely apparent and arbitrarily fixed positions. Choisnard quite correctly says: "Le belier reste toujours à la 12° partie du zodiaque,"[3] etc., obviously meaning that the "sun in Aries" is not an astronomical statement but an indication of time. It is "spring-time" that contains the active forces no matter in which real astronomical zodion the sun is standing. In a few thousand years, when we say it is Aries time, the sun will be in reality in Capricorn, a deep winter sign, though the spring will not have lost its powers.

The fact that astrology nevertheless yields valid results proves that it is not the apparent positions of the stars which work, but rather the times which are measured or determined by arbitrarily named stellar positions. Time thus proves to be a stream of energy filled with qualities and not, as our philosophy would have it, an abstract concept or precondition of knowledge.

The validity of the results of the *I Ching* oracle points to the same peculiar fact. Careful investigation of the unconscious shows that there is a peculiar coincidence with time, which is also the reason why the ancients were able to project the succession of unconsciously perceived inner contents into the outer astronomical determinants of time. This is the basis for the connection of psychic events with temporal determinants. So it is not a matter of an indirect connection, as you suppose, but a direct one. Conjunctions, oppositions, etc., are not in the least affected by the fact that we arbitrarily designate Pisces 1 as Aries 1.

From: "8 June 1932," *Visions II*

So the real connection with astrology is time, and therefore the most striking aspect of our connection with the stars is that of fate. Fate evolves with time, and it is identical with time. When one says the time has not yet come, it means that fate has not yet fulfilled itself; fate fulfills itself only in time, time being only another aspect of fate. Fate and time are absolutely identical, fate being the more human aspect and time the more energic aspect. And time is another aspect of energy, for without time there is no energy, and without energy there is no time. Time is measured energy. In winding up a clock, a certain store of energy is given it, so that it can run its course, and that is called the movement of time, because by that energic process as a measure, time can be appreciated. Life is another aspect of time; it is fate, it is energy, and it is the movement of the stars. It can express itself either by the watch, or by the course or position of the stars, or by the process of energy running down. So there are really many reasons for the connection of our innermost psychology with the movement of the stars, and it is therefore almost to be expected that in just this moment an astrological picture would turn up.

From: "4 December 1929," *Dream Analysis*

Therefore we have to conclude that what we call psychological motives are in a way identical with star positions. Since we cannot demonstrate this, we must form a peculiar hypothesis. This hypothesis says that the dynamics of our psyche is not just identical with the positions of the stars, nor has it to do with vibrations – that is an illegitimate hypothesis. It is better to assume that it is a phenomenon of time. In the concept of time the two come together. Time, or the moment understood as a peculiar form of energy, coincides with our psychological condition. The moment is unique, so that whatever has its origin at a certain moment has the energy and qualities of that particular moment. It must be so, because a thing originating a hundred years ago has the character of that age. In this conception of time we have a mediating concept, which helps us to avoid the irrational explanations of astrology.

The stars are simply used by man to serve as indicators of time, and our psychology has little to do with the stars as a clock, which is merely an instrument used to measure a certain moment – say 10:45. It is exactly the same as if one said the sun is in Aquarius, the moon in Sagittarius, and Gemini is coming over the horizon with an elevation of 5 degrees. This is a particular moment. Four minutes are necessary for a degree of a sign to rise above the horizon. You can even find the very instant by dividing that degree into seconds. Such a constellation during a very long space of time is unique. In the lapse of 26,000 years we have one such position, the year, the month, day, hour, and seconds. The important fact is that it is this particular situation and not that the stars indicate it. One could use other constellations to establish time. The thing that matters is that the present moment is what it is – the particular moment and the actual condition of the world, and its energy and its movement at that moment. Whatever originates at that time will be marked by that particular moment, so the psychological factors are determined by the actual position and all its qualities.

From: "27 November 1929," *Dream Analysis*

So, as I said, it is obvious that the active element is time. People born at a certain time of the year may have certain qualities. The relative position of the stars is only the means for counting time. Then here is a new paradox. What is time? How can it be an active principle? Time is an abstract conception of duration and is perfectly arbitrary at that; one could make an entirely different division. A second might be half a minute, why is a minute sixty seconds? It is not at all convincing, it is merely a conventional arbitrary conception. Then if one tries to boil it down, one comes to the conclusion that time is in the flux of things, like the water-clock or the sand-clock, it is the running down, dividing the day into four parts, each part being one quarter of that day, between sunrise and sunset. To observe time, one observes the movement of things lasting a certain time, as the hands of a watch; it is the duration of a certain flux. This is abstract, but the flux of things is not abstract, it is perfectly concrete and tangible. That is what we term energy because nothing moves without energy. One must wind one's watch or turn the hour-glass. It takes energy to produce the flux, and what we measure is energy; and this is another abstract conception in so far as it means a changing condition of things. When one says time is merely an aspect of energy, one makes it more tangible, because everyone can observe it and measure it. Time and energy are correlated concepts. If there is no energy nothing moves and there is no longer any time. They are identical, a certain movement of time is a certain movement of energy. When we observe energy we really observe time, because it is through energy that we measure time. So I say, with no time there is no possibility of measurement.

Take a stone just before it rolls down hill. It is in a particular position of energy, it will crash but it hasn't. It is latent energy, the energy of position, *potential* energy. It may break loose at any time with terrific vigour. Then it crashes down manifesting *mechanical* energy. It lands in the valley, crashes, splinters, and then where is the energy? It is in the *warmth* of the stone and the stone against which it hurled itself. It has been transformed. This is a new movement of energy. Now, you can describe that whole transformation in terms of time. If nothing happens, there is no time. Time begins when that thing gets loose. There is a certain amount of time until the warmth is dissipated again, and then it becomes unobservable. The specific warmth has completely vanished, so time is only between the breaking loose of the stone and the last trace of warmth of the splintered rock.

Energy was in three forms, latent energy, mechanical energy, and warmth. You can translate this into the terms of water falling on a turbine and creating electricity. As long as the process lasts, there is time, simply different moments expressed through different forms.

Now consider the universal energy of the world, the life energy. It is unknown to us, but we must understand it under those terms. It is not observable if nothing happens. For instance, an egg is latent, nothing moves, but if it develops, time develops, age begins. Now take the energy of the universe and the solar system. In winter there is less radiation, in summer there is more. So someone who was born at a certain moment of the year naturally has a certain quality, because his origin was in those conditions. Nothing to be done about it, it is just so. The peculiar thing is that one should be able to trace the age of a thing to the exact time of its origin.[4] There are certain archaeologists, for instance, who have such a refined sense of the age of an object that they can tell it within ten years, just as an antiquarian knows by the print, quality of the paper, etc. of a book that it suggests a time between 1460 and 1470, let us say. So an etching can be traced. The expert will tell you it is of the French school but influenced by the Dutch. He judges by the actual qualities of the materials used – the paper, the ink, the objects depicted, etc. When you see an old man, white-haired and decrepit, you say he was born about 1850. Often I guess within two years. One can do that without any trouble, it is the same as saying that one was born under Aquarius but a bit more accurate. This is merely a technical method, like looking behind the screen of a clever antiquarian who has certain little helps – for instance, he knows when a certain varnish was introduced into Europe, or that the first pipe is not older than the discovery of North America.

Astrology consists of all these little tricks that help to make the diagnosis more accurate. So the astrologer, though he does not know the year or the month of your birth, may guess by your qualities. Now, the unfortunate thing is that we can designate the condition of energy, universal energy, in no other way than by time. Instead of saying the time of the falling stone, we say it was ten seconds ago that the stone has fallen. We call this year 1929, because once upon a time we began counting, assuming that we knew when Christ was born – although there is a controversy about that, Christ may have been born 100 B.C. Mead has written a very interesting book about that.[5] In China the years have names. In Rome they were named for the consuls, reckoned from the beginning of Rome in 750 B.C. After the French Revolution, they began to count the years as if it were the beginning of a new epoch. We indicate the conditions of the times by a number. For instance, 1875 might be called the time of crinolines, the first railways, newspapers twice a week with pages, corsets for ladies, top-hats for men, bad taste generally. They knew nothing of Nietzsche, Schopenhauer was the most recent news. Chicago was then the most ridiculous little place, and imagine New York in 1875! Four years after the Franco-German War, everything was moving in a different way, the way that was characteristic for that year, and nothing before or after it will be like it.

So, in 1929, everything has the cast and brand of this year. And the children born in this year will be recognizable as part of a great process and marked by a particular condition.[6]

From: "4 December 1929," *Dream Analysis*

Time is the essential identity with creative energy. There is a Greek aphorism, "Wherever there is creation, there is time." Chronos was the god of light, creation, and time. Also the Stoic conception of primordial warmth is practically identical with time. The Greek *Heimarmenē*, meaning astrological compulsion, is identical with primordial warmth, the primordial creative force. I admit that this is strange, and if you are not sufficiently acquainted with the facts, it is not easy. Our Western mind refuses to function along Chinese lines. It is difficult to feel the creative wave of time that moves the winds, the clouds, the birds, and even the streetcars. We should realize the tremendous importance of everything that is *now*. To the Chinese this means everything, but to us it is nothing but chance – chance that we are here, chance that the bird sings and the dog barks. It is the unique characteristic of this moment. Whatever takes its origin in this moment carries the mark of this moment for ever.

From: "To André Barbault, 26 May 1954," *Letters II*

In response to the following question on the connections between astrology and psychology: In what way, physical, causal, or synchronous, do you think these connections can be established?

2. *The modus operandi of astrological constellations.* It seems to me that it is primarily a question of that parallelism or "sympathy"[7] which I call *synchronicity*, an acausal connection expressing relationships that cannot be formulated in terms of causality, such as precognition, premonition, psychokinesis (PK), and also what we call telepathy. Since causality is a *statistical truth*, there are exceptions of an acausal nature bordering on the category of synchronistic (not synchronous) events. They have to do with "qualitative time."

Jung's response to the following question: Astrology introduces the concept of qualitative time ("temps qualitatif") in the universe. Do you recognize its role in the individual psyche (problem of cycles and transits)?

4. *Qualitative time.* This is a notion I used formerly[8] but I have replaced it with the idea of synchronicity, which is analogous to sympathy or *correspondentia* (the *συμπάθεια* of antiquity), or to Leibniz's *pre-established harmony*. Time itself consists of nothing. It is only a *modus cogitandi* that is used to express and formulate the flux of things and events, just as space is nothing but a way of describing the existence of a body. When nothing occurs in time and when there is no body in space, there is neither time nor space. Time is always and exclusively "qualified" by events as space is by the extension of bodies. But "qualitative time" is a tautology and means nothing, whereas synchronicity (not synchronism) expresses the parallelism and analogy between events in so far as they are noncausal. In contrast, "qualitative time" is a hypothesis that attempts to explain the parallelism of events in terms of *causa et effectus*. But since qualitative time is nothing but the flux of things, and is moreover just as much "nothing" as space, this hypothesis does not establish anything except the tautology: the flux of things and events is the cause of the flux of things, etc.

Synchronicity does not admit causality in the analogy between terrestrial events and astrological constellations (except for the deflection of solar protons and their possible effects on terrestrial events),[9] and denies it particularly in all cases of nonsensory perception (ESP), especially precognition, since it is inconceivable one could observe the effect of a nonexistent cause, or of a cause that does not yet exist.

What astrology can establish are the analogous events, but not that either series is the cause or the effect of the other. (For instance, the same constellation may at one time signify a catastrophe and at another time, in the same case, a cold in the head.) Nevertheless, astrology is not an entirely simple matter. There is that deflection of solar protons caused on the one hand by the conjunctions, oppositions, and quartile aspects, and on the other hand by trine and sextile aspects, and their influence on the radio and on many other things.[10] I am not competent to judge how much importance should be attributed to this possible influence.

In any case, astrology occupies a unique and special position among the intuitive methods, and in explaining it there is reason to be dubious of both a causal theory and the exclusive validity of the synchronistic hypothesis.[11]

NOTES

1 He [H. J. Barrett] and Percy had both swallowed a fruit stone at the age of 13 and been convinced they would die of appendicitis.

2 The precession of the equinoxes (reportedly discovered by the Greek astronomer Hipparchus, born *ca.* 190 B.C.) is the slow western motion of the equinoctial points along the ecliptic, caused by the conical motion of the earth's axis; a complete revolution takes about 26,000 years, called the "Platonic Year." As a consequence, the vernal equinox moves clockwise through the twelve zodiacal signs, the precession through each taking about 2,000 years, a "Platonic Month." Thus at the beginning of our era the vernal equinox entered the sign of Pisces and is now moving into Aquarius. Astrology, in its horoscopic calculations, does not take account of the precession but bases them on the vernal equinox fixed by Hipparchus at 0° Aries. This discrepancy is a main objection to astrology (Cf. Corti, 12 Sept. 29, n. 3). [KLG: Jung's statement is true of the tropical zodiac, the system used by most Western astrologers, in which the vernal equinox (the first degree of Aries) coincides with the onset of spring in the northern hemisphere on or around March 20. In the sidereal zodiac, however, the signs of the zodiac are based on the actual positions of the constellations on the ecliptic and thus take into account the precession of the equinoxes against the background of the fixed stars.]

3 Paul Flambart (= Paul Choisnard), *Preuves et bases de l'astrologie scientifique* (2nd edn., 1921), p. 162: ". . . aujourd'hui comme dans l'antiquité on peut appeler Bélier la douzième partie du zodiaque que traverse le soleil aussitôt après l'equinoxe de printemps." [KLG: "Today, as in antiquity, one can call Aries the twelfth part of the zodiac that crosses the sun immediately after the spring equinox.".]

4 "Carbon dating" in archaeology became possible only in the mid-1950s: cf. W. F. Libby, *Radioactive Dating* (1955).

5 G. R. S. Mead, *Did Jesus Live 100 B.C.? An Inquiry into the Talmud Jesus Stories, the Toldoth Jeschu, and Some Curious Statements of Epiphanius* (London and Benares: Theosophical Publication Society, 1903).

6 Some of the ideas Jung was trying out in this lecture reappeared in his memorial address for Richard Wilhelm (1930), CW 15, pars. 81–82, where he first published a reference to "synchronicity," his theory later developed in the monograph "Synchronicity" (1951–52), CW 8, pars. 816ff., but first mentioned (as "synchronism") in the lecture of 28 Nov. 1928 (above, n. 1). See also the next lecture, at n. 8. [KLG: Jung, "Lecture IX, 4 December 1929," in *Dream Analysis*, p. 417.]

7 Cf. Kling, 14 Jan. 58, n. 2.

8 Cf. "Richard Wilhelm: In Memoriam," CW 15, par. 82: "Whatever is born or done at this particular moment of time has the quality of this moment of time." Also "Foreword to the *I Ching*," CW 11, pars. 970f.

9 Cf. Jaffé, 8 Sept. 51, n. 2.

10 "Synchronicity," CW 8, par. 875.

11 Cf. Bender, 10 Apr. 48.

16 Number and archetypes

From: "An Astrological Experiment" (1958) (*CW* 18), pars. 1182–1183

1182 Since most people believe that numbers have been *invented* or thought out by man, and are therefore nothing but concepts of quantities, containing nothing that was not previously put into them by the human intellect, it was naturally very difficult for me to put my question in any other form. But it is equally possible that numbers were *found* or discovered. In that case they are not only concepts but something more – autonomous entities which somehow contain more than just quantities. Unlike concepts they are based not on any psychic assumption but on the quality of being themselves, on a "so-ness" that cannot be expressed by an intellectual concept. Under these circumstances they might easily be endowed with qualities that have still to be discovered. Also one could, as with all autonomous beings, raise the question of their behaviour; for instance one could ask what numbers do when they are intended to express something as archetypal as astrology. For astrology is the last remnant, now applied to the stars, of that fateful assemblage of gods whose numinosity can still be felt despite the critical procedures of our scientific age. In no previous age, however "superstitious," was astrology so widespread and so highly esteemed as it is today.

1183 I must confess that I incline to the view that numbers were as much found as invented, and that in consequence they possess a relative autonomy analogous of the archetypes. They would then have, in common with the latter, the quality of being pre-existent to consciousness, and hence, on occasion, of conditioning it rather than being conditioned by it. The archetypes too, as *a priori* forms of representation, are as much found as invented: they are *discovered* inasmuch as one did not know of their unconscious autonomous existence, and *invented* by the mind in as much as their presence was inferred from analogous representational structures. Accordingly it would seem that natural numbers must possess an archetypal character. If that is so, then not only would certain numbers have a relation to and an effect on certain archetypes, but the reverse would also be true. The first case is equivalent to number magic, but the second is equivalent to my question whether numbers, in conjunction with the numinous assemblage of gods which the horoscope represents, would show a tendency to behave in a special way.

From: "Synchronicity: An Acausal Connecting Principle" (1952) (*CW* 8), par. 870

870 Since the remotest times men have used numbers to establish meaningful coincidences, that is, coincidences that can be interpreted. There is something peculiar, one might even say mysterious, about numbers. They have never been entirely robbed of their numinous aura. If, so a text-book of mathematics tells us, a group of objects is deprived of every single one of its properties or characteristics, there still remains, at the end, its *number*, which seems to indicate that number is something irreducible. (I am not concerned here with the logic of this mathematical argument, but only with its psychology!) The sequence of natural numbers turns out to be unexpectedly more than a mere stringing together of identical units: it contains the whole of mathematics and everything yet to be discovered in this field. Number, therefore, is in one sense an unpredictable entity. Although I would not care to undertake to say anything illuminating about the inner relation between two such apparently incommensurable things as number and synchronicity, I cannot refrain from pointing out that not only were they always brought into connection with one another, but that both possess numinosity and mystery as their common characteristics. Number has invariably been used to characterize some numinous object, and all numbers from 1 to 9 are "sacred," just as 10, 12, 13, 14, 28, 32, and 40 have a special significance. The most elementary quality about an object is whether it is one or many. Number helps more than anything else to bring order into the chaos of appearances. It is the predestined instrument for creating order, or for apprehending an already existing, but still unknown, regular arrangement or "orderedness." It may well be the most primitive element of order in the human mind, seeing that the numbers 1 to 4 occur with the greatest frequency and have the widest incidence. In other words, primitive patterns of order are mostly triads or tetrads. That numbers have an archetypal foundation is not, by the way, a conjecture of mine but of certain mathematicians, as we shall see in due course. Hence it is not such an audacious conclusion after all if we define number psychologically as an *archetype of order* which has become conscious.[1] Remarkably enough, the psychic images of wholeness which are spontaneously produced by the unconscious, the symbols of the self in mandala form, also have a mathematical structure. They are as a rule quaternities (or their multiples).[2] These structures not only express order, they also create it. That is why they generally appear in times of psychic disorientation in order to compensate a chaotic state or as formulations of numinous experiences. It must be emphasized yet again that they are not inventions of the conscious mind but are spontaneous products of the unconscious, as has been sufficiently shown by experience. Naturally the conscious mind can imitate these patterns of order, but such imitations do not prove that the originals are conscious

inventions. From this it follows irrefutably that the unconscious uses number as an ordering factor.

From: "To Dr. H., 30 August 1951," *Letters II*

This remarkable effect [of acausal synchronicities] points to the "psychoid"[3] and essentially transcendental nature of the archetype as the "arranger" of psychic forms inside and outside the psyche. . . .

Although the psychoid archetype is a mere model or postulate, archetypal effects have just as real an existence as radioactivity. . . . Archetypes are not mere concepts but are entities, exactly like whole numbers, which are not merely aids to counting but possess irrational qualities that do not result from the concept of counting, as for instance prime numbers and their behaviour.

From: "To E. L. Grant Watson, 9 February 1956," *Letters II*

The coincidence of the Fibonacci numbers[4] (or *sectio aurea*) with plant growth is a sort of analogy with synchronicity inasmuch as the latter consists in the coincidence of a psychic process with an external physical event of the same character or meaning. But whereas the *sectio aurea* is a static condition, synchronicity is a coincidence in time, even of events that, in themselves, are not synchronous (f.i., a case of precognition). In the latter case one could assume that synchronicity is a property of energy, but in so far as energy is equal to matter it is a secondary effect of the primary coincidence of mental and physical events (as in the Fibonacci series). The bridge seems to be formed by the *numbers.*[5] Numbers are just as much *invented* as they are *discovered* as natural facts, like all true archetypes. As far as I know, archetypes are perhaps the most important basis for synchronistic events.

I am afraid this is all rather involved and very difficult. I don't see my way yet out of the jungle. But I feel that the root of the enigma is to be found probably in the peculiar properties of whole numbers. The old Pythagorean postulate![6]

From: "To Robert Dietrich, 27 May 1956," *Letters II*

Mathematicians are not agreed whether numbers were *invented* or *discovered.*[7]

"In the Olympian host Number eternally reigns" (Jacobi).[8] Whole numbers may well be the discovery of God's "primal thoughts," as for instance the significant number four, which has distinctive qualities. But you ask in vain for speculations on my part concerning the "development of this principle of order." I cannot presume to say anything about this transcendental problem which is ingrained in the cosmos. The mere attempt to do so would strike me as intellectual inflation. After all, man cannot dissect God's primal thoughts. Why are whole numbers individuals? Why are there prime numbers? Why have numbers inalienable qualities? Why are there discontinuities like quanta, which Einstein would have liked to abolish?

Your dream seems to me a genuine revelation: God and Number as the principle of order belong together. Number, like Meaning, inheres in the nature of all things as an expression of God's dissolution in the world of appearances. This creative process is continued with the same symbolism in the Incarnation. (Cf. *Answer to Job*.)

From: "To Werner Nowacki, 22 March 1957," *Letters II*

Your ideas [in an article sent to Jung] go back, in modern form, to the familiar world of Plato's *Timaeus*, which was a sacrosanct authority for medieval science – and rightly so! Our modern attempts at a unitary view, to which your article makes very important contributions, do indeed lead to the question of the cosmic demiurge and the psychic aspect of whole numbers.

From the fact that matter has a mainly quantitative aspect and at the same time a qualitative one, you draw the weighty conclusion, which I heartily applaud, that, besides its obviously qualitative nature, the psyche has an as yet hidden quantitative aspect. Matter and psyche are thus the terminal points of a polarity. The still largely unexplored area between them forms the *terra incognita* of future research. Here tremendous problems open out which you have approached from the physical side.

It seems to me that for the time being I have exhausted my psychological ammunition. I have got stuck, one the one hand, in the acausality (or "synchronicity") of certain phenomena of unconscious provenance and, on the other hand, in the qualitative statements of numbers, for here I set foot on territories where I cannot advance without the help and understanding of other disciplines. In this respect your article is uncommonly valuable and stimulating. I am particularly grateful to you for your appreciation of the transcendent "arranger."

From: "To Patrick Evans, 1 September 1956," *Letters II*

The fact is that the numbers pre-existing in nature are presumably the most fundamental archetypes, being the very matrix of all others. Here Pythagoras was certainly on the right track and we modern men have forgotten this aspect of the pre-existing numbers because we were only busy manipulating numbers for the sake of counting and calculating. But Number is a factor pre-existent to man, with unforeseen qualities yet to be discovered by him.

From: "To Fritz Lerch, 10 September 1956," *Letters II*

Like all inner foundations of judgment, numbers are archetypal by nature and consequently partake of the psychic qualities of the archetype. This, as we know, possesses a certain degree of autonomy which enables it to influence consciousness spontaneously. The same must be said of numbers, which brings us back to Pythagoras. When we are confronted with this dark aspect of numbers, the unconscious gives an answer, that is, it compensates their darkness by statements which I call "indispensable" or "inescapable." The number 1 says that it is one among many. At the same time it says that it is "the One." Hence it is the smallest and the greatest, the part and the whole. I am only hinting at these statements; if you think through the first five numbers in this way you will come to the remarkable conclusion that we have here a sort of creation myth which is an integral part of the inalienable properties of whole numbers. In this respect Number proves to be a fundamental element not only of physics but also of the objective psyche. . . .

I do not doubt that quite fundamental connections exist between physics and psychology, and that the objective psyche contains images that would elucidate the secret of matter. These connections are discernible in synchronistic phenomena and their acausality.

NOTES

1 Cf. "On the Psychology of Eastern Meditation," par. 942.
2 Cf. "A Study in the Process of Individuation" and "Concerning Mandala Symbolism."
3 A term coined by Jung to describe "quasi-psychic 'irrepresentable' basic forms," i.e., the archetypes *per se* in contradistinction to archetypal images (cf. Devatmananda, 9 Feb 37, n. 1 [in *Letters I*]). They belong to the transconscious area where psychic processes and their physical substrate touch. Cf. "On the Nature of the Psyche," CW 8, pars. 368, 417.
4 This and the following paragraph are reprinted in W.'s book (p. 48) but with one serious mistake. He has ". . . the coincidence of a *physical* process with an external physical event . . . ," thus completing vitiating Jung's argument.
5 The function and archetypal role of numbers is discussed at some length in "Flying Saucers," CW 10, pars. 776ff, and "Synchronicity," CW 8, par. 871.
6 To the Pythagoreans the whole universe was explicable in terms of the relation of numbers to one another.
7 Cf. Jung, "Ein astrologisches Experiment," *Zeitschrift für Parapsychologie und Grenzgebiete der Psychologie* (Bern), I: 2/3 (1958), 88f. . . . Also cf. Watson, 9 Feb 56, n. 4.
8 Karl Jacobi (1804–51), German mathematician. Cf. "Synchronicity," CW 8, par. 942.

17 Acausal orderedness and the unus mundus

From: "To J.B. Rhine, 9 August 1954," *Letters II*

The main difficulty with synchronicity (and also with ESP) is that one thinks of it as being produced by the subject, while I think it is rather in the nature of objective events.

From: "To Fritz Künkel, 10 July 1946," *Letters I*

Your view that the collective unconscious surrounds us on all sides is in complete agreement with the way I explain it to my pupils. It is more like an atmosphere in which we live than something that is found *in* us. It is simply the unknown quantity of the world. Also, it does not by any means behave merely psychologically; in the cases of so-called synchronicity it proves to be a universal substrate present in the environment rather than a psychological premise. Wherever we come into contact with an archetype we enter into relationship with transconscious, metapsychic factors which underlie the spiritualistic hypothesis as well as that of magical action.

From: "To John Raymond Smythies, 29 February 1952," *Letters II*

It looks as if the collective character of the archetypes would manifest itself also in meaningful coincidences, i.e., as if the archetype (or the collective unconscious) were not only inside the individual, but also outside, viz. in one's environment. . . . As in the psychic world there are no bodies moving through space, there is also no time. The archetypal world is "eternal," i.e., outside time, and it is everywhere, as there is no space under psychic, that is archetypal conditions. Where an archetype prevails, we can expect synchronistic phenomena, i.e., *acausal correspondences*, which consist in a parallel arrangement of facts in time.

From: "To Enrique Butelman, July 1956," *Letters II*

We are actually investigating accidents, i.e., fractures with their preceding dreams and the corresponding results of other chance-methods of mediaeval origin as f.i.

geomantics, horoscopy, playing cards, etc. We have some encouraging results. Owing to the traditional psychological nature of the said methods they permit a certain insight into the underlying unconscious constellations and their archetypal structure. I have observed personally quite a number of synchronistic events where I could establish the nature of the underlying archetype. The archetype itself (nota bene *not* the archetypal representation!) is psychoid,[1] i.e., transcendental and thus relatively beyond the categories of number, space, and time. That means it approximates to oneness and immutability. Owing to the liberation from the categories of consciousness the archetype can be the basis of meaningful coincidence.

From: "To H. Rossteutscher, 3 May 1958," *Letters II*

You mention the archetype as a basis [of synchronicity], and as a matter of fact an archetypal basis can be demonstrated in most cases of meaningful coincidence. But no causal nexus is thereby expressed, since from what we know of the archetype it is a psychoid content which cannot with certainty be said to exert a simultaneous effect on external events. We have only a very remote conjecture that psychic patterns fall in with the fundamental forms of the physical process in general. ("Psychoid" archetype!) But this is a possibility that must remain open.

From: "To Karl Schmid, 11 June 1958," *Letters II*

. . . In itself the archetype is an irrepresentable configuration whose existence can be established empirically in a number of forms. The archetype of the "mother," for instance, manifests itself in infinitely many forms and yet the one common characteristic of the mother-idea always remains intact. The same is true of the "father." At the same time the archetype is always of an objective nature since it is an *a priori* ideational pattern which is everywhere identical with itself. Thus it can appear as the image of the real mother but also as Sophia, or matter, which, as the name shows, also contains the mother-idea although it refers to a scientific concept.

The archetype, then, is a modality that represents visual forms, and synchronicity is another modality representing events. The concept "event" cannot be included under the concept "form," since form and event cannot be made to coincide. Hence you cannot describe synchronicity as an archetype but only as a modality *sui generis*. The concept of synchronicity says that a connection exists which is not of a causal nature. The connection consists firstly in the fact of coincidence and secondly in the fact of parallel meaning. It is a question of meaningful coincidences. Therefore it would only be confusing to throw together two entirely different concepts. . . .

Synchronistic phenomena are very often connected with archetypal constellations. This much can be determined by experience.

In so far as both modalities, archetype and synchronicity, belong primarily to the realm of the psychic, we are justified in concluding that they are psychic phenomena. In so far, however, as synchronistic events include not only psychic but also physical forms of manifestation, the conclusion is justified that both modalities transcend the realm of the psychic and somehow also belong to the physical realm. This can be expressed in other words by saying that there is a relativity of the psychic and physical categories – a relativity of being and of the seemingly axiomatic existence of space and time.

From: "Synchronicity: An Acausal Connecting Principle" (1952) (*CW* 8), pars. 938, 942–943

938 The synchronicity principle thus becomes the absolute rule in all cases where an inner event occurs simultaneously with an outside one. As against this, however, it must be borne in mind that the synchronistic phenomena which can be verified empirically, far from constituting a rule, are so exceptional that most people doubt their existence. They certainly occur much more frequently in reality than one thinks or can prove, but we still do not know whether they occur so frequently and so regularly in any field of experience that we could speak of them as conforming to law.[2] We only know that there must be an underlying principle which might possibly explain all such (related) phenomena.

942 Synchronicity postulates a meaning which is *a priori* in relation to human consciousness and apparently exists outside man.[3] Such an assumption is found above all in the philosophy of Plato, which takes for granted the existence of transcendental images or models of empirical things, the *είδη* (forms, species), whose reflections (*είδωλα*) we see in the phenomenal world. This assumption not only presented no difficulty to earlier centuries but was on the contrary perfectly self-evident. The idea of an *a priori* meaning may also be found in the older mathematics, as in the mathematician Jacobi's paraphrase of Schiller's poem "Archimedes and His Pupil." He praises the calculation of the orbit of Uranus and closes with the lines:

> What you behold in the cosmos is only the light of God's glory;
> In the Olympian host Number eternally reigns.

943 The great mathematician Gauss is the putative author of the saying: "God arithmetizes."[4]

From: "Synchronicity: An Acausal Connecting Principle" (1952) (*CW* 8), pars. 965, 967–968

965 The question now arises whether our definition of synchronicity with reference to the equivalence of psychic and physical processes is capable of expansion, or rather, requires expansion. This requirement seems to force itself on us when we consider the above, wider conception of synchronicity as an "acausal orderedness." Into this category come all "acts of creation," *a priori* factors such as the properties of natural numbers, the discontinuities of modern physics, etc. Consequently we would have to include constant and experimentally

reproducible phenomena within the scope of our expanded concept, though this does not seem to accord with the nature of the phenomena included in synchronicity narrowly understood. The latter are mostly individual cases which cannot be repeated experimentally. This is not of course altogether true, as Rhine's experiments show and numerous other experiences with clairvoyant individuals. These facts prove that even in individual cases which have no common denominator and rank as "curiosities" there are certain regularities and therefore constant factors, from which we must conclude that our narrower conception of synchronicity is probably too narrow and really needs expanding. I incline in fact to the view that synchronicity in the narrow sense is only a particular instance of general acausal orderedness – that, namely, of the equivalence of psychic and physical processes where the observer is in the fortunate position of being able to recognize the *tertium comparationis*. But as soon as he perceives the archetypal background he is tempted to trace the mutual assimilation of independent psychic and physical processes back to a (causal) effect of the archetype, and thus to overlook the fact that they are merely contingent. This danger is avoided if one regards synchronicity as a special instance of general acausal orderedness. In this way we also avoid multiplying our principles of explanation illegitimately, for the archetype is the introspectively recognizable form of *a priori* psychic orderedness. If an external synchronistic process now associates itself with it, it falls into the same basic pattern – in other words, it too is "ordered." This form of orderedness differs from that of the properties of natural numbers or the discontinuities of physics in that the latter have existed from eternity and occur regularly, whereas the forms of psychic orderedness are *acts of creation in time.* That, incidentally, is precisely why I have stressed the element of time as being characteristic of these phenomena and called them *synchronistic*.

967 Synchronicity is no more baffling or mysterious than the discontinuities of physics. It is only the ingrained belief in the sovereign power of causality that creates intellectual difficulties and makes it appear unthinkable that causeless events exist or could ever occur. But if they do, then we must regard them as *creative acts*, as the continuous creation[5] of a pattern than exists from all eternity, repeats itself sporadically, and is not derivable from any known antecedents . . .

968 For these reasons it seems to me necessary to introduce, alongside space, time, and causality, a category which not only enables us to understand synchronistic phenomena as a special class of natural events, but also takes the contingent partly as a universal factor existing from all eternity, and partly as the sum of countless individual acts of creation occurring in time.

From: "To Stephen Abrams, 21 October 1957," *Letters II*

We conclude therefore that we have to expect a factor in the psyche that is not subject to the laws of space and time, as it is on the contrary capable of suppressing them to a certain extent. In other words: this factor is expected to manifest the qualities of time-and spacelessness, i.e., "eternity" and "ubiquity." Psychological experience knows of such a factor; it is what I call the archetype, which is ubiquitous in space and time, of course relatively speaking. It is a structural element of the psyche we find everywhere and at all times; and it is that in which all individual psyches are identical with each other, and where they function as if they were the one undivided Psyche the ancients called *anima mundi* or the *psyche tou kosmou*[6]. . . . [T]here is no outside to the collective psyche. In our ordinary mind we are in the worlds of space and time and within the separate individual psyche. In the state of the archetype we are in the collective psyche, in a world-system whose space-time categories are relatively or absolutely abolished. . . .

I think you are correct in assuming that synchronicity, although in practice a rare phenomenon, is an all-pervading factor or principle in the universe, i.e., in the Unus Mundus,[7] where there is no incommensurability between so-called matter and so-called psyche. Here one gets into deep waters, at least I myself must confess that I am far from having sounded these abysmal depths.

In this connection I have always come upon the enigma of the *natural number*. I have a distinct feeling that Number is a key to the mystery, since it is just as much discovered as it is invented. It is a quantity as well as meaning.

From: Mysterium Coniunctionis (*CW* 14), par. 662

662 If mandala symbolism is the psychological equivalent of the *unus mundus*, then synchronicity is its parapsychological equivalent. . . . Everything that happens, however, happens in the same "one world" and is a part of it. For this reason events must possess an *a priori* aspect of unity. . . . This [synchronistic] principle suggests that there is an inter-connection or unity of causally unrelated events, and thus postulates a unitary aspect of being which can be very well described as the *unus mundus*.

From: Mysterium Coniunctionis (*CW* 14), pars. 767–769

767 Undoubtedly the idea of the *unus mundus* is founded on the assumption that the multiplicity of the empirical world rests on an underlying unity, and that not two or more fundamentally different worlds exist side by side or are mingled with one another. Rather, everything divided and different belongs to one and the same world, which is not the world of sense but a postulate whose probability is vouched for by the fact that until now no one has been able to discover a world in which the known laws of nature are invalid. That even the psychic world, which is so extraordinarily different from the physical world, does not have its roots outside the one cosmos is evident from the undeniable fact that causal connections exist between the psyche and the body which point to their underlying unitary nature.

768 All that *is* is not encompassed by our knowledge, so that we are not in a position to make any statements about its total nature. Microphysics is feeling its way into the unknown side of matter, just as complex psychology is pushing

forward into the unknown side of the psyche. Both lines of investigation have yielded findings which can be conceived only by means of antinomies, and both have developed concepts which display remarkable analogies. If this trend should become more pronounced in the future, the hypothesis of the unity of their subject-matters would gain in probability. Of course there is little or no hope that the unitary Being can ever be conceived, since our powers of thought and language permit only of antimonian statements. But this much we do know beyond all doubt, that empirical reality has a transcendental background – a fact which, as Sir James Jeans has shown, can be expressed by Plato's parable of the cave. The common background of microphysics and depth psychology is as much physical as psychic and therefore neither, but rather a third thing, a neutral nature which can a most be grasped in hints since its essence is transcendental.

769 The background of our empirical world thus appears to be in fact a *unus mundus*. This is at least a probable hypothesis which satisfies the fundamental tenet of scientific theory: "Explanatory principles are not to be multiplied beyond the necessary." The transcendental psychophysical background corresponds to a "potential world" in so far as all those conditions which determine the form of empirical phenomena are inherent in it. This obviously holds good as much for physics as for psychology, or, to be more precise, for macrophysics as much as for the psychology of consciousness.

NOTES

1 Cf. Dr. H., 30 Aug. 51, n. 5 [KLG: In *Letters II*].

2 I must again stress the possibility that the relation between body and soul may yet be understood as a synchronistic one. Should this conjecture ever be proved, my present view that synchronicity is a relatively rare phenomenon would have to be corrected. Cf. C. A. Meier's observations in *Zeitgemässe Probleme der Traumforschung*, p. 22.

3 In view of the possibility that synchronicity is not only a psychophysical phenomenon but might also occur without the participation of human psyche, I should like to point out that in this case we should have to speak not of *meaning* but of equivalence or conformity.

4 "*ὁ θεὸς ἀριθμητίζει.*" But in a letter of 1830 Gauss says: "We must in all humility admit that if number is merely a product of our mind, space has a reality outside our mind." (Leopold Kronecker, *Über den Zahlenbegriff*, in his *Werke*, III, p. 252.) Hermann Weyl likewise takes number as a product of reason. ("Wissenschaft als symbolische Konstruktion des Menschen," p. 375). Markus Fierz, on the other hand, inclines more to the Platonic idea. ("Zur physikalischen Erkenntnis," p. 434.)

5 Continuous creation is to be thought of not only as a series of successive acts of creation, but also as the eternal presence of the *one* creative act, in the sense that God "was always the Father and always generated the Son" (Origen, *De principiis*, I, 2, 3), or that he is the "eternal Creator of minds" (Augustine, *Confessions*, XI, 31, trans. F. J. Sheed, p. 232). God is contained in his own creation, "nor does he stand in need of his own works, as if he had place in them where he might abide; but endures in his own eternity, where he abides and creates whatever pleases him, both in heaven and earth" (Augustine, on Ps. 113: 14, in *Expositions on the Book of Psalms*). What happens successively in time is simultaneous in the mind of God: "An immutable order binds mutable things into a pattern, and in this order things which are not simultaneous in time exist simultaneously outside time" (Prosper of Aquitaine, *Sententiae ex Augustino delibatae*, XLI [Migne,

P.L., LI, col. 433]). "Temporal succession is without time in the eternal wisdom of God." (LVII [Migne, col. 455]). Before the Creation there was no time – time only began with created things: "Rather did time arise from the created than the created from time" (CCLXXX [Migne, col. 468]). "There was no time before time, but time was created together with the world" (Anon, *De triplici habitaculo*, VI [Migne, *P.L.*, XL, col. 995]).

6 = cosmic psyche.

7 Cf. Anon, 2 Jan 57, n. 1. [KLG: According to Jung, the *unus mundus* is the "original, non-differentiated unity of the world or of Being" (Jung, *Mysterium Coniunctionis*, par. 660).]

Appendix

Gret Baumann-Jung

INTRODUCTION

Jung's second daughter, Gret Baumann-Jung, began studying astrology when she was sixteen and became a highly respected practitioner as well as lecturer on the subject at the Jung Institute in Zürich.[1] In addition, she both provided the initial idea for, and worked on, the astrological experiment by which Jung endeavoured to test his theory on synchronicities or acausal connections.[2] The results of that experiment are documented and discussed in his essay "Synchronicity" (1952).

Her essay on her father's horoscope is an early example of a depth psychological approach to astrology. She articulates this orientation in the opening of her essay with her aim to "illustrate how intensively *we experience the world according to the position of our planets*, which, as it were, represent the archetypal structure."[3] Thus, she relied on Jung's descriptions of his life experiences as shared in *Memories, Dreams, Reflections* and demonstrated how the symbolism of his birth chart and the planetary transits bore a meaningful correspondence to his biographical experiences, revealing the archetypal forces in his life.

Safron Rossi

NOTES

1 Bair, *Jung: A Biography*, p. 318, note 11.
2 Ibid., p. 549.
3 Baumann-Jung, "Some Reflections on the Horoscope of C. G. Jung," p. 35.

BIBLIOGRAPHY

Bair, Deirdre. *Jung: A Biography*. Boston, MA: Little, Brown and Company, 2003.

Baumann-Jung, Gret. "Some Reflections on the Horoscope of C. G. Jung." *Spring: An Annual of Archetypal Psychology and Jungian Thought* (1975): pp. 35–55.

Appendix

Gret Baumann-Jung, "Some Reflections on the Horoscope of C. G. Jung" *Spring* (1975), 35–55[1]

This is not to present a detailed reading of my father's horoscope,[2] but I would like to show, by drawing parallels between his horoscope and his autobiography, how deeply the cosmic imprint marks us, that we experience the world accordingly, and that our activity bears an archetypal stamp.

First I would like to illustrate how intensively *we experience the world according to the position of our planets*, which, as it were, represent the archetypal structure.

It is known that a child projects the archetypes, especially the mother and father archetypes, onto his parents. The Moon and Venus are projected onto the mother. One experiences the mother in a positive or negative manner in accordance with the condition of these planets in the birth chart.

In my father's chart, the Moon is in Taurus, thus feminine, fixed, and stable in the earth sign. Venus is in Cancer, a water, feeling sign. Let us hear how he expresses himself about his mother:

> . . . she was somehow rooted in deep, invisible ground [Moon in earthy Taurus], though it never appeared to me as confidence in her Christian faith [Taurus is connected more with nature than with logos]. For me it was somehow connected with animals, trees, mountains, meadows, and running water [these corresponding with Venus in Cancer], all of which contrasted most strangely with her Christian surface and her conventional assertions of faith. This background corresponded so well to my own attitude that it caused me no uneasiness; on the contrary, it gave me a sense of security and the conviction that here was solid ground on which one could stand.[3]

Further:

> My mother was a very good mother to me [experienced through his Moon sextile Venus]. She had a hearty animal warmth [that is the Moon in Taurus. The way I remember my grandmother, she must have had a Taurus Ascendant] . . . she was most companionable and pleasant. She was very stout, and a ready listener [with Venus in Cancer one listens to people as well as to music]. She also liked to talk, and her chatter was like the gay plashing of a fountain. She had a decided literary gift [Venus conjunct Mercury], as well as taste and

Horoscope of C.G. Jung

Born: 7.32 p.m., 26.July 1875 at Kesswil Thurgau

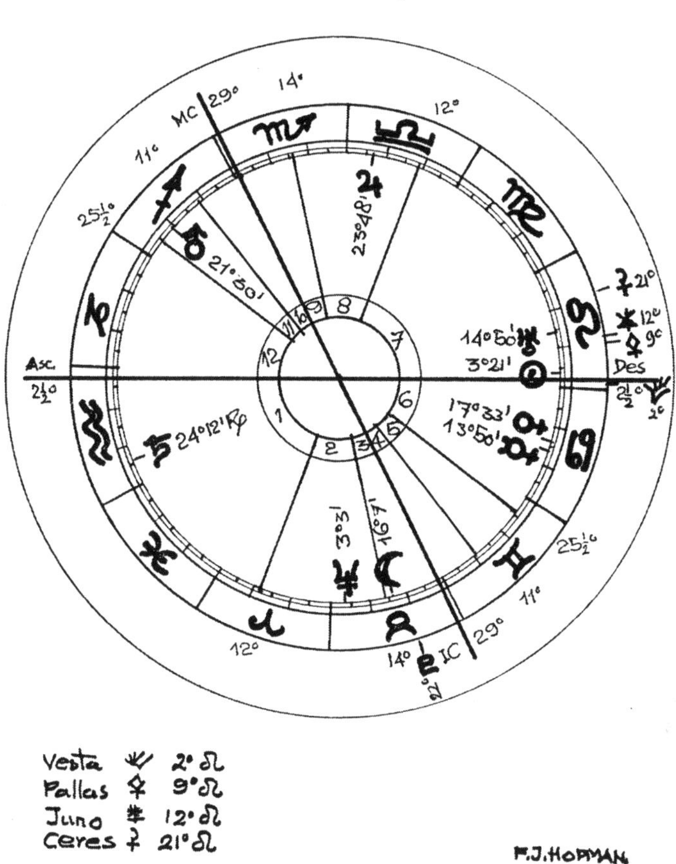

Figure A.1 C.G. Jung's birth chart

Source: Reproduced from *Spring* (1975).

> depth [because his Moon is in the third house, the house of talents, he must have seen her like that; i.e., he himself had a most talented anima].[4]

"But this quality," writes Jung, "never properly emerged" (the Moon being threatened by Pluto; i.e., the unconscious held her):

> it remained hidden beneath the semblance of a kindly, fat old woman, extremely hospitable [Venus in Cancer], and possessor of a great sense of

> humor. She held all the conventional opinions a person was obliged to have, but then her unconscious personality would suddenly put in an appearance. That personality was unexpectedly powerful: a sombre, imposing figure [seen through his Moon conjunct Pluto; with the latter the whole potential of the unconscious is connected] possessed of unassailable authority – and no bones about it. I was sure that she consisted of two personalities, one innocuous and human, the other uncanny. This other emerged only now and then, but each time it was unexpected and frightening.[5]

The unexpected and frightening comes from the square between Uranus and the Moon. Uranus always brings the unexpected, and therefore frightens. Later I shall come back to this in greater detail.

The female planets also indicate what we love. With the Moon in Taurus, my father was a great nature lover. We also sense his Venus in Cancer (water) in his writing; for instance in his fascination with Lake Constance when his mother took him there as a child. "At that time the idea became fixed in my mind that I must live near a lake; without water, I thought, nobody could live it all."[6] Now this water – Venus rules the fourth house (because Venus rules Taurus), which tells us something about his home and property. Thus he built both his houses on a lake.

The father archetype is constituted by the Sun, Jupiter, and Saturn. In Jung's chart, the Sun has no good aspects, but only a square from Neptune which, to say the least, is an element of uncertainty in the relationship to the father. Neptune makes things unreal.

> At that time, too, there arose in me profound doubts about everything my father said . . . what he said sounded stale and hollow, like a tale told by someone who knows it only by hearsay and cannot quite believe it himself.[7]

Now that does not mean that the faults were all with the father. Another child in the same family, with a good Sun, would have heard and understood things very differently. For instance, my sister and I experienced our parents completely differently, and partly heard opposite facts.

There is one father planet, namely Jupiter, in the eighth house, the house of death. Jupiter, as supreme God of heaven, is connected with religion. If a child has Jupiter in the eighth house, the father cannot, with the best intentions, appease its religious needs. This position of Jupiter also contains the possibility that the father could not evolve properly and had to die young. Planets in the eighth house compel one to turn to the unconscious, to go through the house of "dying and becoming," in order to find the archetype and bring it to life.

> With my father it was quite different. I would have liked to lay my religious difficulties before him and asked him for advice, but I did not do so because it seemed to me that I knew in advance what he would be obliged to reply out of respect for his office.[8]

"Out of respect for his office." This characteristic of his father, which corresponds to Saturn, must be obvious to the son, as his Saturn is located in the first house, the house of the ego. In keeping with the splendid Jupiter trine Saturn, which gave Jung a sense of duty and reliability, he could write, "I admired my father's honesty," but in accordance with this Sun square Neptune, which leads to disappointments, he is moved to add: "but on the other hand I was profoundly disappointed and said to myself, 'there we have it; they know nothing about it and don't give it a thought'."[9]

To Jupiter in the eighth house, we can also credit the following passage:

> Later, when I was 18 years old I had many discussions with my father, always with the secret hope of being able to let him know about the miracle of grace [Jupiter] and thereby help to mitigate his pangs of conscience. I was convinced that if he fulfilled the will of God everything would turn out for the best. But our discussions invariably came to an unsatisfactory end. They irritated him, and saddened him. "Oh, nonsense," he was in the habit of saying, "you always want to think. One ought not to think, but believe." I would think, "No, one must experience and know," but he would say, "Give me this belief," whereupon he would shrug and turn resignedly away.[10]

This is how a son with his Sun square Neptune not only is disillusioned by his father but, in fact, himself deludes the father by withholding his thoughts from him.

It is also interesting that in Jung's relation to Freud and his work, the religious aspect was absent. Due to the position of Jupiter in the house of death, this religious aspect seldom appeared. I, at least, always thought my father was the most ungodly man and therefore I did not dare to pray any more for fear it might displease him. In my case, Jupiter is not the house of death, but in that of prison, which is not much better. It is only from my father's books that I learned he obviously had been a religious man.

"I began making friendships, mostly with shy boys of simple origins."[11] Because Jupiter rules the house of friendship, when he is in the house of death one has few or retiring friends. In the third house, we see the relations of everyday life; its ruler, Venus, is in the sixth house, the house of service, connected with inferiors. That is why Jung's friends were of modest origins.

The following passage is significant for Mars in Sagittarius, on the cusp (within 4 degrees) of the twelfth house, the house of prisons, secrets, and seclusion. Mars has to do with our activity. Here this gets a religious coloring through Sagittarius, and something secretive because of being in the twelfth house.

> I also recall from this period (seven to nine) that I was fond of playing with fire [fiery Mars]. In our garden there was an old wall built of large blocks of stone, the interstices of which made interesting caves. I used to tend a little fire in one of these caves, with other children helping me; a fire that had to burn forever and therefore had to be constantly maintained by our united efforts, which consisted in gathering the necessary wood. No one but myself was allowed to attend this fire. Others could light other fires in other caves, but these fires were profane and did not concern me. My fire alone was living and had an unmistakable aura of sanctity.[12]

In later life as well, my father loved to play with little fires. We also recognize his Mars in the twelfth house on account of his writing in secluded rooms and in the passion with which he worked. Activity must have meaning, so to speak, higher meaning, indicated by Mars in Sagittarius.

The secret about the carved manikin in the stone he hid in the attic[13] also belongs here, namely to Jupiter in the house of death and the secretiveness of Mars in the house of seclusion.

* * *

The original impulse for this article came to me as I puzzled over my father's letter of December 19, 1947, to Father Victor White.

> You remember my unsympathetic dream figure of the dry Jesuit logician [Saturn]? Not very long after I wrote to you, I simply had to write a new essay I did not know about what. It occurred to me I should discuss some of the finer points about anima, animus, shadow [subjects belonging to the seventh house, the you, the Du within us as well as without], and last but not least the self. I was against it, because I wanted to rest my head. Lately I had suffered from severe sleeplessness and I wanted to keep away from all mental exertions. In spite of everything, I felt forced [Saturn] to write on blindly, not seeing at all what I was driving at. Only after I had written about 25 pages in folio, it began to dawn on me that Christ – not the man but the divine being – was my secret goal. It came to me as a shock, as I felt utterly unequal to such a task. A dream told me that my small fishing boat had been sunk and that a giant (whom I knew from a dream about 30 years ago) had provided me with a new, beautiful seagoing craft about twice the size of my former boat. Then I knew – nothing doing! I had to go on.

Here you can sense his obedience. The dream of 30 years ago reads:

> A large ocean liner should be pulled to the pier by a little horse. A hardly feasible task. At this moment a giant appeared, and without further ado slayed the little horse and himself pulled the steamer into port.[14]

At that time my father was working on *Psychological Types*. It suddenly struck me that the giant who reappeared after 30 years must be Saturn. Saturn, the planet of fate, has a rotation through the zodiac of 29 1/2 years. Under its influence we must carry additional burdens, and lucky we are if we can carry these burdens as work instead of becoming ill. Saturn is not only a slow, lethargic planet, it also promotes civilization.

In mythology the child-devouring Kronos was dethroned by his son Zeus. Zeus-Jupiter wants us not to limit ourselves in a saturnine manner but to evolve freely in accordance with the laws of our own uniqueness. Under the rulership of Jupiter, Saturn becomes a peaceful agricultural and culture-promoting God.

In my father's horoscope, Mercury and Venus are in the house of service. Close by, in the seventh house, are the Sun and Uranus as well as all the female planetoids.[15] With Saturn's transit occurring every 29 1/2 years, its passage through these houses become very noticeable for a period of about 2 1/2 years. Especially Mercury, the first planet affected, would have burdened my father with a heavy task or an illness, as that planet is the ruler of the house of work and illness (Gemini[16]).

I asked myself what happened astrologically in 1947 when my father felt compelled to write his book *Aion*. Actually it had already started in 1945, at the time when transiting Saturn went over natal Mercury and Venus. The effect of this is shown in my father's letter of February 13, 1946, to Father White:

> There are certain reasons, however, that may excuse my long silence. For a number of weeks I felt very low on account of the grippe in the head and in the intestines and besides this ailment I was caught in the grips of a book that eats me alive if I don't write it.

This clearly shows the influence of Saturn: illness and work, and even its devouring nature. Saturn, however, becomes a helpful giant if one does not refuse the burden of work.

At the beginning of July, 1945, when the pressure of work began, transiting Uranus, the creative planet, was also in exact sextile to natal Uranus at 14° 50′ Gemini. Transiting Saturn was exactly conjunct natal Mercury and sextile natal Pluto, as well as conjunct Pallas. Up until the letter of December 19 to Father White, Saturn was passing over natal Mercury, Sun, and Uranus, and all the planetoids in the seventh house. The seventh house is opposite the first house, the house of the ego. It is the "other" (or the "thou"), within and without. No wonder my father was obliged to write about the shadow, anima, and animus. Significantly, all for female planetoids – Ceres, Pallas, Juno, and Vesta – occupy my father's house of partnership and contributed to his being constantly surrounded by women.

The giant dream of about 30 years earlier coincided with the Saturn transit over these planets. Transiting Saturn was conjunct natal Sun in July, 1917. At that time my father was working on *Psychological Types*. Simultaneously, creative Uranus was over natal Saturn and allowed the ego to be particularly productive.

Naturally I asked myself what happened at the time of the first Saturn transit. I found the following:

> My twelfth year was indeed a fateful one for me [anything fateful, of course, reminds us of Saturn]. One day in the early summer of 1887 [when transiting Saturn was exactly on Mercury, ruler of the house of illness] I was standing in the cathedral square, waiting for a classmate who went home by the same route as myself. It was twelve o'clock, in the morning classes were over. Suddenly another boy gave me a shove [this sudden, unexpected shove came from Uranus, which in early summer 1887 had a sesqui-square[17] to Saturn, one of the rulers of the chart] that knocked me off my feet. I fell, striking my head against the curbstone so hard that I almost lost consciousness. For about half an hour afterward I was a little dazed. At the moment I felt the blow the thought flashed [Uranus!] through my mind: "now you won't have to go to school anymore." I was only half unconscious, but I remained there are few

> moments longer than was strictly necessary, chiefly in order to avenge myself on my assailant. Then people picked me up and took me to a house nearby, where two elderly spinster aunts lived. From then on I began to have fainting spells whenever I had to return to school, and whenever my parents sent me to doing my homework. For more than six months I stayed away from school, and for me that was a picnic. I was free, could dream for hours, be anywhere I liked, in the woods or by the water, or draw.[18]

Further on, he writes that he distanced himself from the world and dreamt away his time. He had vague presentiments of fleeing from himself. "One doctor thought I had epilepsy. I knew what epileptic fits were like and I inwardly laughed at such nonsense. My parents became more worried than ever."[19]

At that time, in 1887, not only was Saturn moving through his house of illness, but Neptune, planet responsible for pretence, hysteria, and daydreaming, made an exact semi-square[20] to natal Mercury, ruler of the house of illness, which tends to diseases with a psychic background.

The houses of the natal horoscope can be progressed as if four minutes make a year; i.e., for each year of life, four minutes are added to the time of birth. In 1887, progressed Pluto had come to be semi-square to the cusp of the sixth house, thereby causing a spate of incidents. Simultaneously (according to the "day for a year" method of calculating progressions), there was a progressed square from Saturn to Pluto exact to the second. A Saturn-Pluto square in the birth chart indicates an inborn tendency for the unconscious to break through the conscious limits. At the same time, transiting Pluto (3° Gemini) formed an exact sextile to the Sun at 3° Leo, so that consciousness could integrate the invasion from the unconscious. One bit of devilry was to occur nevertheless. "One fine summer day that same year," writes my father, "I came out of school at noon and went to the cathedral square."[21]

Then follows the story where he was beset by an impertinent thought (Pluto) which he only dared to think after an intense altercation with God.

> I gathered all my courage, as though I were about to leap forthwith into hell-fire [Pluto], and let the thought come. I saw before me the cathedral, the blue sky. God sits on His golden throne, high above the world – and from under the throne an enormous turd falls upon the sparkly new roof, shatters it, and breaks the walls of the cathedral asunder.[22]

That was the effect of Pluto in semi-square to natal Venus, ruler of the third house, from which we read the conscious attitudes. He also writes about the anxiety of his parents:

> And one day a friend called on my father. They were sitting in the garden and I hid behind a shrub, for I was possessed of an insatiable curiosity. I heard the visitor saying to my father, "and how is your son?" "Ah, that's a sad business," my father replied. "The doctors no longer know what is wrong with him. They think it may be epilepsy. It would be dreadful if he were incurable. I have lost what little I had, and what will become of the boy if he cannot earn his own living?"

I was thunderstruck. This was the collision with reality. "Why, then I must get to work!" I thought suddenly.

From that moment on I became a serious child.[23]

"They were sitting in the garden . . ." it must therefore have been early autumn, a time when one can still sit outside. The neurosis which had started early in summer had already lasted a few months. In September, 1887, Saturn, the planet of reality, stood on my father's Sun. That was the "collision with reality."

The following experience is connected with the same transit:

> I had another important experience at about this time. I was taking the long road to school from Klein-Hüningen, where we lived, to Basel, when suddenly for a single moment I had the overwhelming impression of having just emerged from a dense cloud. I knew all at once: now I am *myself*! It was as if a wall of mist were at my back, and behind that wall there was not yet an "I." But at this moment *I came upon myself*. Previously I had existed too, but everything had merely happened to me. Now I happened to myself. Now I knew: I am myself now, now I exist.[24]

So much, then, for the first transit of Saturn over the natal Sun.

Uranus has a cycle of 84 years. My experience is that Uranus especially constellates the unconscious and can force a completely new conscious attitude, particularly during a transit over the Ascendant or Sun. This is often accompanied by dramatic or absurd events and synchronicities. At such times people can come completely unhinged and seek astrological advice, hoping thereby to straighten out their derangement. The Greeks venerated in Uranus that force in nature that apparently creates out of nothing. He is the first Creator and inventor of lightning. Evidently, according to the "big bang" theory, he has been around since the beginning, when with a great bolt of lightning our world is supposed to have come into existence. From a psychological point of view, he corresponds to intuition. Personified in fairytales you can find him as the faithful John, in the Bible as John the Baptist, as the disciple John and the apocalyptic John.

As an illustration I would like to mention a dream I had when Uranus was on my Ascendant: I was sitting in a church in which, at certain times, the miracle-working picture came into action. It depicted the 12 apostles. The miracle commenced with a terrific shock – lightning darted out of the picture and the apostle John stepped out. One had to put into his hands whatever one was carrying, and make a solemn tour round the church, past the picture.

John the Baptist appears in the gospel where it is said: "and the light shineth in the darkness and the darkness apprehends it not. There came a man sent from God, whose name was John. The same came for witness that he might bear witness of the light."

This is how Uranus functions. Because of that we have to take him, our intuition, seriously, since he may connect us with the Self. Not taking Uranus seriously may cause him to plague us with such things as hay fever and other allergies.

Saturn and Uranus are the rulers of Aquarius, my father's rising sign. Accordingly his horoscope has two rulers. Saturn is in the first house, where the conscious ego is formed. Uranus is on the opposite side of the chart, in the seventh house, the house of partnership. The effect of these two planets was evident to my father:

> The play and counterplay between personalities No. 1 and No. 2 [Saturn and Uranus], which has run through my whole life, has nothing to do with a "split" or dissociation in the ordinary medical sense. On the contrary, it is played out in every individual [more or less, I would like to add]. In my life No. 2 [Uranus, the inner John] has been of prime importance and I have always tried to make room for anything that wanted to come to me from within. He is a typical figure but he is perceived only by the very few. Most people's conscious understanding is not sufficient to realize that he is also what they are.[25]

That is because Uranus corresponds more to the unconscious. At my father's birth, Saturn was retrograde at 24° Aquarius and Uranus direct 14° 50′ Leo. Progressed according to the rule one day equals one year, both rulers of the horoscope approached exact opposition. The moment this became exact, my father died. Probably the aged body could not take such inner tension anymore.

The dream of December 18–19, 1947, as told by my father to Father White in the December 19 letter, also illumines the nature of Uranus:

> Last night I dreamt of at least 3 Catholic priests who are quite friendly and one of them had a remarkable library. I was the whole time under a sort of military order and I had to sleep in the barracks. There was a scarcity of beds, so the two men had to share one bed. My partner [my father calls him *senex venerabilis* in a letter to Father White on January 30, 1948] had already gone to bed. The bed was very clean, white, and fresh and he was a most venerable looking, very old man with white locks and a long flowing white beard. He offered me graciously one half of the bed and I woke up when I was just slipping into it.

In my experience Uranus repeatedly appears as the venerable wise old man with a white beard. On the day this was dreamt, Uranus was in a 24° Gemini and completed a grand airy trine with natal Saturn and Jupiter. One might say that No. 1 personality made a harmonious visit to No. 2. The simultaneous trine of transiting Uranus to natal Jupiter underlines the religious significance. On the objective level one feels how the relationship with Father White must have been most stimulating for my father's religious thinking.

Moreover, transiting Pluto, who connects one with the collective unconscious, stood just near natal Uranus. Consequently a connection must have been made between No. 2 personality and the collective unconscious.

Continuing with the effects of Uranus, we read: "during the summer holidays, however, something happened that was destined to influence me profoundly."[26]

There follows the dramatic account of the detonating table and the exploding knife. During the summer holidays of 1898, from July until roughly September 10, transiting Uranus stood exactly at my father's MC,[27] at 29° Scorpio. The transit of Uranus over the Zenith is usually accompanied by a sudden, unexpected change in one's job. As a result of these events my father decided to go in for psychiatry. That these Uranus incidents were connected with the tremendous explosive effect may be accounted for by the fact that transiting Pluto was at 14° 50′ Gemini, therefore in exact sextile to natal Uranus, No. 2 personality. Obviously it was of tremendous importance that my father should find his way to psychiatry.

Now I would like to give some details about Pluto, who also plays an important role in my father's horoscope. Usually astrologers say too little about Pluto: for instance, that he signifies transformation and has to do with sub- and superhuman events. He was discovered (1930) at a time when Nazism was rising, and the discovery of the atom bomb belongs to him. In fact the atom bomb contains Plutonium, an element that can change matter into energy. Pluto has enormous strength; in his negative form he also represents destructive forces. In our case of the exploding table and knife this force ultimately had a positive effect, on account of the sextile to Uranus. This enabled my father to accept the hint he received and to make up his mind in favor of his true occupation.

In my father's chart we find Pluto in the third house, called Fratres (three or four of his brothers and sisters died soon after birth). The third house has to do with our conscious attitudes, our inborn mentality, our talents and creative power. Thus he was born with a strong spiritual, creative power. Moreover, Pluto is in Taurus, which is an earthy sign signifies creation from matter. My father once dreamt Pluto to be a sculptor (statistically Taurus belongs to the chart of sculptors) and that in fact he was the devil. It was fascinating to observe how my father would fashion his thoughts and matter, so to speak, by sculpting, woodcarving, building towers, or canalizing brooks.

In mythology Pluto represents Hades, who stole Persephone and desired her to remain with him during one third of the year. According to Kerényi, the unspoken mystery in Eleusis consisted of a birth in the underworld, the birth of Dionysos. Already in the fifth century B.C. Heraclitus said: "If this procession had not been in the honor of Dionysos and the phallus-song sung for him, it would have been a very impudent act. However, Hades and Dionysus, for whom these feasts are celebrated, are one and the same."

In nature it is Demeter, the corn-goddess, who produces the grain. Persephone corresponds to the seed absorbed by the earth. It is there that the transformation to new life and growth takes place. This occurrence is in direct relation to Pluto. Unintentionally one is reminded of *John 12:24*: "Except a corn of wheat fall into the earth and die it abideth alone, but if it die, bringeth forth much fruit." This saying also reminds us of the "dying and becoming" of Goethe, of introversion and the temporary descent into one's own depths in order that life may renew itself. If we do not do that, Pluto takes an awful revenge by banning us to dungeons of dark depression or, concretely, by blasting us into the underworld with his weapon the atom bomb.

There is also the parallel – Pluto, Dionysus, Christ – because Christ too is a transformer. Just as Dionysos, and his metamorphosis of the grape vine could change water into wine, so could Christ, at the marriage feast at Kana, effect this transformation.

Perhaps it is a little bold to assert that Pluto corresponds to at least some aspects of Christ. But let's look again at the letter of December 19, 1947 to Father White:

> Lately I had suffered from severe sleeplessness and I wanted to keep away from all mental exertions. In spite of everything, I felt forced [this reminds us of the transit of Saturn over the Sun] to write on blindly, not seeing at all what I was driving at. Only after I had written about 25 pages in folio, it began to dawn on me that Christ – not the man but the divine being – was my secret goal.

At this time transiting Pluto – moving only about 1° a year – stood exactly on natal Uranus, the No. 2 personality of my father. This conjunction was exact to the minute at the end of October, 1947, and again, because of retrogression, on December 9; thereafter once again in the middle of August, 1948. The book *Aion* appeared in 1951, when incidentally progressed Uranus arrived at 19° Leo.

Returning to my father's autobiography, we read: "On 10th December, 1900, I took up my post as assistant at the Burghölzli Mental Hospital, Zürich."[28]

On that day Mercury, the ruler of the house of work, came to the M.C., i.e., to the cusp of the house of career. When in 1903–04 the progressed Sun moved from Leo to Virgo (ruled by Mercury), my father started on his proper scientific work, his association experiments. He writes:

> As early as 1900 I had read Freud's *The Interpretation of Dreams*. I had laid the book aside, at the time, because I did not yet grasp it. At the age of 25 I lacked the experience to appreciate Freud's theories. Such experience did not come until later. In 1903 I once more took up *The Interpretation of Dreams* and discovered how it all linked up with my own ideas.[29]

In 1900, transiting Uranus (with a cycle of 84 years) came to the cusp of the 11th house, the house of friendship. Moreover, an autumn 1903 transiting Uranus formed an exact sextile to natal Saturn, one of the rulers of the horoscope, and to natal Jupiter who, as ruler of Sagittarius, governs the 11th house.

In 1906, at the time of the initial correspondence between Freud and Jung, transiting Jupiter, the auspicious planet, came to an exact trine to natal Saturn and Jupiter, which would have favored the transference of a positive father-image. As we know, it did not last. "The year 1909," writes Jung, "proved decisive for our relationship."[30] In 1909 transiting Saturn formed an evil square to natal Venus, giving rise to difference of opinion. Moreover, the progressed Ascendant had just reached 0° Aries and the progressed M.C. was at 0° Capricorn. The result was that my father could not subordinate himself any longer but had to become independent. In a letter written to Jung on April 16, 1909, Freud formulated the situation thus:

> . . . It is remarkable that on the same evening that I formally adopted you as an eldest son, anointing you was my successor and Crown Prince – *in partibus infidelium* – that then and there you should have divested me of my paternal dignity . . .[31]

Yet another astrological event took place in 1909. Transiting Pluto had arrived to 24° Gemini, hence in good aspect to natal Saturn, carrier of the ego. That signifies a time when the ego can establish positive relations to the collective unconscious. Of course, not everybody would react similarly so this aspect. But my father, through his Pluto conjunct Moon, had a door open, so to speak, to the collective unconscious. He writes:

> . . . Freud was able to interpret the dreams I was then having only incompletely or not at all. They were dreams with collective contents, containing a great deal of symbolic material. One in particular was important to me, for it led me for the first time to the concept of the "collective unconscious . . ."[32]

The dream:

> I was in a house I did not know, which had two stories. It was "my house." I found myself in the upper story, were there was a kind of salon furnished with fine old pieces in rococo style. On the walls hung a number of precious old paintings. I wondered that this should be my house, and thought, "Not bad." But then it occurred to me that I did not know what the lower floor looked like. Descending the stairs, I reached the ground floor. There everything was much older, and I realize that this part of the house must date from about the fifteenth or sixteenth century. The furnishings were medieval; the floors were of red brick. Everywhere it was rather dark. I went from one room to another thinking, now I really must explore the whole house. I came upon a heavy door, and opened it. Beyond it, I discovered a stone stairway that led down into the cellar. Descending again, I found myself in a beautifully vaulted room which looked exceedingly ancient.[33]

He recognized that the walls dated from Roman times. However, he descended still further and there discovered to very ancient, decomposed skulls. Then he awoke.

Here you see how Pluto is connected with the entire collective unconscious potential. The separation from Freud occurred in 1912, when transiting Saturn moved through the third house (over the Moon conjunct Pluto), which is a relationship house, and led to the break. With Uranus transits, new contents force their way into consciousness without yet being fully comprehended. So consciousness must grow and this process is usually accompanied by synchronicity and all sorts of absurd incidents, in the inner as well as in the outer world. When Uranus goes over our Ascendant we feel most insecure, all our previous concepts seem to have lost validity. Nothing tallies any longer. Many people fear they might crack up.

Regarding this transit my father writes:

> After the parting of the ways with Freud, a period of inner uncertainty began for me. It would be no exaggeration to call it a state of disorientation. I felt totally suspended in mid-air, for I had not yet found my own footing . . . then, around Christmas of 1912, I had a dream.[34]

It was the end of December, 1912, when Uranus stood exactly on father's Ascendant. The dream was about being on a magnificent Italian loggia when suddenly a beautiful white bird, gull or dove settled down and "spoke slowly in a human voice: 'Only in the first hours of the night can I transform myself into a human being, while the male dove is busy with twelve dead'."[35] Jung remarks, "All I knew with any certainty was that the dream indicated an unusual activation of the unconscious."[36]

Here Uranus availed himself of a bird in order to announce himself. For our present state of consciousness this incident, so typical for Uranus, is incomprehensible.

Being retrograde, Uranus remained close to the Ascendant during all of 1913. To help himself during this grievous time, my father resorted to active imagination. This is probably the best one can do during a Uranus transit.

> Towards the autumn of 1913 the pressure which I had felt was in *me* seemed to be moving outwards, as though there were something in the air. The atmosphere actually seemed to me darker than it had been.[37]

During October, 1913, transiting Pluto was an exact semi-square to the Moon, which can make an invasion of the unconscious possible. Pluto corresponds to the collective, in the world as well as in us. The following vision of my father's typifies such a Pluto transit. (During 1917 Pluto continued going backward and forward over this aspect.)

The vision reads:

> I saw a monstrous flood covering all the northern and low-lying lands between the North Sea and the Alps. When it came up to Switzerland I saw that the mountains grew higher and higher to protect our country. I realized that a frightful catastrophe was in progress. I saw the mighty yellow waves, the floating rubble of civilization and the drowned bodies of uncounted thousands. Then the whole sea turned to blood. This vision lasted about one hour. I was perplexed and nauseated, and ashamed of my weakness.[38]

The following experience dates from those days when Uranus was conjunct my father's Ascendant and Pluto was semi-square the Moon:

> It was during Advent of the year 1913 – December 12, to be exact – that I resolved upon the decisive step. I was sitting at my desk once more, thinking over my fears. Then I let myself drop. Suddenly it was as though the ground literally gave way beneath my feet, and I plunged down into dark depths. I could not fend off the feeling of panic. But then, abruptly, at not too great a depth, I landed on my feet in a soft, sticky mass. I felt great relief, although I was apparently in complete darkness.[39]

The vision continues, but what I want to point out is that on that day, fortunately, Saturn, the planet of reality, was exactly sextile to natal Uranus (No. 2 personality). That must have been a great help. Without it my father could have lost his balance.

In July, 1914, transiting Saturn entered the house of work and brought extra burdens, partly caused by the war.

> Very gradually the outlines of an inner change began making their appearance within me. In 1916 I felt an urge to give shape to something. I was compelled

> from within, as it were, to formulate and express what might have been said by Philemon. This was how the *Septem Sermones ad Mortuos* with its peculiar language came into being.[40]

This inner compulsion to formulate was given by Mars, which was transiting natal Mercury during May and June; Mercury has to do with writing and language. These *Sermones* originated partly through the invasion from the unconscious, indicated by the semi-square between transiting Pluto and the Moon, and transiting Saturn over Mercury, giving the possibility to comprehend and formulate.

> Today I can say that I have never lost touch with my initial experiences. All my works, all my creative activity, has come from those initial fantasies and dreams which began in 1912 [with the transit of Uranus over the Ascendant] . . . everything that I accomplished in later life was already contained in them, although at first only in the form of emotions and images.[41]

Much credit for my father's work, then, must go to Uranus, who uses the figure of Philemon, among others, to express himself.

After this grave period, my father reports: "It was only toward the end of the First World War that I gradually began to emerge from the darkness."[42] At the end of the war, in 1918, transiting Uranus came over Saturn, the carrier of the ego, and brought clarity.

> During those years, between 1918 and 1920, I began to understand that the goal of psychic development is the self. There is no linear evolution; there is only a circumambulation of the self. Uniform development exists, at most, only at the beginning; later, everything points toward the center. This insight gave me stability, and gradually my inner peace returned. I knew that in finding the mandala as an expression of the self I had attained what was for me the ultimate. Perhaps someone else knows more, but not I.[43]

Jupiter, the supreme God in heaven, has to do with religion and stimulates us to develop our wholeness. Jupiter arrived in the house of work in the middle of April, 1918, and in 1919 went over Mercury, Venus, Vesta, Sun, Pallas, Juno, and Uranus, and finally, in July, over Ceres. It therefore does not surprise me that my father had to occupy himself with the divine in man. In 1919, transiting Saturn was also in harmony with Jupiter and with Mars, who stands in a Jupiter sign and rules the house of religion.

In 1922 my father bought the land in Bollingen, just when transiting Saturn made an exact sextile to the cusp of the fourth house. The fourth house tells something about the ownership of property. If one acquires real estate under a good Saturn aspect, such possession will endure. However, the fourth house has to do with ancestors as well, and it was my father's wish that Bollingen should remain in possession of the family, so that the ancestral spirits would have a residence. During the summer holidays of 1923, while we did construction work on the tower, transiting Jupiter, carrier of good fortune, was in harmony with Venus, ruler of the fourth house – because Taurus, ruled by Venus, is on the cusp of the fourth – and in autumn 1923, transiting Saturn made a trine to natal Jupiter and Saturn.

I have mentioned that Uranus always brings unexpected and extraordinary incidents. Regarding this we read:

> When we began to build at Bollingen in 1923, my eldest daughter came to see the spot, and explained, "What, you're building here? There are corpses about!" naturally I thought, "Ridiculous! Nothing of the sort!" But when we were constructing the annex four years later, we did come upon a skeleton [8/22/'27]. It lay at a depth of seven feet in the ground. An old rifle bullet was embedded in the elbow. From various indications it seemed evident that the body had been thrown into the graves in an advanced state of decay. It belongs to one of the many dozens of French soldiers who were drowned in the Linth in 1799 and were later washed up on the shores of the upper lake. These men were drowned when the Austrians blew up the bridge of Grynau which the French were storming.[44]

On August 22, 1927, transiting Uranus was to the minute exactly sextile to my father's Ascendant, in fact in the martial sign Aries. Because of this it is really very likely that the skeleton was that of a soldier. Moreover, this Uranus in Aries caused my father to give the soldier a military funeral by shooting thrice over the grave.

* * *

"All my writings," wrote my father, "may be considered tasks imposed from within; their source was a fateful compulsion. What I wrote were things that assailed me from within myself."[45]

It therefore does not surprise me that especially Saturn and Uranus were a help in his literary creations. The following are only a few examples of their influence:

1938–40: *Psychology and Religion*; transiting Saturn trine natal Mars, who stands in the religious sign of Sagittarius and rules the ninth house, the house of religion.
1942: *Paracelsica*; transiting Uranus trine natal Ascendant.
1944: *Psychology and Alchemy*; transiting Saturn trine natal Saturn and natal Jupiter, and opposition natal Mars; transiting Uranus sextile natal Sun.
1946: "Analytical Psychology and Education," "Essays on Current Events," "The Psychology of the Transference"; transiting Saturn conjunct natal Mercury and Venus; transiting Jupiter conjunct natal Jupiter; transiting Uranus sextile natal Uranus.
1948: *Symbolik des Geistes*; transiting Uranus trine natal Saturn and Jupiter.
1955–56: *Mysterium Coniunctionis*; transiting Uranus in the house of partnership; transiting Saturn square natal Saturn. The *progressions* show: progressed Sun trine progressed Uranus and progressed Saturn; progressed Mars trine progressed Pluto; progressed Venus conjunct natal Jupiter and trine natal Saturn. (Unfortunately the year 1955 also brought the sudden death of my mother when Uranus came to the cusp of the

house of marriage, while transiting Saturn was square natal Saturn. Pluto, the Prince of death, had at the time of my mother's operation in spring squared the natal Saturn of my father, and at the moment of her death had arrived over her Moon.)

1951: *Aion* (published); transiting Saturn in Libra, conjunct natal Jupiter.

"Why," I asked myself, "should the 'Answer to Job' have been written with such vehemence?" Incidents occur when two progressed planets make exact aspects. That happens seldom, because the slow-moving planets do not change their original position much. In Jung's 77th year (1952), the square between progressed Venus and Mars was exact, and his progressed Moon was opposite progressed Uranus. Thus both female planets (Anima) were negatively constellated, irritated and had to explode. Moreover, the progressed Ascendant was in sesqui-square to natal Jupiter; i.e., the ego was in conflict with the religious urge.

On January 26, 1944, my father broke his leg and subsequently suffered a stroke. In those days transiting Jupiter was an exact opposition to natal Saturn. The cusp of the progressed house of illness was square natal Mars, and the progressed Ascendant had arrived at 0° Gemini to cause an inner change. Gemini is ruled by Mercury, who has to do with writing. After his illness my father wrote virtually nonstop. Again we see how he was true to his horoscope.

Shortly before his death, as we talked about horoscopes, my father remarked: "The funny thing is that the darned stuff even works after death." And in fact, soon after his death his progressed M.C. made an exact trine with natal Jupiter. At such a moment one can become famous. His recently published *Memories, Dreams, Reflections* became a bestseller. What a pity it did not happen during his lifetime – he would not have complained that nobody read his books.

Recently someone came to me so worked up he could hardly get it out how strongly he felt the presence of my father. He was afraid I would not understand this. This man has Neptune, planet of the medium mystic, the visionary, on his Ascendant at 3 1/2° Cancer. My calculations showed that the progressed Ascendant of my father had arrived at exactly 3 1/2° Cancer. Only then did I realize that this is the degree of my Ascendant as well. Was it because of this that I was moved to occupy myself with my father's horoscope?

To sum up, it can be said that my father was especially influenced to create major works during transits of Saturn and Uranus. What is not visible in his birth chart is that he was someone who absolutely had to fulfill his mission, for the chart says nothing about what we bring into the world with us in our genes, nor does it indicate the quality of the soul which receives its imprint at the moment of the first breath.

NOTES

1 This paper was delivered in German at the Psychological Club Zürich in October 1974. It has been translated into English by F. J. Hoffman, with the editorial assistance of Daryl Sharp. Throughout quotations are taken from Jung's autobiography, *Memories,*

Dreams, Reflections, recorded and edited by Aniela Jaffé, translated from the German by Richard and Clara Winston (New York: Random House, 1961; London: Collins and Routledge & Kegan Paul, 1963). Here, the page numbers cited refer to the American edition. [KLG: Amendments have been made to the formatting of the article for its inclusion in this book. Comments within the square brackets in the text are Gret Baumann-Jung's own.]

2 [SR: There are varying birth times recorded for C. G. Jung. He is most famously recalled for saying that he was born "when the last rays of the setting sun lit the room" which some have calculated to have occurred at 7:41 pm. See Astro Databank entry for C. G. Jung, www.astro.com/astrodatabank (accessed 17 December 2016).]
3 Jung, *Memories, Dreams, Reflections*, p. 90.
4 Ibid., p. 48.
5 Ibid., pp. 48–49.
6 Ibid., p. 7.
7 Ibid., p. 43.
8 Ibid., p. 52.
9 Ibid., p. 53.
10 Ibid., p. 43.
11 Ibid., p. 43.
12 Ibid., pp. 19–20.
13 Ibid., pp. 21–23. For a long discussion of Jung's carved manikin and stone hidden in the attic, see Daniel C. Noel, "Veiled Kabir: C. G. Jung's Phallic Self-Image," *Spring* 1974, Eds.
14 Quoted from note 5 to the letter to Father White, December 19, 1947.
15 [SR: The original drawing of C. G. Jung's horoscope included the four major asteroids: Vesta, Pallas, Juno, and Ceres. It is generally understood that the asteroids correspond to feminine archetypal principles related to the Greek goddesses: Hestia and the sacred, Athena and creative intellectual work, Hera and equality in relationships, and Demeter and nurturing and cycles of time. Hence, they have to do with more refined aspects of feminine consciousness.]
16 [SR: Gemini is not a house but a sign, and in Jung's chart Gemini is the ruler of the fourth and fifth houses. The house of work and illness is the sixth house.]
17 [SR: A sesqui-square is a 135° angle.]
18 Jung, *Memories, Dreams, Reflections*, p. 30.
19 Ibid., p. 31.
20 [SR: A semi-square is a 45° angle.]
21 Jung, *Memories, Dreams, Reflections*, p. 36.
22 Ibid., p. 39.
23 Ibid., p. 31.
24 Ibid., pp. 32–33.
25 Ibid., p. 45.
26 Ibid., p. 104.
27 [SR: MC is the abbreviation for the *medium coeli* or midheaven point in a chart.]
28 Jung, *Memories, Dreams, Reflections*, p. 111.
29 Ibid., pp. 146–147.
30 Ibid., p. 156.
31 Ibid., p. 361.
32 Ibid., p. 158.
33 Ibid., p. 182.
34 Ibid., pp. 170–171.
35 Ibid., p. 172.
36 Ibid., p. 172.
37 Ibid., p. 175.
38 Ibid., p. 175.

39 Ibid., p. 179.
40 Ibid., pp. 189–190.
41 Ibid., p. 192.
42 Ibid., p. 195.
43 Ibid., pp. 196–197.
44 Ibid., pp. 231–232.
45 Ibid., p. 211.

Index